SMALL BUSINESS ACCOUNTING

SMALL BUSINESS ACCOUNTING

MELVIN A. MONTGOMERY

Prentice Hall
Upper Saddle River, NJ 07458

Library of Congress Cataloging-in-Publication Data
Montgomery, Melvin A.
Small business accounting / Melvin A. Montgomery.
p. cm.
Includes index.
ISBN 0-13-628793-X
1. Small business--Acounting. I. Title.
HF5657.M647 1998 97-11601
657'.9042--dc21 CIP

Acquisitions Editor: *Elizabeth Sugg*
Production Editor: *Tally Morgan/WordCrafters*
Director of Manufacturing & Production: *Bruce Johnson*
Manufacturing Buyer: *Marc Bove*
Printer/Binder: *Banta Harrisonburg*
Marketing Manager: *Danny Hoyt*

Printed in the United States of America

10 9 8 7 6 5 4 3 2 1

ISBN 0-13-628793-X

Prentice-Hall International (UK) Limited, *London*
Prentice-Hall of Australia Pty. Limited, *Sydney*
Prentice-Hall Canada Inc., *Toronto*
Prentice-Hall Hispanoamericana, S.A., *Mexico*
Prentice-Hall of India Private Limited, *New Delhi*
Prentice-Hall of Japan, Inc., *Tokyo*
Simon & Schuster Asia Pte. Ltd., *Singapore*
Editora Prentice-Hall do Brasil, Ltda., *Rio de Janeiro*

To all who seek knowledge will be given wisdom...

Table of Contents

Preface

The purpose of this book is to enable you to learn *small business accounting* quickly and easily. After studying this book and working on the problems and exercises you will be able to do the accounting and you will be able to prepare financial statements for your own small business without any difficulty whatsoever. Coverage of the material in this book is complete and little, if anything, has been left to your imagination.

This book is the product of several years work which includes my own personal experience as a businessman and is also the result of having taught thousands of business men and women *small business accounting* in my classes at Robson Square and Simon Fraser University, as well as other locations.

In order to run a business efficiently you must have a knowledge of accounting. Accounting is more than simple bookkeeping. By learning accounting you will gain a complete understanding of absolutely every kind of business transaction. With this knowledge you will be able to make business decisions quickly and effectively. In addition you will save a large amount of money by keeping your own books and records, and by doing your own accounting, including preparation of financial statements for your own business.

Accounting is *easy* to learn. The time that you spend studying this book will yield benefits that will last you a lifetime. Thank you for undertaking to read this book. May your career and business prosper.

Mel Montgomery

July 17, 1997

SMALL BUSINESS ACCOUNTING

CHAPTER ONE

Balance Sheet and Ledger Accounts

INTRODUCTION

Accounting deals with money and the earning of profit by a small business. Most business men and women have only a vague idea of what *small business accounting* involves. They have some notion that books must be kept, a set of financial statements must be prepared at the end of each year and an income tax return must be filed shortly after the end of each year. They also realize that accounting, from their point of view, involves spending hours or days trying to locate receipts and trying to explain the nature and reasons for expenditures to an accountant. After this usually frustrating exercise they then end up having to empty their bank accounts to the tune of several hundred dollars at the very least, to as much as several thousand dollars, to pay the accountant. And this they must do on a yearly basis. This is what accounting seems to mean to many small business owners and managers. But it need not be this way.

You can eliminate all of the frustration associated with accounting by simply learning *small business accounting.* Did you realize that if you know how to do accounting you can keep your own books and records, do your own accounting, and prepare a set of financial statements for your own small business in less time than it takes attempting to explain transactions to an accountant to whom you are paying a handsome fee on an annual basis? In this book you will learn how to do all of these things. This includes keeping the books and records, doing the accounting and preparing financial statements for your own small business. And the upper limit to the size of business you can handle is not that small after all. This system of double entry accounting, in universal use, may be used for a business with sales as large as several million dollars without any modifications whatsoever. It is applicable to every business situation and every kind of business.

You need to know accounting in order to manage a business efficiently and earn a profit. Without a knowledge of accounting it will take you much longer to make even routine decisions. And a knowledge of accounting allows the owner of a business to control the direction and rate of profitability of his or her business venture. Try explaining financial plans to a banker, shareholder or investor without a complete grasp of accounting terminology and without an understanding of the true nature of accounting transactions. It can be difficult. But all of these difficulties can easily be eliminated by simply learning *small business accounting.*

ACCOUNTING IS *EASY* TO LEARN

If you know how to read and can do elementary arithmetic you can learn accounting. With the use of cheaply available electronic calculators even the need to know how to do arithmetic can almost be dispensed with. Accounting itself involves only a very simple system of logic, similar to the logic involved in driving an automobile on the right hand side of the road. Once you know how to drive and know the rules of the road you can drive anywhere. The fact that one encounters thousands of streets in a city does not make driving any more difficult. Similarly with *small business accounting.* It is really quite *easy* to learn and do. If you have the ability to distinguish between left and right, you have the ability to learn small business accounting.

ACCOUNTING TRANSACTIONS

Accounting transactions are also known as *financial transactions.* These are simply events in the course of the life of a business that can be recorded in terms of *money.* If an event cannot be expressed and recorded in terms of money, then for accounting purposes, it is not a transaction. For example, if a person invests money in a business venture, if a business purchases equipment, buys merchandise for resale, sells merchandise, or pays the salaries of employees hired by the business, these are all financial transactions for accounting purposes. A thank you note, on the other hand, received by the business from a satisfied customer is not a transaction for accounting purposes. All accounting transactions are recorded in terms of dollars and cents.

DEVELOPING AN ACCOUNTING SYSTEM BY FOLLOWING YOUR INSTINCTS

Accounting deals with *transactions* or events of a *financial* nature that can be expressed in terms of *money.* If you knew nothing whatsoever about accounting and were asked to develop an accounting system for a business, what could you possibly do? To begin with, about the only thing that you could do is simply list each transaction as it takes place. Your information would likely include the date, nature and amount of each transaction. Thus, you would end up with a list of transactions in chronological order. In listing these transactions you would undoubtedly notice that certain transactions appear over and over again. Sales are made regularly, certain expenses such as the cost of telephone service and salaries occur regularly, and so on. A list of transactions, in chronological order, may be thought of as an elementary accounting system. The problem with this elementary system is that it does not really provide much useful information on which to base management decisions.

Because many of the same transactions are repeated over and over again, our system can be made more efficient by assembling transactions of the same kind into groups. To do this we go through our list and enter all of the transactions involving *telephone expense* on one sheet of paper, all of the transactions involving *salaries expense* on another sheet of paper, and so on. These groups of transactions of the same kind become our accounts. By adding up the entries in each account we can obtain the results for the full year. By making up a list of transactions, which includes the sum of transactions in each account, we end up with a statement of results for the full year in summarized form. This summary of results, which is only one page in length, can more easily be interpreted by the business owner than dozens of pages of individual entries. That is the nature of an elementary accounting system; a system in embryo form. In this system, transactions are recorded, sorted and summarized.

The system of accounting that we are going to learn to use is in advanced form and is in use throughout the civilized world. That is the universal system of double entry accounting. With it you can easily handle even the most complicated accounting transactions. It provides for, among other things, the proper recording, interpretation and control of financial events in the course of the life of a business. It is designed to enable us to rapidly calculate the financial position and operating results of any small business.

THE ACCOUNTING CYCLE

Analyzed transactions are first recorded, in chronological order, in a book of account called the *journal.* These entries are then transferred to a second book of account, called a *ledger,* where the balance of results of each type of transaction is determined. From these account balances the financial position and profitability of a small business is presented in a set of standardized *financial statements* called the *balance sheet* and *income statement.* A pair of each of these statements—each only one page in length—describes a business. No business is so small, nor so large, that it is incapable of being described by a balance sheet and an income statement. Every business, from the smallest to the largest, must file a set of financial statements with its income tax return, every year. Shareholders, investors, creditors, and suppliers are also all interested in the financial position and profitability of a business as presented in these two statements, the balance sheet and income statement.

THE FIRST STEP IN LEARNING ACCOUNTING

Because accounting procedure consists of recording transactions in a journal, transferring these transactions to a ledger, and then producing a set of financial statements from the account balances in the ledger, it is natural to expect that the first step in learning accounting is to make entries to the journal. But, this is not the case. If you tried to learn accounting by first entering transactions into the journal you would find the whole process very confusing and next to impossible to understand.

In order to make the process simple and easy we are going to look at the end product first—that is, one of the pair of financial statements that every business must produce—the balance sheet. After we see how a balance sheet is constructed we will then take a look at the ledger, etc. Last of all, we will learn how to make journal entries! We learn accounting in the reverse order to which we do accounting. Does this seem a bit confusing? Actually, this reverse sequence makes accounting very easy to understand so that just about anyone can learn how to do accounting.

Accounting Process:

1: Journal

2: Ledger

3: Financial Statements

- **Income Statement**
- **Balance Sheet**

Exhibit 1-1: The accounting cycle is a three-stage process.

BALANCE SHEET

A typical balance sheet is shown in Exhibit 1-2. It consists of three main elements—a *heading,* a *left-hand side* and a *right-hand side.* Every balance sheet is constructed in this manner, although a second variation in format is permitted, for practical purposes, as we will discover later on.

HEADING

We are going to examine each of these three elements that make up a balance sheet, in turn. First of all, the heading identifies the business, Pacific Printers Mart, which is simply the trade name under which this business is operating. Underneath the name of the business is the title of the statement*Balance Sheet.* We must always include the title of the statement even though it is obvious to anyone with only a little knowledge of accounting that this statement is a balance sheet. Because a firm's financial position changes every day—in fact, its financial position changes each time a transaction occurs—we must indicate a cut-off point. In our example this is at the close of the business day on December 31, 1997. Our balance sheet gives us this firm's financial position at that point in time.

The remainder of the balance sheet includes the body which consists of a left-hand side and a right-hand side. On the left-hand side of the balance sheet are listed the assets and on the right-hand side are listed the liabilities of the business and the owner's equity in the business.

PACIFIC PRINTERS MART
Balance Sheet
December 31, 1997

Assets:		*Liabilities and Owner's Equity*	
Cash	$3,600	*Liabilities:*	
Accounts Receivable	1,400	Accounts Payable	$6,500
Automobile	7,700		
Office Equipment	1,800	*Owner's Equity:*	
Furniture and Fixtures	2,000	Jack Fraser, Capital	10,000
	$16,500		$16,500

Exhibit 1-2: A balance sheet is comprised of three principal elements.

ASSETS

Assets consist of property owned by a business, which has monetary value, and is kept by the business usually with the intention that money be earned by employing these items of property in the business. Typical assets of any small business might include cash, accounts receivable, inventory, equipment, buildings, land, patents, corporate charter, etc. Some assets, like an automobile, for example, are tangible in nature, while other assets are intangible and only consist of legal rights, such as accounts receivable and patents. Notice that whereas all financial transactions are expressed and recorded in terms of dollars and cents, *cash* is a specific asset. In our example, Exhibit 1-2, Pacific Printers Mart has $3,600 in cash available. For sales made on credit it has accounts receivable in the amount of $1,400. Other assets on this balance sheet include an automobile, office equipment, and furniture and fixtures.

All assets are recorded at *cost* and their monetary value as recorded in the books is not changed to reflect changing market values. Some assets, perhaps most assets, decline in value over time while other assets appreciate in value over time. The balance sheet simply lists the historical cost of each asset as recorded in the books of account. It is important to be aware of this accounting principle when studying the balance sheet of a firm. For example, a business may have purchased a lot for $10,000 twenty years earlier. Today, this same parcel of land has a market value of $50,000. The balance sheet is not altered to reflect current market value of this land, that is $50,000 but continues to indicate the asset *land* at cost, that is, *$10,000.* In spite of this shortcoming the balance sheet is still a very useful statement. By employing cost as the basis for recording transactions involving assets, uniformity in recording is maintained. Market value involves judgment which typically varies from person to person, that is to say it is subject to individual interpretation. By using cost as the basis for recording assets all elements of subjective judgment are eliminated and this practice proves to be the most efficient when all things are considered.

As already mentioned, assets may be tangible or intangible. Tangible assets are the ones we are most familiar with and include cash, inventory, furniture, equipment, land, etc. Intangible assets are just as important to the profitability of a small business and include various legal rights such as accounts receivable, goodwill, patent rights and the costs of organizing the business, which is referred to as the company's charter.

LIABILITIES

Liabilities are *debts.* Every operating business incurs liabilities, regardless of the attitude of its owners towards debt, simply as a matter of business practice and convenience. Like it or not, if the business has a telephone—and virtually all businesses have telephones—then that business incurs a liability every month in the form of a telephone bill. That bill remains a liability until it is paid and a business owner cannot avoid this liability by tendering money to the telephone company in advance. Other liabilities are incurred simply as a matter of trade practice. Goods are ordered by telephone and delivered by the supplying firm. The supplying firm then bills the retailer shortly afterwards.

Most liabilities resulting from the operations of a small business are short-term in nature. These include accounts payable for purchases of goods or services on credit. Other short-term liabilities include salaries payable, interest payable, dividends payable and taxes payable. When credit results from borrowing money, as opposed to purchasing goods or services on credit, the liability that results is typically called a note payable. That is to say the business owner signs a document promising to pay back the money in accordance with agreed upon terms and conditions. Notes payable may be either short-term or long-term. Long-term liabilities resulting from borrowing money include other credit devices such as a mortgage resulting in a mortgage payable or bonds resulting in bonds payable.

OWNER'S EQUITY

Owner's equity is equal to *total assets minus total liabilities.* It originates from two sources—investment in the business by the owner and profitable operation of the business. In the balance sheet for Pacific Printers Mart, Exhibit 1-2, owner's equity is expressed as *Jack Fraser, Capital* and amounts to $10,000. You might think of owner's equity as that fraction of the business interest that belongs to the owner after the claims of all creditors are taken into consideration. If the operations of the small business are profitable, and if these profits are not withdrawn by the owner but are allowed to remain in the business, then the owner's equity in the business will grow along with the business.

BALANCE SHEET EQUATION

By examining both sides of the balance sheet in Exhibit 1-2, we notice that the sum of the figures on the left-hand side is equal to the sum of figures on the right-hand side. The sum of figures on each side *balance.* Hence the title *Balance Sheet.* The sum of figures on each side equals $16,500. From the relationship of the elements of the balance sheet we can derive the balance sheet equation. This equation is simply expressed, as illustrated in Exhibit 1-3, as total assets equals total liabilities plus owner's equity.

ASSETS = LIABILITIES + OWNER'S EQUITY

Exhibit 1-3: The balance sheet equation.

Inserting the data for total assets, liabilities and owner's equity from our balance sheet in Exhibit 1-2 into the balance sheet equation, we obtain:

Assets = Liabilities + Owner's Equity
$16,500 = $6,500 + $10,000

As expected, the two sides do indeed balance, as they must, provided that we have not made any errors in arithmetic.

Aside from the fact that the two sides of the balance sheet must balance because the balance sheet simply presents a detailed expression of the balance sheet equation, there is a natural reason why the balance sheet must balance. This will become clearer when we develop a balance sheet on a transaction-by-transaction basis.

TWO PERCEPTIONS OF THE SAME BUSINESS

Each side of the balance sheet is a virtually complete picture of the business—each entirely complete by itself, but viewed from a different perspective. The natural reason why the balance sheet must balance is that every asset that the business owns was paid for with money supplied by the owner or credit supplied by creditors.*Absolutely every asset that the business owns—listed on the left-hand side of the balance sheet—was acquired with credit supplied by creditors or funds supplied by the owner—which are listed on the right-hand side of the balance sheet as liabilities and owner's equity.* Thus a balance sheet must balance because it simply consists of two different ways of perceiving the very same business. The picture we obtain of the left-hand side of the balance sheet is one of what the business owns in the way of assets and is easily visualized. We can actually see, feel, or handle the money in the till, the equipment, furniture, and automobile, etc. A snapshot of the right-hand side of the balance sheet indicates where the funds came from to obtain the property listed on the left-hand side. The right-hand side tells us what amount of funds was supplied by creditors and what amount of funds was supplied by the owner, including the funds derived from profitable operation of the business which belong to the owner of the business. As absolutely everything the business owns was acquired from funds from these two sources the two sides must balance. Thus, a balance sheet, simply expresses two different ways of perceiving the very same business, so both sides must be equal and balance.

DEVELOPING A BALANCE SHEET FROM TRANSACTIONS

Now that we are familiar with the nature of a balance sheet, let us develop one for Pacific Printers Mart on a transaction-by-transaction basis. Jack Fraser, the owner of the business, is a printing equipment broker. He earns a commission by listing used printing equipment that printers wish to sell. The list is circulated among all printers, some of whom wish to buy. For each sale made, the printer listing the equipment pays Pacific Printers Mart a commission of ten percent of the selling price. At the moment, no inventory is kept on the premises of Pacific Printers Mart. It is simply a brokerage business where a fee is earned by providing a service.

JACK FRASER INVESTS CASH IN THE BUSINESS

On March 1st, Jack Fraser opens a bank account for his new business, Pacific Printers Mart. He deposits $10,000 of his own money into the bank account for Pacific Printers Mart. Let us produce a balance sheet for Pacific Printers Mart at the completion of this transaction. Our first balance sheet is illustrated in Exhibit 1-4 below.

PACIFIC PRINTERS MART
Balance Sheet
March 1, 1997

Assets:		*Owner's Equity:*	
Cash	$10,000	Jack Fraser, Capital	$10,000
	$10,000		$10,000

Exhibit 1-4: Opening balance sheet.

At the top of the balance sheet is the heading, containing the name of the business, *Pacific Printers Mart;* the title of the financial statement, *Balance Sheet;* and the date of this statement, *March 1, 1997.* At the close of the business day on March 1, 1997 the business owns only one asset *Cash* in the amount of $10,000. What this business owns is listed on the left-hand side of the balance sheet. These are its assets. Where did the funds come from to acquire the asset *Cash* listed on the left-hand side of the balance sheet? No money was borrowed—that is to say, no funds were supplied by creditors.

These funds were supplied by the owner of the business, and accordingly, under the owner's equity section we indicate the amount of funds supplied by the owner as *Jack Fraser, Capital* and list the amount supplied which is *$10,000.* Owner's equity then is a measure of the amount of capital supplied by the owner. So the left-hand side of the balance sheet reveals what assets the business owns, at the close of business on the date of the statement, and the right-hand side reveals who supplied the funds to acquire these assets. Both sides of the balance sheet balance, as they must, as the balance sheet employs two different approaches to describing the very same business.

AN ASSET IS PURCHASED WITH CASH

Every time a transaction occurs, the financial position of a business changes. This means that with every transaction we will have a new balance sheet to reflect the change in financial position resulting from our latest transaction.

On March 5th, a truck, complete with canopy, costing $7,700 is purchased from Surrey Motors Inc. and is paid for with cash. The balance sheet for Pacific Printers Mart, after this transaction is completed is illustrated in Exhibit 1-5.

PACIFIC PRINTERS MART
Balance Sheet
March 5, 1997

Assets:		*Owner's Equity:*	
Cash	*$2,300*		
Automobile	*7,700*	Jack Fraser, Capital	$10,000
	$10,000		$10,000

Exhibit 1-5: Asset purchased with cash.

Notice how the balance sheet has changed as a result of our second transaction. The business now has two kinds of assets, cash and an automobile, but the total dollar value of assets remains the same at $10,000. However, only $2,300 remains in the cash account and we now have a second asset, automobile, listed at cost, which is $7,700. No change occurs to the right-hand side of the balance sheet because no additional funds were contributed by the owner or creditors.

AN ASSET IS PURCHASED ON CREDIT

On March 11th a photocopier and typewriter costing $1,800 are purchased from Dandy Discounts Inc., on credit. Payment need not be made until April 30th. The balance sheet for Pacific Printers Mart, after this transaction is completed, is illustrated in Exhibit 1-6.

With the addition of this new asset, office equipment, to the balance sheet, total assets increase to $11,800 from $10,000. The size of the business, as measured by total assets, has increased due to this purchase on credit. On the right-hand side of the balance sheet we have a new entry, accounts payable, in the amount of $1,800. Owner's equity remains unchanged and the total on the right-hand side of the balance sheet is now $11,800 which balances with the total of assets on the left-hand side. All of the assets listed on the left-hand side were obtained from funds supplied by creditors (in this case the creditor did not actually lend Pacific Printers Mart money with which to buy the equipment, but rather sold the equipment to this firm on credit) and funds supplied by the owner. These two sources of capital are listed on the right-hand side

PACIFIC PRINTERS MART
Balance Sheet
March 11, 1997

Assets:		*Liabilities and Owner's Equity*	
Cash	$2,300	*Liabilities:*	
Automobile	7,700	Accounts Payable	*$1,800*
Office Equipment	*1,800*	*Owner's Equity:*	
		Jack Fraser, Capital	10,000
	$11,800		$11,800

Exhibit 1-6: Office equipment purchased on credit.

of the balance sheet. The increase in assets on the left-hand side of the balance sheet is offset by a corresponding increase in liabilities on the right-hand side of the balance sheet and the two sides of the balance sheet remain in balance.

AN ASSET IS PURCHASED WITH A DOWN PAYMENT

On March 15th, desks and chairs costing $2,400 are purchased from Superior Office Products Inc. A down payment of $500 is made with the balance to be paid in three installments of $500 and a final installment payment of $400. Installment payments are to be made every second month with the first installment to be made at the end of March. After the purchase of office furniture with a down payment, with the balance to be paid in installments, the balance sheet for Pacific Printers Mart appears as shown in Exhibit 1-7.

Our latest acquisition is listed in the asset section as *Furniture and Fixtures $2,400.* The asset cash is reduced $500 from its previous balance of $2,300 to its current balance which is $1,800. The sum of assets is now $13,700 which is $1,900 more than the total on the previous balance sheet. In acquiring this latest asset, its acquisition resulted partially from the exchange of one asset for another and partially by obtaining credit from a supplier. Cash is reduced by $500 which is the amount of the down payment. The balance of the purchase price came from credit supplied by the creditor, Superior Office Products Inc. Accordingly, the liability account, accounts payable, on the right-hand side of the balance sheet, increases by $1,900 from its previous balance $1,800 to its present balance $3,700.

PACIFIC PRINTERS MART
Balance Sheet
March 15, 1997

Assets:		*Liabilities and Owner's Equity*	
Cash	*$1,800*	*Liabilities:*	
Automobile	7,700	Accounts Payable	*$3,700*
Office Equipment	1,800	*Owner's Equity:*	
Furniture and Fixtures	2,400	Jack Fraser, Capital	10,000
	$13,700		$13,700

Exhibit 1-7: Furniture purchased with a down payment.

AN ASSET IS SOLD ON CREDIT

On March 20th it was decided that the canopy on the truck was not needed and would be sold. A friend, Don Robson, offered to buy the canopy for $500 and his offer was accepted. Don Robson agreed to pay for the canopy in two equal installments of $250 each, with the first payment to be made at the end of March. The second payment would be made one month later, at the end of April. Exhibit 1-8 shows us what the balance sheet for Pacific Printers Mart looks like after this transaction is completed.

No change in total assets results from the sale of an asset on credit. Here, the sale of the canopy, purchased as part of and considered a part of the truck, merely results in the exchange of one asset for another. The balance in the automobile account has been reduced $500 from its previous balance of $7,700 to the current balance $7,200. In the asset section, we now have a new asset listed, *accounts receivable* with a balance of $500 which is identical to the amount by which the balance in the automobile account has been reduced. The right-hand side of the balance sheet is not affected by this transaction.

PACIFIC PRINTERS MART
Balance Sheet
March 20, 1997

Assets:		*Liabilities and Owner's Equity*	
Cash	$1,800	*Liabilities:*	
Accounts Receivable	*500*	Accounts Payable	$3,700
Automobile	*7,200*		
Office Equipment	1,800	*Owner's Equity:*	
Furniture and Fixtures	2,400	Jack Fraser, Capital	10,000
	$13,700		$13,700

Exhibit 1-8: Sale of an asset on credit.

COLLECTION OF AN ACCOUNT RECEIVABLE

No further transactions occurred until March 31st when Don Robson remitted his first installment payment on the canopy. On March 31st a check for $250 was delivered to Pacific Printers Mart. When this transaction is completed the balance sheet for Pacific Printers Mart appears as shown in Exhibit 1-9.

PACIFIC PRINTERS MART
Balance Sheet
March 31, 1997

Assets:		*Liabilities and Owner's Equity*	
Cash	*$2,050*	*Liabilities:*	
Accounts Receivable	*250*	Accounts Payable	$3,700
Automobile	7,200		
Office Equipment	1,800	*Owner's Equity:*	
Furniture and Fixtures	2,400	Jack Fraser, Capital	10,000
	$13,700		$13,700

Exhibit 1-9: Collection of an account receivable.

Collecting an account receivable has no effect on total assets. Total assets remain unchanged at $13,700. Collecting an account receivable simply results in the exchange of one asset for another. The balance in the cash account increased by $250 from $1,800 to its current level $2,050 while a corresponding reduction, in the amount of $250 occurred to the balance of accounts receivable. Previous to this transaction the balance in accounts receivable stood at $500. It now stands at $250.

PAYING AN ACCOUNT PAYABLE

On March 31st a payment in the amount of $500 was made to Superior Office Products Inc. for office furniture purchased earlier. The balance sheet at the end of the month, when this last transaction is completed, is illustrated in Exhibit 1-10.

Paying a bill reduces total assets. Here, the cash balance is reduced from $2,050 to $1,550 and total assets are now $13,200. On the right-hand side of the balance sheet a reduction in liabilities occurred. Accounts Payable was reduced to $3,200 from its previous balance $3,700.

No additional transactions occurred during March, the month during which the business was being set up. At this stage of the business all of the transactions involved only balance sheet accounts, that is, *assets, liabilities, and owner's equity.* When the business becomes operational two other kinds of accounts will be considered, *revenue* and *expense* accounts.

PACIFIC PRINTERS MART
Balance Sheet
March 31, 1997

Assets:		*Liabilities and Owner's Equity*	
Cash	*$1,550*	*Liabilities:*	
Accounts Receivable	250	Accounts Payable	*$3,200*
Automobile	7,200		
Office Equipment	1,800	*Owner's Equity:*	
Furniture and Fixtures	2,400	Jack Fraser, Capital	10,000
	$13,200		$13,200

Exhibit 1-10: Payment of an account payable.

LEDGER ACCOUNTS

By constructing a new balance sheet after every transaction we can see clearly how the financial position of a business changes after each transaction. The previous illustration employing Pacific Printers Mart served a useful purpose in acquainting us with the nature of a balance sheet, however, in practice it would be very impractical to construct a new balance sheet every time a transaction occurred. In only one day hundreds of sales might be made, for example, and every sale is a transaction.

To collect data on transactions, especially those that are repetitive in occurrence, it is useful to employ a device called *a ledger*. The ledger account for cash is illustrated in Exhibit 1-11.

Cash **101**

Date		JP	Debit	Date		JP	Credit

Exhibit 1-11: The Cash ledger account.

Besides being labeled with the name and number of the account, a typical ledger account consists of two sides with identical rulings—a left-hand side and a right-hand side. Each side consists of four columns—a date column, an explanation column, a reference column, and a money column. In our illustration (Exhibit 1-11) the heading in the explanation column is left blank, the reference column is titled JP, the money column on the left-hand side of the ledger is titled debit, and the money column on the right-hand side of the ledger is titled credit.

A separate page is used for each ledger account and each page bears an account number and a title. For example, the first page is the cash account with the title *Cash* written at the top of the page together with the account number which is *101* in our example, but which could be 1, 01, 001, or 101, depending upon the scheme for numbering accounts that is employed. The cash account is followed by the remaining accounts such as accounts receivable, office equipment, land, etc. Each of these accounts is assigned a number. A complete list of accounts with assigned numbers is presented in the Appendix of this book. A loose leaf binder containing all of the individual ledger accounts for a business is simply referred to as the *Ledger*.

Ignoring column rulings for the moment, the elements of a ledger account appear as shown in Exhibit 1-12.

The ledger account is in the shape of a capital T and, other than its title (including the account number), consists of a left-hand side, which is called the *debit* side, and a right-hand side, which is called the *credit* side.

MEANING OF DEBIT AND CREDIT

Most people have erroneous, preconceived, notions of the meanings of the terms debit and credit. In the minds of many people, the term credit, for example, carries a favorable connotation. For instance, if a shopper receives a letter from Wal Mart Department Store indicating that the store has credited her account in the amount of $200 she feels pleased. That means that she can buy $200 worth of additional merchandise from Wal Mart or receive that amount back in cash. But what about a letter saying that her account has been debited? It might trigger panic or feelings of alarm in the mind of the unfortunate customer. Most people think of *credit* as something good and *debit* as something bad.

Debit and credit simply mean *left* and *right* respectively. A debit entry means that the amount has been entered in the money column on the left-hand side of the ledger

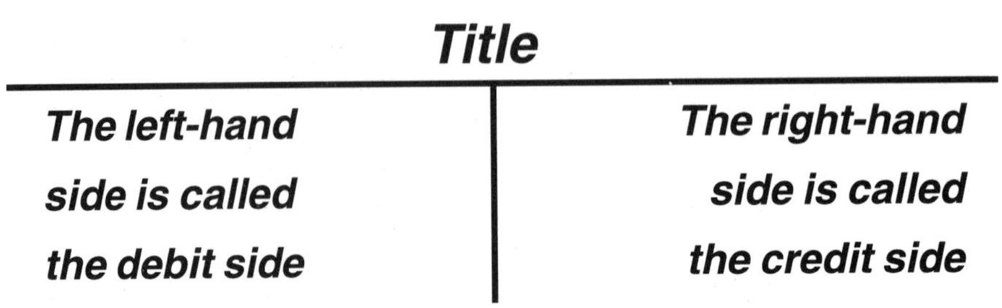

Exhibit 1-12: Elements of a ledger account.

account whereas a credit entry means that the amount has been entered in the money column on the right-hand side of the ledger account.

Using the terms debit and credit, derived from Latin, for left and right, and the term *folio* instead of page, makes an accountant sound impressive to the client who does not know what these terms mean. If an accountant used the phrase left-hand entry instead of the term debit the client would know what he was talking about. In fact, the client might conclude that—if that is all there is to accounting—he might as well make the left-hand entry himself! So by using terms such as debit, credit, and folio (derived from Latin) and acronyms such as A/R for accounts receivable, A/P for accounts payable, etc., the accountant usually succeeds in convincing the client that he is getting his money's worth. Now that you know their meaning, you, too, can use these terms. But be careful that you do not use them too often. Industrial psychologists have determined that frequent usage of acronyms—where ordinary everyday terms would do—may be a sign of incompetence.

RULES OF DEBIT AND CREDIT

In order to know whether to make entries to the left-hand side or to the right-hand side of an account for a given transaction it is necessary to formulate rules of debit and credit. In order to formulate rules of debit and credit it is necessary to refresh our memories with respect to the components that make up a balance sheet. Remember, a balance sheet contains only three types of accounts—assets, liabilities, and owner's equity accounts. Assets are listed on the left-hand side of the balance sheet while liability accounts and owner's equity accounts are listed on the right-hand side of the balance sheet. Here, the English terms left and right are retained for use in describing the two sides of this financial statement. We never say debit side when referring to the left-hand side of the balance sheet. Also, recall that the sum of assets on the left-hand side of a balance sheet is equal to the sum of liabilities and owner's equity on the right-hand side.

Ledger accounts, as we have just seen, consist of two sides which have identical column rulings, with a money column on each side. The left-hand side is the debit side and the right-hand side is the credit side. In deciding upon which side to enter a given transaction into a ledger account we must have rules for debiting and crediting accounts. At the moment it may seem that both sides are available for entry, but by considering various situations that we will have to deal with we can devise a logical and orderly way of recording transactions.

In the course of running a business, assets are going to be acquired—which is an increase in assets. Assets are also likely to be sold from time to time. This represents a decrease in assets. Thus, our rules must accommodate both increases and decreases to asset accounts. Moving to the right-hand side of the balance sheet, liabilities will be incurred, representing an increase in liabilities. When payments are made on outstanding debts a decrease in liabilities results. Our rules must accommodate both increases and decreases to liability accounts. Similarly with owner's equity accounts. When the owner invests money in the business, or allows profits to remain in the business, owner's equity will increase. If the owner withdraws cash or other assets from the business, or if the business suffers an operating loss, owner's equity will decrease. Thus, our rules of debit and credit must accommodate both increases and decreases to owner's equity accounts. In addition, our rules of debit and credit must be formulated in such a way so as to ensure that every time a transaction is entered the balance sheet remains in balance.

This is easier to achieve than it sounds. All we need to do is devise rules of debit and credit in the same manner as we have devised rules of the road for drivers. So long as everyone sticks to the rules consistently the system works. This is so because even after millions of transactions have been entered the balance sheet will balance to the very penny, provided, of course, that no errors in arithmetic have occurred. Our rules of the road for drivers of automobiles stipulate that we must drive on the right-hand side. The system would work just as well if the rules stipulated that we must drive on the left-hand side, so long as everyone follows the rules consistently. Similarly with accounting. We devise rules of debit and credit for analyzing and recording financial transactions and follow these rules consistently. Be certain to keep a mental picture of the balance sheet, such as that shown in Exhibit 1-13, in the back of your mind as we proceed to state the rules of debit and credit.

RULES FOR ASSET ACCOUNTS

Because asset accounts are located on the left-hand side of the balance sheet, as a matter of convention, we enter increases to asset accounts in the left-hand money column, the debit side, of the ledger account. Formulating the rule in this manner appeals to our sense of consistency and logic. If we debit increases to asset accounts, then we must do the opposite for decreases to asset accounts. Accordingly, we credit decreases to asset accounts. These are the rules of debit and credit as they apply to asset accounts and we must follow them consistently in order for our system to work.

RULES FOR LIABILITY AND OWNER'S EQUITY ACCOUNTS

As both liability and owner's equity accounts are located on the right-hand side of the balance sheet, any rule formulated for one of these kinds of accounts will also apply to the other kind. When we formulated our rules of debit and credit for asset accounts we related our rules to the location of assets on the balance sheet. We can apply the same principle to liability and owner's equity accounts, that is, we relate the rules of

---

BALANCE SHEET

Assets	=	***Liabilities***
		+
		Owner's Equity

Exhibit 1-13: A balance sheet contains three kinds of accounts; both sides must balance.

debit and credit to the position of liability and owner's equity accounts on the balance sheet.

Liability and owner's equity accounts are located on the right-hand side of the balance sheet. Increases to liability and owner's equity accounts are recorded by right-hand, or credit entries. Decreases to liability and owner's equity accounts are recorded by debit entries. This is exactly the opposite to the rules of debit and credit for asset accounts.

The rules of debit and credit for any account are directly related to the location of that account—either left-hand side or right-hand side—on the balance sheet. The rules of debit and credit are shown in schematic form in Exhibit 1-14.

If we wish we can simply memorize the rules of debit and credit, but it is best to remember how they were formulated, especially when we apply them in practice.

APPLYING THE RULES OF DEBIT AND CREDIT

Consider what happens when we apply the rules of debit and credit to specific accounts. If an automobile is purchased it means that the business has an asset that it did not have before. Applying the rules of debit and credit as these rules apply to asset accounts, means that we debit the asset account, automobile, with the amount of the purchase price. Similarly if the business purchases equipment (or any other kind of asset). The asset account, equipment, is debited with the amount it cost. Thus, asset accounts will always end up with debit balances. At times we may make individual credit entries to asset accounts, such as when some of the assets in the account are disposed of, but the net balance remaining in the account will always be a debit balance.

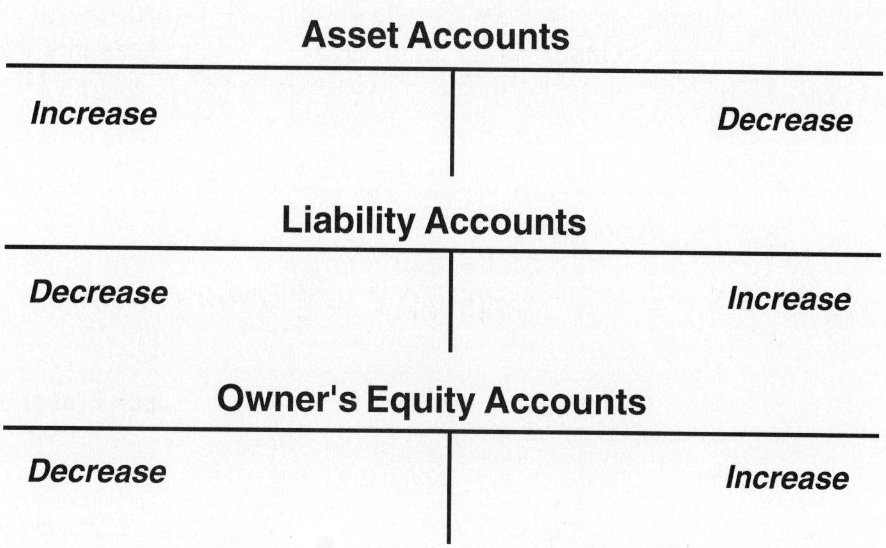

Exhibit 1-14: Rules of debit and credit for balance sheet accounts.

When the telephone bill is received, we apply the rules of debit and credit to this transaction as these rules apply to liability accounts, and we credit the liability account, accounts payable, with the amount of the bill. This is an increase in liabilities. When the bill is paid this results in a decrease in liabilities and we debit accounts payable. Whenever we incur a liability we credit the account; when we pay the bill we debit the account. If any balance at all remains in a liability account it will be a credit balance. If we were to end up with a debit balance in a liability account, which is unlikely, it would mean that we paid our creditors more than the amounts they billed us for. Thus, liability accounts virtually always have net credit balances.

Just like liability accounts, owner's equity accounts almost always have credit balances. When the owner invests money in the business, for example, the owner's equity account is credited. When the owner withdraws cash or other assets the owner's equity account is debited. For a debit balance to result would mean that the owner has withdrawn more assets than he has contributed to the business or the business has suffered operating losses resulting in a decrease in equity greater than the amount contributed to begin with. Sometimes this happens to be the case.

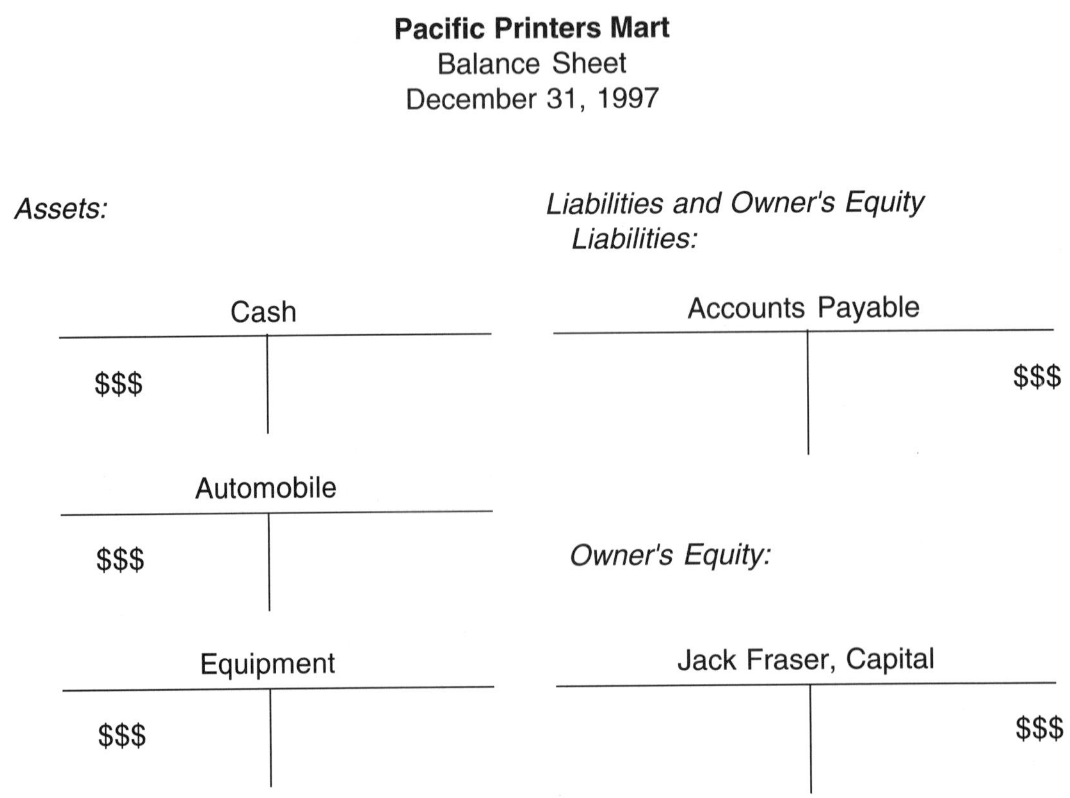

Exhibit 1-15: Ledger accounts superimposed on a balance sheet.

Normally, asset accounts have debit balances; liability accounts have net credit balances; and owner's equity accounts also have net credit balances. If we superimpose individual ledger accounts into their positions on the balance sheet we will obtain a better understanding of why the rules of debit and credit were formulated the way they were. Such a superimposition of ledger accounts on a balance sheet, with the normal balance of each account marked with $s, is illustrated in Exhibit 1-15. Notice how each kind of net balance, debit or credit, relates to the position of each account on the balance sheet. Asset accounts, which are on the left-hand side of the balance sheet, normally have debit balances. Liability accounts and owner's equity accounts, which are located on the right-hand side of the balance sheet, normally have credit balances.

USING THE LEDGER

Let us analyze each transaction for Pacific Printers Mart using the rules of debit and credit that we have just learned and enter the results into ledger accounts. To avoid cluttering up the ledger accounts with data that is not essential for our illustration we will not assign numbers to the accounts nor will we enter the dates of transactions. All we will do is enter the dollar amount of each transaction in the appropriate side of each account.

OWNER INVESTS CASH IN THE BUSINESS

On March 1st, Jack Fraser opens a bank account in the name of the business, Pacific Printers Mart, and deposits $10,000 of his own money into the account. Now, let us analyze this transaction using the rules of debit and credit that we have just learned. The business now has an asset, $10,000 worth of cash, whereas previously it had no cash at all. *Increases in assets are recorded by debits,* so we *debit* the *Cash* ledger account *$10,000.*

But that is not the end of our analysis. Our entry to the cash ledger is only part of this transaction. Every asset that a business owns is acquired from funds supplied by the owner or from credit supplied by a creditor. Where did this $10,000 in cash come from? It was supplied to the business by the owner, Jack Fraser. A measure of funds supplied by the owner is owner's equity. *Increases in owner's equity are recorded by credits,* so we *credit* the *owner's equity* account, *Jack Fraser, Capital* with *$10,000.* Below are the ledger accounts for our first transaction:

Cash

10,000	

Jack Fraser, Capital

	10,000

In analyzing any transaction, first identify the specific accounts to which entries are to be made. In this case the accounts are *Cash* and *Jack Fraser, Capital.* Then, referring to a balance sheet, such as that illustrated in Exhibit 1-10 or Exhibit 1-15, decide what type of account each of these accounts in our transaction is, that is whether it is an *asset, liability,* or *owner's equity* account. Having identified the type of account, then apply the rules of debit and credit to the specific account to complete your analysis. After your analysis is complete make your entries to the appropriate ledger accounts.

In our first transaction we have two entries. At least two entries for each transaction will always be the case. Because of the way in which the balance sheet is formulated—it consists of two sides, each side with a separate approach to describing the same business—there will be at least two entries for every transaction. And, the debit entry will always be equal to the credit entry. In a compound transaction with more than two entries the sum of the debit entries will always be equal to the sum of the credit entries.

DOUBLE-ENTRY ACCOUNTING

Most people have a vague notion that businesses keep two sets of books. And most people have heard the term *double-entry bookkeeping.* What you are learning in this text is the system of *double-entry accounting* which is in universal use. Bookkeeping usually involves keeping specific financial records such as payroll records, or involves collecting and recording financial data, without the bookkeeper necessarily knowing how to analyze transactions or knowing how to prepare financial statements. If you are diligent in following the material in this text, and do the problems at the end of each chapter, you should have no difficulty in analyzing transactions, making entries to the books of account and preparing financial statements. Although it is essential to provide the tax department with a set of properly prepared financial statements at the end of each year, it is not necessary to employ an accountant to prepare them. Chances are, that as your business grows you will not bother to do the accounting yourself. However, a knowledge of accounting will provide you with a clearly defined framework within which to make all of your financial decisions.

ASSET ACQUIRED WITH CASH

Let us continue our example involving Pacific Printers Mart. On March 5th, a second-hand truck, complete with canopy, was purchased with cash. The total purchase price was $7,700. To analyze this transaction we have to identify the specific accounts involved, decide which group of accounts each specific account belongs to, and then apply the rules of debit and credit to each of these accounts. A truck was purchased so one specific account is the *Automobile* account. The automobile account belongs to the asset group of accounts. *Increases in assets are recorded by debits,* so we *debit* the *Automobile* account *$7,700.*

The truck was paid for with cash, so the other specific account involved in this transaction is the *Cash* account. Cash is an asset. Increases in assets are recorded by debits; *decreases in assets are recorded by credits.* We have decreased the asset, *Cash,* so we *credit* the *Cash* account *$7,700.* When our analysis is completed we post these results to the appropriate ledger accounts as shown in the illustration on the following page.

Cash

10,000	
	7,700

Automobile

7,700	

Again, the debit and credit entries are equal, as they must be in every transaction. Also note that ledger accounts serve to accumulate data on each kind of transaction. In the Cash ledger the $10,000 debit entry remains from our previous transaction which took place on March 1st. The net balance in the Cash ledger is now $2,300 and this is the amount that would appear on the balance sheet if we were to prepare one from the balances in the ledger accounts at this point in time.

ASSET PURCHASED ON CREDIT

On March 11th, office equipment costing $1,800 was purchased on credit. In the back of our minds we must visualize the impact of this transaction on the balance sheet. First , we identify the specific accounts involved. They are *Office Equipment* and *Accounts Payable. Office Equipment* is an *asset.* Assets are located on the left-hand side of the balance sheet. Increases in assets are recorded by left-hand entries, known as debits. So we *debit* the asset account, *Office Equipment $1,800.*

Accounts Payable is a *liability.* Liabilities are located on the right-hand side of the balance sheet. Increases in liabilities are recorded by right-hand entries, known as credits. So we *credit* the liability account, *Accounts Payable $1,800.*

The debit entry equals the credit entry so we know that our analysis is correct. Even though we know that the entry to Accounts Payable must be a credit entry in order to offset the debit entry to the asset account, Office Equipment, it is nevertheless important to obtain this result by analyzing the complete transaction. This way we gain a complete and thorough understanding of the rules of debit and credit rather than simply take advantage of the fact that the debit entry and credit entry must be equal. The ledger accounts appear as shown below:

Office Equipment

1,800	

Accounts Payable

	1,800

ASSET PURCHASED WITH DOWN PAYMENT

On March 15th office furniture costing $2,400 was purchased with a $500 down payment and the balance is to be paid later. First, we identify the specific accounts involved in this transaction. They are *Furniture and Fixtures, Cash,* and *Accounts Payable.* Although no "fixtures" have been installed, this is the traditional name of the account to which furniture belongs, so we use it. Next, we determine which group of accounts each of these specific accounts belongs to. This may be done by referring to a balance sheet, or, after a little practice, by keeping a mental picture of the balance sheet in the back of our minds. Anyway, by now we realize that there are only three kinds of accounts on the balance sheet—*asset* accounts on the left-hand side of the balance sheet and *liability* accounts and *owner's equity* accounts on the right-hand side of the balance sheet. So each of the specific accounts identified must be one of those three kinds of accounts as there are no other kinds of accounts that belong to the balance sheet.

Office furniture, or using the proper name of the account, *Furniture and Fixtures,* is an asset. Assets are located on the left-hand side of the balance sheet. Increases in assets are recorded by left-hand entries, known as debit entries, so we debit Furniture and Fixtures $2,400. That is the sort of analysis you should go through in the back of your mind. Visualize Furniture and Fixtures among the assets on the balance sheet; visualize the location of asset accounts on the balance sheet; and finally, apply the rules of debit and credit by remembering how they were formulated, that is increases to assets are debited because assets are located on the left-hand side of the balance sheet.

A cash down payment of $500 was made. Cash is an asset. Assets are located on the left-hand side of the balance sheet. Increases in assets are recorded by debits. Do we have an increase in assets this time? No, we do not. A down payment was made meaning that cash was spent. The business now has less cash than it did before as a result of this transaction. Decreases in assets are recorded by credits, so we credit Cash $500.

Nineteen hundred dollars is the amount left owing on the purchase. This means that we have an Account Payable of $1,900. An Account Payable is a liability. Liability accounts are located on the right-hand side of the balance sheet. Increases in liabilities are recorded by right-hand entries, otherwise known as credit entries, so we credit the liability account, Accounts Payable $1,900. The ledger accounts after the results of our analysis have been entered are shown below. Notice that the debit entry is equal to the sum of the credit entries in this compound transaction.

Furniture and Fixtures

2,400	

Cash

10,000	7,700
	500

Accounts Payable

	1,800
	1,900

SALE OF AN ASSET ON CREDIT

On March 20th, the canopy on the truck was sold to a friend, Don Robson, on credit, for $500. Don Robson promised to make the first payment, in the amount of $250 at the end of the month. By examining the facts at hand, we identify the Automobile account and Accounts Receivable as the accounts being affected. The canopy on the truck is part of the asset*Automobile*. Assets are located on the left-hand side of the balance sheet. Reductions in assets are recorded by right-hand entries, so we credit the Automobile account $500.

The first payment is expected at the end of the month. At the time of this transaction, when the deal was closed, no money whatsoever was received as the sale was on credit. A sale on credit results in an account receivable. Accounts Receivable is an asset account, located on the left-hand side of the balance sheet. Increases in assets are recorded by debits. We debit the asset account, Accounts Receivable $500. Later, when payment is received, a credit entry corresponding to the amount of payment will be entered to Accounts Receivable and a debit entry will be entered in the Cash account. The ledger accounts, which include the transaction we have just analyzed, are shown below:

Automobile

7,700	
	500

Accounts Receivable

500	

COLLECTION OF AN ACCOUNT RECEIVABLE

On March 31st, the first installment was received from Don Robson. A check for $250 arrived in the mail as first payment for the canopy from the truck. In analyzing this transaction we must be careful to identify the correct accounts. A check for $250 was received, so Cash is one of the accounts to which we must make an entry. Why did Pacific Printers Mart receive a check? It is the first payment due on the canopy that was sold earlier, but it is not the Automobile account that is affected this time. When the canopy was sold we credited the Automobile account at that time and debited

Accounts Receivable. Accordingly, this payment was received in partial settlement of the account receivable.

Accounts Receivable is an asset account. Assets are on the left-hand side of the balance sheet. Reductions in assets are recorded by right-hand, that is, credit entries, so we credit Accounts Receivable $250.

Payment was received in the form of a check. Nevertheless, whatever form the money is in is not important, the account that is affected is the Cash account. Cash is an asset. Assets are located on the left-hand side of the balance sheet. By this time we realize where assets are located, but by repetition we can make the process of analysis virtually automatic. Increases in assets are recorded by debits, so we debit the Cash account $250. After you have had sufficient practice you will simply form a mental image of the entire balance sheet in the back of your mind and automatically debit increases to asset accounts and credit decreases to these same accounts. You will also be able to automatically handle liability and owner's equity accounts. Here are the ledger accounts immediately after this transaction has been entered.

Cash

10,000	
	7,700
	500
250	

Accounts Receivable

500	
	250

PAYMENT OF A LIABILITY

As our final transaction during the month, on March 31st, a payment was made on the office furniture that had been purchased from Superior Office Products Inc. earlier in the month. A check for $500 was issued.

In analyzing this transaction we have to be very careful in identifying the accounts involved. One account is easy to identify. That is the Cash account. You might jump to the wrong conclusion and decide that the other account in this transaction is Furniture and Fixtures. It is not. We do not make entries to Furniture and Fixtures unless furniture is purchased or disposed of. What are we really doing at this stage? We are remitting a payment on a liability that was incurred when office furniture was purchased partially on credit at an earlier date. So the second account in this transaction is *Accounts Payable.*

The asset Cash was reduced so we credit Cash $500. The liability Accounts Payable was reduced so we debit Accounts Payable $500. These accounts appear as follows:

Cash

10,000	
	7,700
	500
250	
	500

Accounts Payable

	1,800
	1,900
500	

Notice that both the Cash and Accounts Payable ledger accounts have several entries in them. That is the purpose of a ledger account. It is used to accumulate financial data on transactions. If we compute the net balance from the data collected in each account we can produce a balance sheet for the end of March which will be identical to that in Exhibit 1-10 which was produced by preparing a new balance sheet after each transaction. Obviously, with a large number of transactions involved, it is much more efficient to enter transactions into ledger accounts, and produce a balance sheet from this data, than it is to produce a balance sheet after every transaction. After all of the transactions for the month of March have been entered to ledger accounts, the ledger appears as shown in Exhibit 1-16.

Exhibit 1-16: Complete ledger at the end of March.

Cash

10,000	
	7,700
	500
250	
	500

Accounts Receivable

500	
	250

Office Equipment

1,800	

Furniture and Fixtures	
2,400	

Automobile	
7,700	
	500

Accounts Payable	
	1,800
	1,900
500	

Jack Fraser, Capital	
	10,000

TRIAL BALANCE

Because entries have been made to several accounts and several transactions are involved it is a good idea to check and see if the ledger as a whole is in balance. This is easily done by copying the net balance from each account onto a sheet of scratch paper. What we do is write down the name of each account, as we come to it in the ledger, and enter its net balance in one of two columns, either debit or credit, in accordance with whether its net balance is a net debit balance or a net credit balance.

Pacific Printers Mart
Trial Balance
March 31, 1997

Cash	$1,550	
Accounts Receivable	250	
Office Equipment	1,800	
Furniture and Fixtures	2,400	
Automobile	7,200	
Accounts Payable		$ 3,200
Jack Fraser, Capital		10,000
	$13,200	$13,200

Exhibit 1-17: Trial balance at the end of March.

Then we add up the entries in each column to arrive at the column totals, which should balance. If the totals do not balance then we must go back and find our error and correct it so that the column totals do balance. What we have produced is called a *trial balance.* Its main purpose is to simply ascertain that the sum of all debit entries is equal to the sum of all credit entries. The trial balance at the end of March, for Pacific Printers Mart, is illustrated in Exhibit 1-17.

BALANCE SHEET

A balance sheet may be prepared directly from the balances in the ledger accounts or by referring to the trial balance. Unlike the trial balance which is simply produced on scratch paper, and often discarded when the exercise is over, the balance sheet is a formal financial statement which is retained permanently. The balance sheet, prepared from the balances in the ledger accounts, is illustrated in Exhibit 1-18.

Pacific Printers Mart
Balance Sheet
March 31, 1997

Assets:		*Liabilities and Owner's Equity*	
Cash	$1,550	*Liabilities:*	
Accounts Receivable	250	Accounts Payable	$ 3,200
Office Equipment	1,800		
Furniture and Fixtures	2,400	*Owner's Equity:*	
Automobile	7,200	Jack Fraser, Capital	$10,000
	$13,200		$13,200

Exhibit 1-18: Balance sheet at the end of March.

SUMMARY

Every business must prepare a set of financial statements at the end of each year for income tax purposes. These statements are the product of accounting. In addition to the income tax department, other parties are interested in the financial position and earnings of a business as well. These two statements—the balance sheet and income statement are capable of describing any business, both large and small.

Every person who runs a business should have a knowledge of accounting. A knowledge of accounting enables the small business owner to make financial decisions in an organized, efficient, manner. Organized financial data is perhaps the most important tool that the small business owner can have for controlling the direction and rate of growth of his or her business enterprise.

In this chapter we were introduced to the first of the two financial statements that describe a business—a balance sheet. We produced a balance sheet on a transaction-by-transaction basis and became familiar with the elements that make up this statement. In addition, we formulated rules of debit and credit and learned how to enter transactions directly to ledger accounts. From the data in the ledger accounts we produced the very same balance sheet as we did previously on a transaction-by-transaction basis. As we continue the study of small business accounting we will learn how to make use of additional tools which will make the process easier and which will enable us to handle the financial affairs of even a fairly complicated business. Working on problems is an essential part of learning small business accounting. To facilitate the solution of problems, a computer template is included with this textbook to enable you to concentrate on learning the language and concepts in small business accounting without engaging in an excessive amount of chore work. Remember, small business accounting is easy to learn.

Exercises

1. What is the purpose of accounting?

2. Define a transaction. List two examples.

3. List the books used in the accounting process. Name the two financial statements that are produced as a result.

4. List the three kinds of accounts that are found on a balance sheet.

5. What information is contained in the heading of a balance sheet?

6. What are assets? Give three examples.

7. Define liabilities. Give two examples.

8. What is owner's equity? What are its sources?

9. State the balance sheet equation.

10. Why must the two sides of a balance sheet always balance? Explain.

11. Land on which a business is located was purchased in 1970 for only $40,000. It now has a market value of three times that amount but is still listed on the firm's balance sheet at its original cost. Should the figure for land on the balance sheet be changed to reflect current market value? Explain.

12. To which of the three types of accounts on the balance sheet, that is, assets, liabilities, or owner's equity, does each of the following accounts belong?
    a. Cash.
    b. Land.
    c. Salaries Payable.
    d. Furniture and Fixtures.
    e. Jack Fraser, Capital.
    f. Accounts Payable.
    g. Accounts Receivable.
    h. Automobile.
    i. Patents.
    j. Income Taxes Payable.
    k. Interest Payable.
    l. Building.
    m. Office Equipment.
    n. Mortgage Payable.
    o. Shop Supplies.
    p. Notes Payable.

q. Company Charter.
r. Bonds Payable.

13. List the four column headings that are found on each side of a ledger account.

14. Define the terms debit and credit.

15. State the rules of debit and credit for asset accounts, liability accounts, and owner's equity accounts. With the aid of a diagram of a balance sheet and ledger accounts illustrate how the rules of debit and credit for balance sheet accounts were formulated.

16. What is the minimum number of entries for a given transaction? Can there be more entries than the minimum number? Explain.

17. What is a trial balance? State its purpose.

Problems

1. Arrange the data below into balance sheet format for Busy-Busy Weed Control as of December 31, 1997.

Accounts Payable	$15,000
Building	20,000
Cash	2,000
B.B. Jones, Capital	110,000
Equipment	30,000
Land	60,000
Furniture and Fixtures	13,000

2. Prepare a balance sheet from the data below for Rodent Control Service as of December 31, 1997.

Cash	$1,200
Accounts Receivable	800
Equipment	40,000
Furniture and Fixtures	5,000
I.M. Faste, Capital	50,000
Automobile	10,000
Accounts Payable	7,000

3. Prepare a balance sheet for Great Star Lighting Service. Using your knowledge of the balance sheet fill in any missing data. This firm's fiscal year ends on June 30, 1997.

Land	$90,000

J.R. Flash, Capital	200,000
Furniture and Fixtures	50,000
Cash	?
Accounts Payable	15,000
Equipment	10,000
Building	60,000

4. Prepare a new balance sheet after each transaction, from the data below, for Olympic Auctioneers.

March 1	The proprietor, H.E. Chant, opened a bank account in the name of the business, depositing $50,000.
March 3	A lot was purchased for $30,000 cash.
March 5	A building left over from the 1986 World Exposition was purchased for $2,000 and was moved to the site of the lot. It was estimated that this building was worth $25,000. The full amount was paid for in cash.
March 14	Office furnishings were purchased from Royal Oak Office Suppliers Inc. on credit. This furniture cost $2,500 and the full amount was to be paid in 90 days.
March 23	A truck was purchased from Marpole Motors Inc. for $10,000. A down payment of $3,000 was made with the balance to be paid in equal monthly installments of $500 each.
March 31	The first installment payment was made to Marpole Motors Inc. A check for $500 was issued.

5. From the data below prepare a balance sheet for the Surrey Machine Shop as of September 30, 1997.

B. Smith, Capital	$84,000
Automobile	13,000
Furniture and Fixtures	7,000
Accounts Payable	2,000
Building	10,000
Notes Payable	15,000
Land	40,000
Accounts Receivable	8,000
Equipment	20,000
Cash	3,000

6. Here is the financial data for Delta Delicatessen as of June 30, 1997. Prepare a balance sheet. Also, prepare a new balance sheet after each transaction, listed below.

Cash	$5,000
Accounts Payable	1,000
Building	40,000
H.P. Singh, Capital	?

Equipment	10,000
Land	60,000

July	2	A strip of land was sold for $10,000. Payment in full would be received in 60 days.
July	15	Five thousand dollars was borrowed from the bank. A note (Notes Payable) was signed for this amount.
July	20	Additional equipment, costing $6,000 was purchased and paid for in cash.
July	31	A payment of $500 was made to a creditor.

7. Analyze each transaction below using the rules of debit and credit as they apply to balance sheet accounts, then enter this data into appropriate ledger accounts. Write out your analysis. The first transaction has been done for you to help you get started.

October	1	Ralph Karbendler deposits $50,000 in a bank account, in the name of the business, Ralph's Auto Body Shop.

This is how the above transaction is analyzed: *Cash is an asset. Increases in assets are recorded by debits. Debit Cash $50,000. Ralph Karbendler, Capital is an owner's equity account. Increases in owner's equity are recorded by credits. Credit Ralph Karbendler, Capital, $50,000.*

October	2	Purchased a tow truck for $20,000 with a cash down payment of $5,000 leaving the balance owing.
October	10	Purchased shop equipment for $3,000 paying cash.
October	11	Purchased land with a building on it for $100,000. The building was valued at $20,000. A down payment of $10,000 was made with a note signed for the balance.
October	20	More shop equipment was purchased—this time on credit. It cost $2,000 and was to be paid for in four equal monthly installments beginning with the end of this month.
October	22	An annex to the building was sold for $5,000 and removed from the site. There was neither a gain nor loss on the sale. A down payment of $1,000 was received with the balance to be paid to Ralph's Auto Body Shop in equal monthly installments of $500 each.
October	31	A check for $500 was issued as the first installment to be paid on the equipment which was purchased on October 20th.
October	31	A check for $500 was received in payment for the annex sold on October 22nd.

8. Analyze the transactions given below in terms of increases or decreases to asset, liability, or owner's equity accounts. Enter this data into the appropriate ledger accounts.

November 1	J. Frost deposits $20,000 in a bank account in the name of the business, Superior Home Insulators.
November 2	Purchases a van for $10,000. Makes a down payment of $4,000 with the balance to be paid in equal monthly installments of $1,000 each commencing with the end of the month.
November 7	Buys special equipment for injecting insulation. This equipment cost $4,000 and was paid for in cash.
November 10	Purchases a desk and chair for $500. Agrees to pay for this purchase at the end of the month.
November 20	Buys several ladders at an auction. Paid $1,000 cash.
November 25	Sells on credit, 3 of the ladders purchased previously, for $100 each. The buyer agreed to pay Joan Frost for these at the end of November.
November 30	A check in the amount of $300 was received for the ladders sold on the twenty-fifth of November.
November 30	Issued a check for $500 for office furniture purchased earlier in the month.
November 30	Makes a payment on the van.
November 30	Hires a helper. Agrees to pay him $1,000 a month. The helper is to commence work on December 3rd.

9. Prepare a trial balance and a balance sheet, for the end of the month, for the businesses in problems 7 and 8 above.

10. Analyze each of the events listed below in accordance with correct accounting practice and enter into ledger accounts where appropriate. Where the event is not a financial transaction for accounting purposes state this fact.

August 21	Purchased a truck costing $10,000 on credit.
August 25	Bought a construction trailer for $8,000 paying cash.
September 2	Sold a strip of land for $5,000 to the owner of the adjoining business. Payment would be received in 30 days.
November 3	Remitted payment on equipment purchased earlier. Check number 705 in the amount of $400 was issued.

November	8	Hired an employee at a salary of $1,200 per month. Duties to commence the next day.
November	9	John Smith, the owner of the business, invested $5,000 in the business.
December	3	Receives a real estate appraiser's report indicating that the land purchased five years earlier for $20,000 is now worth $30,000. The president shows you this report and asks you to record the value of this asset properly. A fellow employee confides to you that the president has dismissed members of his staff in the past for failing to comply with his wishes.
December	5	Purchased office furniture, costing $1,000 and paid for immediately.
December	8	Borrowed money from the bank. Signed a note for $20,000.

CHAPTER TWO

The Journal and Income Statement

INTRODUCTION

If the only reason you have hired an accountant to do your accounting and prepare year-end financial statements for your business is because you do not know how to do accounting yourself then you should learn how to do accounting. On the other hand, you may know how to do accounting, but still hire an accountant, in which case you are in an enviable position. Accounting is a powerful tool whereby you may turn seemingly random or only partially understood financial data into a meaningful series of financial transactions, thereby allowing you to exert greater control and direction over the affairs of the business. You cannot run a business efficiently without a knowledge of accounting.

LEDGER ACCOUNT NUMBERS

In the preceding chapter we learned how to analyze transactions and how to enter them into appropriate ledger accounts. At that time we did not bother assigning account numbers to the various ledger accounts because the accounts were few in number and assigning account numbers would only serve to clutter up our illustration with information that we were not going to make use of at that point in time.

Recall, from Chapter One, that we learn the accounting process in the reverse sequence to which we actually do accounting. In practice, we first make entries to a journal, transfer these entries to the ledger, and from the balances in the ledger accounts, produce financial statements. We started out by learning how to produce a balance sheet on a transaction-by-transaction basis and then we learned how to make entries to ledger accounts by analyzing transactions and by applying the rules of debit and credit. Learning accounting in reverse sequence makes the process easy to understand.

Now that we are about to learn how to make entries into the journal we will need to employ account numbers in our ledger accounts. Any numbering scheme may be used. For example, we may assign 1, 10, 100, 101, or any other number to the Cash account. Similarly with other accounts. However, in this book, we will use a numbering scheme whereby the first digit indicates the type of account, that is, asset, liability, etc., and the remaining digits make up the entire account number. Such a scheme is presented in Exhibit 2-1, which we can use to continue our example involving Pacific Printers Mart. An expanded numbering scheme, employing virtually all of the accounts that you will ever need to use, is presented in the Appendix. A scheme with a few accounts, which is presented below in Exhibit 2-1, will serve our purposes for the moment.

Notice that the account numbers of all asset accounts begin with the digit "1"; all liability accounts begin with the digit "2"; and, all owner's equity accounts begin with the digit "3". In our scheme, (see Appendix) asset accounts occupy the range 101 to 129 inclusive; liability accounts occupy the range 230 to 242 inclusive; and owner's equity accounts occupy the range 343 to 354 inclusive. Unassigned numbers are available and may be used for accounts of the same type as required, later on. A complete list of accounts comprises a *ledger index* which is also known as a *Chart of Accounts.*

Assets:

101 Cash

103 Accounts Receivable

112 Office Equipment

114 Furniture and Fixtures

116 Automobile

Liabilities:

230 Accounts Payable

Owner's Equity:

343 Jack Fraser, Capital

Exhibit 2-1: List of ledger accounts.

THE JOURNAL

Unlike a ledger, which consists of a loose-leaf collection of accounts held in a binder, the journal is a bound book with its pages numbered in consecutive sequence like the pages in a textbook. See Exhibit 2-2 for an illustration of the column rulings in a typical journal.

The column rulings shown in Exhibit 2-2 are for a general journal. This is the kind of journal used in small business accounting. Although column headings are included in our illustration, more often than not, journals available at stationery stores omit this information because persons with a knowledge of accounting, who buy these books, know what to include in each column.

The first column is for the date of each transaction. The year is written at the top of the date column on every page. You will see how this is done when we continue our example involving Pacific Printers Mart. In the second column we list the names of the accounts in a particular transaction along with an explanation of why the transaction took place, or additional details of the transaction, particularly if the reason is not obvious. The third column, with the heading LP, is a reference column, while the fourth and fifth columns are money columns. We record the amounts of each transaction in the money columns—debit or credit based on our analysis of a particular transaction. The debit money column is always to the left of the credit money column.

When buying a journal at a stationery store you must examine the column rulings very carefully to be certain that you have selected the proper book. Do not simply buy a journal by name. Examine the column rulings and choose a journal on this basis if you wish to avoid needless frustration later on. If you examine a book of account and it contains three money columns, for example, instead of two, do not buy it despite assurances from the sales clerk (who is working on commission) that three columns are surely better than two. If the pages of the book are not numbered, that is okay, because you can number them yourself, by hand. As mentioned before, column headings are usually not printed in a journal, so do not expect to find printed column headings. Instead, what you want to be certain of is that each column is suitable for its required purpose.

Date	Account Titles and Explanation	LP	Debit	Credit

Exhibit 2-2: Illustration of a page from a general journal.

Most people have no difficulty recognizing the first column, suitable for entering the date—just wide enough to enter the month and day of the month. Examine the second column carefully. The second column must be wide enough to write in the names of accounts with ease and, accordingly, should be three or four times wider than the date column. The reference column is narrow and need only be wide enough to enter a three digit number. Finally, the fourth and fifth columns, for the debit and credit entries, must be ruled as money columns to enable you to easily enter the dollar and cents amount of each transaction. A proper general journal will have columns ruled identical to the rulings in our illustration in Exhibit 2-2.

BACK TO OUR ILLUSTRATION

Going back to our example involving Pacific Printers Mart, let us enter each of those transactions into a general journal. From now on we will simply refer to the general journal as the *journal*. The first transaction occurred on March 1, 1997 when Jack Fraser opened a bank account for Pacific Printers Mart and deposited $10,000 of his own money into this account. Before you begin your analysis, it is helpful to have a sample balance sheet handy to refer to, to remind yourself of the different types of accounts and their arrangement on the balance sheet. That way you can mentally derive the rules of debit and credit for each kind of account as you analyze each transaction and retain a clear image of why each entry is made the way it is in each situation.

Before we actually make an entry to the journal, we analyze the transaction and make entries to ledger accounts drawn on scratch paper. Once we are certain that our analysis is correct we then make entries into the journal. Every transaction is represented by an entry which consists of at least two items, a debit and a credit—a debit to one account and a credit of the same amount to another account. When an entry consists of more than two items the sum of the debits must equal the sum of the credits. If the debits do not equal the credits then our analysis is either in error or is incomplete. After you have had some practice you will be able to analyze transactions by simply referring to the image of a balance sheet in the back of your mind, and make entries directly to the journal. But, for the moment, you are well advised to have some scratch paper handy.

JACK FRASER INVESTS CASH IN THE BUSINESS

Our first transaction occurred on March 1st when Jack Fraser deposited $10,000 into the bank account of Pacific Printers Mart. As in our previous analysis, in which we made entries directly to ledger accounts, the first step is to identify the accounts involved.

Using a sample balance sheet to refer to until we develop a mental picture of a balance sheet in the back of our minds, we identify the accounts involved. The accounts we are dealing with here are Cash and Jack Fraser, Capital. Next, we analyze each account in turn, in the same manner as before. Cash is an asset. Then we apply the rules of debit and credit to this kind of account. Increases in assets are recorded by debits, so we debit Cash $10,000. We quickly draw a simple ledger account for Cash on scratch paper and enter $10,000 on the debit side as shown below:

Cash	
10,000	

Likewise for the remainder of our analysis. The owner contributed money to the business so this item must be entered to Jack Fraser, Capital. Jack Fraser, Capital is an owner's equity account. Increases in owner's equity are recorded by credits, so we credit Jack Fraser, Capital $10,000. We draw another simple ledger account on scratch paper—this time for Jack Fraser, Capital—and enter $10,000 on the credit side as shown below:

Jack Fraser, Capital	
	10,000

A glance at our entries to the simple ledger accounts drawn on scratch paper reveals that the debit item is equal to the credit item, which provided that our accounts were selected properly, means that our analysis is correct. Now we are ready to enter this transaction into the journal. After entering this transaction into the journal the journal entry appears as shown in Exhibit 2-3.

	Journal		**Page 1**
1997			
March 1	Cash	10,000	
	Jack Fraser, Capital		10,000
	Owner invested cash in the business.		

Exhibit 2-3: Journal entry for the first transaction.

Notice that the entry was made in page one of our journal. Every page of the journal must be numbered. At the top of the date column we write in the year, 1997, and on the line below in the same column we write in the date, March 1. The year must be entered in the date column at the top of each page in which entries are made. We enter the names of the accounts in the second column. We write in the name of the account for the first item in our transaction, Cash, and enter the amount $10,000 in the debit money column. For the moment, no entry will be made to the third column, the reference column. Next, we enter the remaining item in our transaction, Jack Fraser, Capital, in the line below, indenting the name of the account, and enter $10,000 in the credit money column. In each transaction,all of the accounts to which debit entries are being made must be listed first, followed by the accounts with credit entries. Names of accounts to which credit entries are being made are indented to help distinguish them from accounts with debit entries. A brief explanation of each transaction is placed in the second column, with no indent, in the line below the last credit item.

COMPLETE JOURNAL FOR MARCH

After all of the transactions for the month of March have been analyzed and each item entered into the journal, the journal appears as shown in Exhibit 2-4.

Exhibit 2-4: Journal for the month of March.

		Journal		**Page 1**
1997				
March	1	Cash	10,000	
		Jack Fraser, Capital		10,000
		Owner invested cash in the business.		
	5	Automobile	7,700	
		Cash		7,700
		Bought a truck from Surrey Motors.		
	11	Office Equipment	1,800	
		Accounts Payable		1,800
		Bought a photocopier and a typewriter from Dandy Discounts Inc.		
	15	Furniture and Fixtures	2,400	
		Cash		500
		Accounts Payable		1,900
		Bought desks and chairs from Superior Office Products Inc.		
	20	Accounts Receivable	500	
		Automobile		500
		Sold the canopy from the truck to Don Robson.		
	31	Cash	250	
		Accounts Receivable		250
		Received the first payment from Don Robson.		

March	31	Accounts Payable	500	
		Cash		500
		Remitted payment to Superior Office Products Inc.		

A blank line is left after each transaction. This makes the journal easier to scan for errors as each transaction stands out as a unit. This is especially the case when we have a compound transaction such as that of March 15th with more than one credit item. When transactions stand out as units we can easily compare the debits to the credits. If we omit an explanation of the transaction, which is frequently done, and if in addition no blank line is left between transactions, then we simply end up with an unbroken series of debit and credit entries. This makes it difficult to detect errors, such as accidentally omitting a debit or a credit entry, especially where compound transactions are involved.

A JOURNAL INCREASES EFFICIENCY

Although it appears that using a journal results in additional and needless work—the reverse is actually the case. By using a journal we prevent most errors from occurring to begin with. This is because the debit and credit items for a given transaction are listed together in a journal entry as opposed to the debit and credit items being located in different parts of the ledger, when we make entries directly to ledger accounts. Thus, with a journal we can compare the debit and credit items for a given transaction, to see if they are equal, at any time. It would be virtually impossible to trace an error resulting from the accidental omission of a debit or credit entry to a ledger account if ledger accounts alone are used, because of numerous entries to each ledger account. With a journal we can trace such errors. In addition, a journal provides us with a complete chronological record of transactions in the business. If desired, we can always look up a transaction if we have some idea as to when it occurred.

POSTING TO THE LEDGER

After transactions have been recorded in the journal they are then posted to the ledger at some convenient point in time. If you wish to prepare financial statements every month then posting must be completed every month before financial statements can be prepared. Every transaction for a given accounting period must be recorded in the journal and posted to the ledger before financial statements can be prepared.

Posting simply refers to the transfer of entries from the journal to appropriate ledger accounts.

POSTING THE FIRST ITEM

First of all, we look up the first item from the first entry in the journal (see Exhibit 2-4). The first item in the journal indicates that Cash was debited $10,000. Next, we

Cash				101
1997				
March 1		1	10,000	

Exhibit 2-5: Item posted to ledger account.

turn to the ledger and look up the Cash account, which is account number 101, and transfer this item from the journal to the Cash ledger account, as illustrated in Exhibit 2-5 above.

The entry to Cash was a debit entry in the journal so we post this item to the debit side of the ledger account. At the top of the date column we write in the year and in the line below we write in the date, March 1. Next we write $10,000 in the debit money column. Then we show that this amount was transferred, or *posted,* from page one of the journal by entering the figure "1" in the reference column. If, at some later date, we want more information on this particular transaction recorded in the ledger we can trace this item back to page one of the journal.

Nothing is entered into the explanation column of the ledger. It is left blank and only used in certain instances as will be explained later on. When posting to the ledger is completed, we go back to page one of the journal and enter in the reference column, the account number of the account in the ledger, to which the item has been posted. In this case it was account number 101. Our entry in the journal now appears as shown in Exhibit 2-6.

	Journal			Page 1
1997				
March 1	Cash	101	10,000	
	Jack Fraser, Capital			10,000
	Owner invested cash in the business.			

Exhibit 2-6: Journal entry after Cash ledger has been posted.

Now that the first item in our journal entry (see Exhibit 2-6) has been posted to the ledger we must post the remaining item to the ledger. Therefore, we post the credit item from the journal to the credit side of the ledger account, Jack Fraser, Capital (account number 343) as shown in Exhibit 2-7.

Jack Fraser, Capital					343
	1997				
	March	1		1	10,000

Exhibit 2-7: Item posted to ledger account.

The posting of this credit item follows a process similar to that of posting the debit item to the Cash account, except of course, this time the posting is to the credit side of account number 343, Jack Fraser, Capital. Always ensure that the posting is to the proper side of the account. Debit items in the journal are posted to the debit side of ledger accounts and credit items in the journal are posted to the credit side of ledger accounts. Our latest item was posted from page one of the journal and this is noted with a "1" in the reference column in the ledger account. Now we go back to page one of the journal and write "343" in the reference column in the journal. This indicates that the item has been posted to account number 343 in the ledger.

When posting always enter account numbers in the reference column of the journal and page numbers in the reference column of ledger accounts. Never use a tick mark (✓) to indicate the posting of an entry. For one thing, tick marks do not allow us to trace entries, which creates a problem if an error in posting has been made. Besides, the tick mark is used for a specific purpose in the ledger as we shall see later on. And, as all entries in the ledger must originate from postings from the journal, the page number in the reference column of a particular ledger account serves to prove that the entry originated from the journal.

Although we made entries directly to ledger accounts, for purposes of illustration in Chapter One, in practice it is never done this way. All transactions must be analyzed and entered into the journal first, and then at some convenient point in time, these entries are transferred to the ledger. After posting to the ledger, the March 1st journal entry for Pacific Printers Mart appears as shown in Exhibit 2-8.

Journal **Page 1**

1997					
March	1	Cash	101	10,000	
		Jack Fraser, Capital	343		10,000
		Owner invested cash in the business.			

Exhibit 2-8: Journal entry after posting is complete.

POST WHEN CONVENIENT

Posting may be done at any convenient time after transactions have been recorded in the journal. Entries are not usually posted at the time they are first made in the journal, but rather are posted at some later point in time when sufficient entries have accumulated to make the procedure worthwhile. You might post the entries in your spare time, and if you happen to be interrupted by the telephone, or by a customer, etc., you need not be concerned. The cross-reference system employed in posting was designed to eliminate omitting a posting or posting the same item twice. You can begin posting on one day and carry on where you left off at a later date without difficulty because of the cross-reference system. After all entries for the month of March have been posted the journal appears as shown in Exhibit 2-9.

Exhibit 2-9: Journal for the month of March after posting is completed.

Journal **Page 1**

1997					
March	1	Cash	101	10,000	
		Jack Fraser, Capital	343		10,000
		Owner invested cash in the business.			
	5	Automobile	116	7,700	
		Cash	101		7,700
		Bought a truck from Surrey Motors.			
	11	Office Equipment	112	1,800	
		Accounts Payable	230		1,800
		Bought a photocopier and a typewriter from Dandy Discounts Inc.			
	15	Furniture and Fixtures	114	2,400	
		Cash	101		500
		Accounts Payable	230		1,900
		Bought desks and chairs from Superior Office Products Inc.			
	20	Accounts Receivable	103	500	
		Automobile	116		500
		Sold the canopy from the truck to Don Robson.			
	31	Cash	101	250	
		Accounts Receivable	103		250
		Received the first payment from Don Robson.			

March	31	Accounts Payable	230	500	
		Cash	101		500
		Remitted payment to Superior Office Products Inc.			

CHECK THE JOURNAL ENTRIES

When posting is complete, quickly peruse the journal to ensure that no items have been omitted. Be especially careful with compound entries such as that for March 15th. As most entries stand out as pairs of items, it is helpful to mentally compare the debit and credit items. If the sum of debit items does not equal the sum of credit items for a particular transaction this means that the analysis is incomplete or incorrect. In this case be on the alert for the possibility that an item from a compound entry might have been left out.

Again, if the sum of debit items does not equal the sum of credit items for a particular transaction it means that an error has been made and the balance sheet will not balance as a result. A businessman who operated a butcher shop hired a bookkeeper, based on the recommendations of a friend, who assured him that this particular bookkeeper would do the job cheaply, at only $12 per hour. To hire an accountant to prepare his financial statements would have cost him a flat rate of $600 at that time. As it happened, this bookkeeper easily prepared the financial statements in one day, except for one little problem. The balance sheet did not balance and the totals on each side differed by 26 dollars. The businessman felt relieved to have gotten the job done so cheaply and was pleased to find that the discrepancy was only twenty-six dollars. After all, thousands of transactions took place over the past year. He was certain that this minor error would easily be rectified within an hour. When the source of error was not tracked down within the time expected the businessman simply pulled out his wallet and produced $26 indicating that he would take care of the "missing money" out of his own pocket and that way the accounts would balance. But the bookkeeper correctly pointed out that money is not necessarily missing and that you cannot make the books balance by giving the firm an amount of cash equal to the amount of the error and that the source of the error must be located and the error corrected. In fact, if the owner of the business was to provide the firm with $26 in cash a debit to the cash account would be exactly offset by a corresponding credit to owner's equity and the error would remain the same—the balance sheet totals would still differ by a factor of twenty-six dollars. Two days later, still receiving his twelve dollars per hour salary, the bookkeeper had not yet located the error. This would not have happened if the bookkeeper had done the accounting in the manner that we are learning to do accounting. It is apparent that he possessed less than a complete knowledge of the accounting cycle. In our system, if the debit equals the credit for each transaction, the balance sheet must balance.

Errors should not be a major problem in accounting. If an error has occurred, check the journal entries carefully to see that they have been analyzed correctly. Ensure that the debits equal the credits, then check to see that all items in every entry have been posted and that they have been posted to the correct side of each ledger account.

Check to ensure that the same figures have been posted to the ledger as were entered in the journal. With simple round numbers this type of mistake will not occur frequently but with a figure such as $4,513.87 it can easily happen. Sometimes a transposition of digits occurs. Instead of posting $4,513.87 we post $4,153.87 and, of course, difficulty arises because the balance sheet refuses to balance even though at first glance all entries appear to be correct. But a careful examination will reveal the source of the error.

Placement of the decimal point can be a source of error. Say, for example, that most of the figures you are dealing with at the moment are two digit dollar figures, such as $35.14, $18.96, etc. If this sequence of two digit dollar figures is interrupted by a four digit dollar figure, especially one that has zeros in it, a decimal error may occur. What do you repeat in the back of your mind when you are posting $17.00 from the journal to a ledger account? Probably something like "seventeen oh-oh". Now you arrive at the figure $1,700 in the journal which you are about to post to the ledger. In the back of your mind do you still say "seventeen oh-oh"? What about when you are exhausted or when your mind is absorbed with other business problems at the same time? Do not be surprised if the $1,700 posted from the journal ends up as $17.00 in the ledger. This sort of error is more likely to occur if two persons are doing the posting with one person reading entries from the journal while the other person enters them into ledger accounts.

Finally, look out for errors in arithmetic. Nowadays, with electronic calculators available cheaply, errors in arithmetic should not be a major problem but can still occur if figures are entered carelessly into the calculator. The best way to ensure against the possibility of errors is to work carefully to begin with.

LEDGER AFTER POSTING

After the posting process has been completed for the month of March, the ledger appears as shown in Exhibit 2-10. If all of our transactions have been analyzed correctly and if no errors have been made in posting then the balance sheet produced from the balances in the ledger accounts will balance.

Exhibit 2-10: Ledger after posting.

Cash — 101

1997				1997			
March	1	1	10,000	March	5	1	7,700
	31	1	250		15	1	500
					31	1	500

Accounts Receivable — 103

1997				1997			
March	20	1	500	March	31	1	250

Office Equipment — 112

1997							
March	11	1	1,800				

Furniture and Fixtures — 114

1997							
March	15	1	2,400				

Automobile — 116

1997				1997			
March	5	1	7,700	March	20	1	500

Accounts Payable — 230

1997				1997			
March	31	1	500	March	11	1	1,800
					15	1	1,900

Jack Fraser, Capital — 343

				1997			
				March	1	1	10,000

THE TRIAL BALANCE

If we wish, we may prepare a formal balance sheet directly from the net balances in the ledger accounts. However, as discussed previously, it is a good idea to prepare a trial balance to ensure that all of the accounts are in balance. This was done, before posting, but to maintain proper sequence, is repeated here. A trial balance, of course, cannot be prepared until all of the entries have been posted from the journal to the ledger. The trial balance at the end of March is illustrated in Exhibit 2-11.

To prepare a trial balance we simply list the net balance of each ledger account in the appropriate debit or credit column as illustrated in Exhibit 2-11. Both sides balance at $13,200 so we know that our accounting is correct. We can now prepare a formal balance sheet from our trial balance.

Pacific Printers Mart
Trial Balance
March 31, 1997

Cash	$ 1,550	
Accounts Receivable	250	
Office Equipment	1,800	
Furniture and Fixtures	2,400	
Automobile	7,200	
Accounts Payable		$ 3,200
Jack Fraser, Capital		10,000
	$13,200	$13,200

Exhibit 2-11: Trial balance at the end of March.

THE BALANCE SHEET

You might be wondering how a trial balance differs from a balance sheet, other than the fact that a trial balance is not a formal financial statement, but is simply produced on scratch paper to prove that the sum of the debit balances equals the sum of the credit balances. The trial balance in Exhibit 2-11 contains only balance sheet accounts, so, except for format, it resembles a balance sheet. Later on, our ledger and hence our trial balance, will contain both balance sheet and income statement

Pacific Printers Mart
Balance Sheet
March 31, 1997

Assets:		*Liabilities and Owner's Equity*	
Cash	$ 1,550	*Liabilities:*	
Accounts Receivable	250	Accounts Payable	$ 3,200
Office Equipment	1,800		
Furniture and Fixtures	2,400	*Owner's Equity:*	
Automobile	7,200	Jack Fraser, Capital	10,000
	$13,200		$13,200

Exhibit 2-12: Balance sheet at the end of March.

accounts. At that time, our trial balance will cease to resemble a balance sheet. A balance sheet for Pacific Printers Mart, prepared from the data in the trial balance, is illustrated in Exhibit 2-12. We end up with the same balance sheet as we produced earlier (see Exhibit 1-18).

THE INCOME STATEMENT

With only a balance sheet to describe a business we do not have a complete picture of the financial affairs of the business. From the information on the balance sheet we know what assets the business owns and we also know what amount of capital was supplied by creditors and what amount of capital was supplied by the owner to acquire the assets that a business owns. A balance sheet gives us the financial position of a business at a given point in time, which is at the end of the last day of a particular accounting period. This may be the end of a month, end of a calendar year, or end of a consecutive twelve month period, called a fiscal year. It is possible, by studying a series of balance sheets for consecutive periods, to see how the financial position of the business has changed over time. In particular, by studying the changes in owner's equity we can determine whether a business has grown from profitable operations or whether the business has shrunk from losses. But, by analyzing the financial situation this way we have no details with which to manage and control the direction of growth and profitability of the business. To manage a business we need specific operating results and not just the end product. It does not help us much in our decision making to know that owner's equity increased $30,000 last year. We need details of how much money was spent on salaries, advertising, etc., to achieve a certain volume of sales, and have to be able to relate these expenditures to end results and objectives. The income statement provides us with the data required to perform such analysis. An income statement is sometimes called a statement of profit and loss.

Whereas one of the things that a balance sheet reveals to us is what assets the business owns at a particular point in time, an income statement reveals how much the business has earned or lost over a certain period of time. From the balance sheet, for example, we know what assets a business owns, etc., on December 31st and from the data on the income statement we know how much money the business has earned from January 1st of the year in question to December 31st of that same year. Earnings only make sense if they relate to a period of time. As an employee, for example, you might earn so much per hour, so much per week, so much per month, or so much per year. So to properly describe a business you must provide details on what it owns, what it owes, and how much it earns. An example of an income statement is presented in Exhibit 2-13.

ELEMENTS OF AN INCOME STATEMENT

Like the balance sheet, an income statement must be presented in formal format. Its main elements consist of a heading and body. The heading includes the title *Income Statement* and the period of time to which it applies, *For the month ending April 30, 1997.* The body contains a detailed list of revenue earned and expenses incurred during the month of April. All revenue earned during April must be recorded and included in the income statement for the month of April. Similarly with expenses. All expenses

Pacific Printers Mart
Income Statement
For the month ending April 30, 1997

Revenue:		
Commissions		$6,400
Expenses:		
Rent Expense	$400	
Telephone Expense	35	
Utilities Expense	70	
Office Supplies Expense	30	
Advertising Expense	250	
Salaries Expense	600	1,385
Net Income:		$5,015

Exhibit 2-13: An example of an income statement.

incurred during the month of April must be recorded and included in the income statement for April. And so on, for all other accounting periods. An income statement is simply a detailed expression of the following equation:

Net Income = Revenue - Expenses

REVENUE

Revenue is a measure of earnings. Revenue is not a measure of all money flowing into a business. Money may flow into a business for a variety of reasons, such as when the owner invests cash in the business, when the business borrows money from a bank, or when the business disposes of a redundant asset for cash. None of these transactions are examples of revenue.

Revenue consists of earnings. Examples include sales of merchandise purchased for resale by a store, fees earned by an attorney, and commissions earned by a real estate sales agent. Sometimes cash is received immediately. At other times, a sale is made on credit or a service is performed on credit, and we end up with an account receivable. Either way, whether we receive payment immediately or not, revenue has been earned. We record revenue when it is earned and not at some date in the future when an account receivable is collected, for example. Whenever revenue is earned, it results in an increase in assets, normally cash or accounts receivable. There is no reason, however, as to why a firm cannot receive other assets, besides cash or accounts receivable, as payment for goods sold or services performed. If the business agrees to accept $100 worth of goods in exchange for $100 worth of goods sold or services performed, that is fine. That barter, nevertheless, results in revenue earned according to the principle that we have just learned and taxation rules have moved in this direction in recent years to affirm this very principle.

Revenue accrues from the operations of a business and always results in an increase in assets, which is almost always in the form of cash or accounts receivable. But every increase in cash, as already mentioned, or accounts receivable, cannot be attributed to the earning of revenue. In addition to the list of items that result in cash flowing into a business, but which are not revenue, we may include collecting an account receivable. An account receivable may result from a sale made on credit as well as from other sources. If merchandise purchased for resale is later sold on credit, we record the sale, that is revenue, at the time the sale is made. We do not count revenue again when the account receivable is collected and cash is received. One of the reasons why everyone in business needs to have a knowledge of accounting is to gain a proper understanding of the distinction between revenue, cash, accounts receivable, etc. Every transaction is measured in terms of money. But, simply expressing something in terms of money does not mean cash. Cash, itself, is an asset. Revenue is recorded in terms of money, but does not necessarily result in cash, at least not right away.

In order to formulate a proper definition of revenue we can do so by considering the impact a transaction has on owner's equity. Recall that owner's equity arises from only two sources, investment by the owner and earnings—profitable operation—of the business. When merchandise, for example, is marked-up in price and sold at a profit, an increase in owner's equity results, and revenue is earned. Revenue is a transaction undertaken expressly for the purpose of earning a profit, such as when a sale is made or service is performed, resulting in an increase in owner's equity. *Revenue consists of earnings and increases owner's equity.* Examples of specific revenue accounts include Commissions, Fees, and Sales.

EXPENSES

Expenses are not the measure of all cash flowing out of a business. Cash may flow out of a business for various reasons, such as when the owner withdraws cash from the business, when the business makes payments on loans, when the business purchases an asset such as an automobile and pays for it in cash, and when the business makes payments to certain creditors. None of the preceding transactions are examples of expenses.

The only way we can simply define expenses is to say that expenses consist of expenses, and then give illustrative examples before arriving at a more profound definition. We cannot state that expenses consist of expenditures. We must record expenses in the period in which they were incurred whether an immediate expenditure was involved or not.

Examples of expenses include items such as the cost of telephone service, utilities, salaries, rent, advertising, insurance, interest, etc. Sometimes we pay for the goods or services that constitute an expense immediately. At other times, the bill will not be paid until a later date, in which case we end up with a liability, an account payable. Either way, whether we pay the bill immediately or not, an expense has been incurred. Some expenses—depreciation expense, for example—involve no expenditure at all. We record expenses in the period in which they are incurred and not at some later point in time, such as when a bill has been paid, for example. When an expense is incurred, it results in either a decrease in assets immediately (if the bill is paid immediately) such as a decrease in cash, or some other decrease in assets, for example, depreciation, as we will learn later. Alternatively, when an expense is incurred, it results in an increase in liabilities which in turn will result in a decrease in assets when the bill is finally paid. Bills are normally taken care of by paying cash. However, there is no reason why a creditor cannot take some other asset in payment, besides cash, for goods sold to the business or services performed for the business. If a creditor agrees to accept a machine worth $200 as payment for $200 worth of services performed for the business, that is fine. That exchange, nevertheless, results in an expense incurred and must be recorded as such. Failure to do so means that the accounting has not been done properly and the business loses a valuable income tax deduction that it is otherwise entitled to.

Expenses accrue from the operation of a business and always result in either an immediate decrease in assets; or in an increase in liabilities, which in turn leads to a decrease in assets when the bill is paid. Every decrease in assets, particularly cash, cannot be attributed to the incurring of an expense. If an expense is incurred and a corresponding liability, an account payable is recorded and the asset cash decreases when we eventually pay the bill. But we do not record an expense again when the bill is paid. If we did, we would be double-counting. Every transaction, and there are no exceptions, is measured in terms of money, but every expenditure of cash is not an expense. Although this may seem confusing at the moment, it will soon all be very clear. That is why accounting is a useful and powerful tool. It enables you to make order out of chaos and thus direct and control activities in a meaningful, purposeful manner so you can achieve your objectives of growth and profitability.

In order to arrive at a proper definition of expenses we can do so by considering the impact that a transaction has on owner's equity. Owner's equity decreases when an owner withdraws assets from the business or when the results of business operations have been unprofitable. If expenses exceed revenue, operations are unprofitable. It is the expense component then that leads to a decrease in owner's equity. Withdrawal of assets by the owner is not an expense, although this action results in a decrease in owner's equity. *Expenses are costs incurred when transactions are undertaken for the purpose of earning a profit,* such as rent and telephone service, *resulting in a decrease in owner's equity.*

RULES OF DEBIT AND CREDIT FOR REVENUE AND EXPENSE ACCOUNTS

From the previous discussion of the nature of income statement accounts, we are now in a position to formulate rules of debit and credit for revenue and expense accounts. Both revenue and expenses were defined in terms of their impact on owner's equity. Owner's equity is one of the components of a balance sheet. Other than from investment by the owner, owner's equity will only increase if revenue is earned. And, other than by withdrawal of assets by the owner, owner's equity will only decrease when expenses are incurred. And when operations are unprofitable, expenses exceed revenue and owner's equity decreases. But in analyzing transactions, we look at the financial event on a transaction basis and only consider the impact of the transaction under consideration to determine its impact on owner's equity. From our discussion, it follows that the rules of debit and credit for income statement accounts must be identical to the rules of debit and credit for owner's equity accounts.

REVENUE IS RECORDED BY CREDITS

EXPENSES ARE RECORDED BY DEBITS

Exhibit 2-14: Rules of debit and credit for income statement accounts.

Recall that increases in owner's equity are recorded by credits. *Revenue increases owner's equity and, therefore, is recorded by a credit.* Decreases in owner's equity are recorded by debits. *Expenses decrease owner's equity and are recorded by debits.* These rules of debit and credit for income statement accounts are summarized in Exhibit 2-14.

INCOME STATEMENT TRANSACTIONS

Let us now apply the rules of debit and credit for income statement accounts to the transactions of Pacific Printers Mart for the month of April. During the month of March all of the transactions in our example involved only balance sheet accounts. Now, commencing with the month of April, we encounter transactions involving income statement accounts as well. During April the following transactions occurred:

April	1	Placed an advertisement in the newspaper. It cost \$100 and was paid for immediately.
April	5	Sold a printing press for a client. A commission of \$1,200 was earned and payment was received the same day.
April	7	Purchased typing paper and other office supplies. Cost was \$30. Paid for at the time of purchase.
April	12	Sold a platemaker for a client. The client agreed to remit the commission, in the amount of \$700 at the end of May.
April	14	Placed another ad in the newspaper. It cost \$150 and was to be paid for by the end of May.
April	21	Sold three printing presses and a typesetting machine. Commissions totaling \$4,500 were received immediately.
April	30	Paid part-time secretary her salary amounting to \$600.
April	30	Paid office rent. Issued a check for \$400.
April	30	Received the telephone bill. Amount \$35. It is not due until the 7th of the following month.
April	30	Bill for electricity consumed during April was received. It amounted to \$70 and payment is due within ten days.

April	30	Jack Fraser withdrew $1,500 for his personal use.
April	30	Remitted payment of $1,800 to Dandy Discounts Inc. for office equipment purchased in March.
April	30	Received a check for $250 from Don Robson as the final installment on the canopy purchased in March.

FIVE KINDS OF ACCOUNTS

Before analyzing each of the transactions for April it is helpful to remind ourselves of the kinds of accounts that we must deal with. The balance sheet contains three kinds of accounts and the income statement contains two kinds of accounts. That is virtually all the kinds of accounts there are in accounting. Only five different kinds of accounts. They are presented in Exhibit 2-15.

As you have learned earlier, in analyzing any transaction, you must first identify the specific accounts involved and then apply the rules of debit and credit to each kind of account. You can easily recognize the kind of account you are dealing with after a little practice. For example, you should immediately recognize Cash as an asset account; Accounts Payable as a liability account, Commissions as a revenue account, and so on.

ANALYZING TRANSACTIONS FOR APRIL

Before making entries to the journal, we may analyze each of our transactions on scratch paper first. It is a good idea to proceed in this manner until you have formed a mental picture of the financial statements in the back of your mind. In time, you will be able to glance at a transaction and immediately realize its impact on the balance sheet and income statement. But in order to reach this stage you must train your mind to analyze transactions in a logical manner. Later on, after you have gained some experience, you may record entries directly in the journal, without resorting to the use of scratch paper on which to perform your analysis. The analysis for each of the transactions during April is presented on the following page:

Balance Sheet:	***ASSETS***
	LIABILITIES
	OWNER'S EQUITY
Income Statement:	***REVENUE***
	EXPENSES

Exhibit 2-15: There are virtually only five different kinds of accounts.

April 1:

First identify the specific accounts involved. These are *Advertising Expense* and *Cash.* Visualize where each of these accounts is located on the financial statements. Advertising Expense belongs to the expense section of the income statement and Cash belongs to the asset section of the balance sheet. Then apply the rules of debit and credit. Be aware of how the rules of debit and credit were formulated as you apply them. Dealing with the first part of the transaction, we would reason our analysis out to ourselves as follows: *An expense was incurred. Expenses (reduce owner's equity and) are recorded by debits. So we debit Advertising Expense $100.* Then we deal with the remainder of the transaction. *Cash is an asset. Decreases in assets are recorded by credits, so we credit the Cash account $100.* Rather than write all of that analysis out on paper, you will probably find it more convenient to quickly draw two simple ledger accounts on scratch paper and, as you go through the analysis in the back of your mind, make entries to the ledger accounts (drawn on scratch paper) as shown below:

Advertising Expense

100	

Cash

	100

Be certain to go through the complete analysis for every transaction in the back of your mind, even though you make entries to simple ledger accounts as shown above. In other words when you apply the rules of debit and credit to income statement accounts, for example, realize what impact revenue and expenses have on owner's equity, which is part of the balance sheet. Let us continue our analysis for the remainder of April. You may wish to round out the analysis for the remaining transactions by drawing simple ledger accounts on scratch paper and by entering entries in them. This will give you an opportunity to compare debit and credit entries to ensure that they are equal and offset each other.

April 5:

The two accounts are Commissions and Cash. Commissions is a revenue account and belongs to the income statement; Cash is an asset account and belongs to the balance sheet. Revenue (increases owner's equity and) is recorded by a credit, so we credit Commissions $1,200. Increases to assets are recorded by debits, so we debit Cash $1,200.

April 7:

The accounts involved are Office Supplies Expense and Cash. Office Supplies Expense belongs to the income statement; Cash is an asset and belongs to the balance sheet. Expenses (reduce owner's equity and) are recorded by debits, so we debit Office Supplies Expense $30. Decreases in assets are recorded by credits so we credit Cash $30.

April 12:

First we identify the accounts that comprise this transaction. They are Commissions and Accounts Receivable. Commissions is a revenue account located on the income statement; Accounts Receivable is an asset account located on the balance sheet. Revenue (increases owner's equity and) is recorded by a credit, so we credit Commissions $700. An increase to an asset account is recorded by a debit, so we debit Accounts Receivable $700. Frequently we find it more convenient to analyze the credit entry item of the transaction before the debit item. Even so, when the transaction is entered into the journal, always record the debit item in the transaction before the credit item.

April 14:

The accounts involved are Advertising Expense and Accounts Payable. By this time we realize as soon as we identify the account that Advertising Expense belongs to the expense section of the income statement. Accounts Payable is a liability account and belongs to the balance sheet. Expenses (decrease owner's equity and) are recorded by debits, so we debit Advertising Expense $150. Increases in liabilities are recorded by credits (liabilities are on the right-hand side of the balance sheet) so we credit Accounts Payable $150.

April 21:

The accounts in this transaction are Commissions, a revenue account, and Cash, an asset account. Revenue (increases owner's equity and) is recorded by a credit, so we credit Commissions $4,500. Increases in assets are recorded by debits, so we debit Cash $4,500.

April 30:

Paid the part-time secretary her salary. The accounts in this transaction are Salaries Expense and Cash. Expenses (located on the income statement) cause a reduction in owner's equity (located on the right-hand side of the balance sheet) and are recorded by debits. So we debit Salaries Expense $600. Cash is an asset (located on the left-hand side of the balance sheet). Decreases in assets are recorded by credits, so we credit Cash $600.

April 30:

Paid office rent. The accounts in this transaction are Rent Expense and Cash. Expenses are recorded by debits, so we debit Rent Expense $400. Reductions in assets are recorded by credits so we credit Cash $400.

April 30:

Received the telephone bill. First we must identify the specific accounts involved. They are Telephone Expense and Accounts Payable. As we know, expenses are recorded by debits, so we debit Telephone Expense $35. Liabilities are located on the right-hand side of the balance sheet. Increases in liabilities are recorded by credits, so we credit Accounts Payable $35.

April 30:

Received the bill for electricity. The accounts involved in this transaction are Utilities Expense and Accounts Payable. Expenses are recorded by debits, so we debit Utilities Expense $70. Accounts Payable is a liability account (located on the right-hand side of the balance sheet). Increases in liabilities are recorded by credits, so we credit Accounts Payable $70.

April 30:

Jack Fraser withdrew $1,500 from the business for his personal use. We must be careful in identifying the accounts this time. When the owner withdraws money from the business this is not an expense; it is a withdrawal of capital. One of the accounts involved is Cash. The other account is obviously an owner's equity account. So far, we are only aware of one owner's equity account which is Jack Fraser, Capital. Decreases in owner's equity are recorded by debits, so we could logically debit Jack Fraser, Capital $1,500. But if we do it this way we will not be able to distinguish this debit representing a withdrawal of capital by the owner from other debits to Jack Fraser, Capital which do not represent withdrawals of capital by the owner. To eliminate this difficulty we open a new account to represent withdrawals by the owner, which is titled *Jack Fraser, Drawings.* Decreases in owner's equity are recorded by debits so we debit Jack Fraser, Drawings $1,500. Decreases in assets are recorded by credits, so we credit Cash $1,500.

April 30:

Remitted payment of $1,800 to Dandy Discounts Inc. The two accounts involved are Cash and Accounts Payable. Decreases in assets are recorded by credits, so we credit Cash $1,800. Decreases in liabilities are recorded by debits, so we debit Accounts Payable $1,800.

April 30:

Received a check for $250 from Don Robson. The accounts in this transaction are Cash and Accounts Receivable. Increases in assets (located on the left-hand side of the balance sheet) are recorded by debits, so we debit Cash $250. Decreases in assets are recorded by credits, so we credit Accounts Receivable $250.

Analysis of every transaction, with the aid of a pad of scratch paper on which to work out the analysis to begin with and mental analysis later on, precedes entry to the journal. This analysis should be carried out in a logical sequence. Identify the accounts involved in the transaction, first of all. Decide what category of account each specific account belongs to, that is, assets, liabilities, owner's equity, revenue, or expenses. Then apply the rules of debit and credit to each account. All of the debit items for a given transaction must be entered before any of the credit items are entered for that transaction.

LEDGER ACCOUNT NUMBERS

A complete *small business ledger accounts index* is presented in the appendix of this book. That index, however, includes a large number of accounts and may prove to be confusing at the moment. So for our present purposes a simplified list of accounts is presented in Exhibit 2-16.

Exhibit 2-16: Small business ledger accounts index.

Assets:

101 Cash
103 Accounts Receivable
112 Office Equipment
114 Furniture and Fixtures
116 Automobile
118 Shop Equipment
120 Leasehold Improvements
122 Building
124 Land
125 Patents

Liabilities:

230 Accounts Payable
231 Salaries Payable
240 Notes Payable

Owner's Equity:

343 Jack Fraser, Capital
344 Jack Fraser, Drawings

Revenue:

455	Commissions
456	Fees

Expenses:

567	Rent Expense
568	Telephone Expense
569	Utilities Expense
572	Office Supplies Expense
573	Shop Supplies Expense
574	Advertising and Promotion Expense
584	Salaries Expense

Each of the transactions for the month of April has been recorded in the journal, as illustrated in Exhibit 2-17 and posted to the ledger, as illustrated in Exhibit 2-18.

Exhibit 2-17: Journal entries for April.

Journal **Page 2**

1997				
April	1	Advertising and Promotion Expense	100	
		Cash		100
		Placed an ad in the newspaper.		
	5	Cash	1,200	
		Commissions		1,200
		Earned a commission on the sale of a printing press.		
	7	Office Supplies Expense	30	
		Cash		30
		Purchased typing paper, etc.		
	12	Accounts Receivable	700	
		Commissions		700
		Earned a commission on the sale of a platemaker for a client.		

April	14	Advertising and Promotion Expense	150	
		Accounts Payable		150
		Placed an ad in the newspaper.		
	21	Cash	4,500	
		Commissions		4,500
		Earned commissions on the sale of four machines.		
	30	Salaries Expense	600	
		Cash		600
		Paid secretary her salary.		
	30	Rent Expense	400	
		Cash		400
		Paid rent for April.		
	30	Telephone Expense	35	
		Accounts Payable		35
		Received telephone bill for April.		
	30	Utilities Expense	70	
		Accounts Payable		70
		Received bill for electricity.		
	30	Jack Fraser, Drawings	1,500	
		Cash		1,500
		Withdrew cash for personal use.		
	30	Accounts Payable	1,800	
		Cash		1,800
		Remitted payment to Dandy Discounts Inc.		
	30	Cash	250	
		Accounts Receivable		250
		Received final payment from Don Robson.		

LEDGER AFTER POSTING

After the entries from the journal for the month of April have been posted to the ledger, the ledger appears as shown in Exhibit 2-18. Notice that the ledger accounts include entries for March, which were posted in the previous month, as well as the entries for the current month, April, which we have just finished posting. That, of course, is the purpose of the ledger. It accumulates data for each kind of transaction.

Exhibit 2-18: Ledger at the end of April.

Cash 101

Date		Balance	Ref.	Debit	Date		Balance	Ref.	Credit
1997					1997				
March	1		1	10,000	March	5		1	7,700
	31		1	250		15		1	500
April	*5*		*2*	*1,200*		31		1	500
	21		*2*	*4,500*	*April*	*1*		*2*	*100*
	30	*16,200*	*2*	*250*		*7*		*2*	*30*
						30		*2*	*600*
						30		*2*	*400*
						30		*2*	*1,500*
						30	*13,130*	*2*	*1,800*

Accounts Receivable 103

Date		Balance	Ref.	Debit	Date		Balance	Ref.	Credit
1997					1997				
March	20		1	500	March	31		1	250
April	*12*	*1,200*	*2*	*700*	*April*	*30*	*500*	*2*	*250*

Office Equipment 112

Date		Ref.	Debit	Date		Ref.	Credit
1997							
March	11	1	1,800				

Furniture and Fixtures 114

Date		Ref.	Debit	Date		Ref.	Credit
1997							
March	15	1	2,400				

Automobile 116

Date		Ref.	Debit	Date		Ref.	Credit
1997				1997			
March	5	1	7,700	March	20	1	500

Accounts Payable 230

1997					1997				
March	31		1	500	March	11		1	1,800
April	*30*	*2,300*	*2*	*1,800*		15		1	1,900
					April	*14*		*2*	*150*
						30		*2*	*35*
						30	3,955	*2*	*70*

Jack Fraser, Capital 343

				1997			
				March	1	1	10,000

Jack Fraser, Drawings 344

1997							
April	*30*	*2*	*1,500*				

Commissions 455

				1997			
				April	*5*	*2*	*1,200*
					12	*2*	*700*
					21	*2*	*4,500*

Rent Expense 567

1997							
April	*30*	*2*	*400*				

Telephone Expense 568

1997							
April	*30*	*2*	*35*				

Utilities Expense 569

1997							
April	*30*	*2*	*70*				

Office Supplies Expense 572

1997							
April	*7*	*2*	*30*				

Advertising and Promotion Expense				574
1997				
April	*1*	*2*	*100*	
	14	*2*	*160*	

Salaries Expense				584
1997				
April	*30*	*2*	*600*	

JOURNAL AFTER POSTING

After all of the entries in the journal, for the month of April, have been posted to the ledger, the journal appears as illustrated in Exhibit 2-19. The journal in our illustration is identical to the journal in Exhibit 2-17 except that it now contains the account number of each ledger to which each item has been posted.

Exhibit 2-19: Journal entries for April, after posting.

Journal **Page 2**

1997					
April	1	Advertising and Promotion Expense	574	100	
		Cash	101		100
		Placed an ad in the newspaper.			
	5	Cash	101	1,200	
		Commissions	455		1,200
		Earned a commission on the sale of a printing press.			
	7	Office Supplies Expense	572	30	
		Cash	101		30
		Purchased typing paper, etc.			
	12	Accounts Receivable	103	700	
		Commissions	455		700
		Earned a commission on the sale of a platemaker for a client.			

April	14	Advertising and Promotion Expense	574	150	
		Accounts Payable	230		150
		Placed an ad in the newspaper.			
	21	Cash	101	4,500	
		Commissions	455		4,500
		Earned commissions on the sale of four machines.			
	30	Salaries Expense	584	600	
		Cash	101		600
		Paid secretary her salary.			
	30	Rent Expense	567	400	
		Cash	101		400
		Paid rent for April.			
	30	Telephone Expense	568	35	
		Accounts Payable	230		35
		Received telephone bill for April.			
	30	Utilities Expense	569	70	
		Accounts Payable	230		70
		Received bill for electricity.			
	30	Jack Fraser, Drawings	344	1,500	
		Cash	101		1,500
		Withdrew cash for personal use.			
	30	Accounts Payable	230	1,800	
		Cash	101		1,800
		Remitted payment to Dandy Discounts Inc.			
	30	Cash	101	250	
		Accounts Receivable	103		250
		Received final payment from Don Robson.			

TRIAL BALANCE AT THE END OF APRIL

A trial balance at the end of April is produced by simply copying the ledger account balances (Exhibit 2-18) into a two column schedule as shown in Exhibit 2-20.

Pacific Printers Mart
Trial Balance
April 30, 1997

Cash	$3,070	
Accounts Receivable	700	
Office Equipment	1,800	
Furniture and Fixtures	2,400	
Automobile	7,200	
Accounts Payable		$1,655
Jack Fraser, Capital		10,000
Jack Fraser, Drawings	1,500	
Commissions		6,400
Rent Expense	400	
Telephone Expense	35	
Utilities Expense	70	
Office Supplies Expense	30	
Advertising and Promotion Expense	250	
Salaries Expense	600	
	$18,055	$18,055

Exhibit 2-20: Trial balance at the end of April.

FINANCIAL STATEMENTS

Our trial balance, Exhibit 2-20, balances, which means that we have not made any errors. By now, quite a few accounts are involved and the trial balance no longer resembles a balance sheet. This time both balance sheet and income statement accounts are included in our trial balance. This is so because a trial balance is simply a list of all of the accounts in the ledger which have a balance, together with the balance of each account. We can easily prepare financial statements from the data in the trial balance, confident that these statements will be correct. The balance sheet will balance and the income statement will tie in with the owner's equity section of the balance sheet.

INCOME STATEMENT

The income statement for the month of April, Exhibit 2-21, reveals that a net income of $5,015 was earned during April. There was no income for the month of March because the business did not actually become operational until April. Remember, none of the transactions during March involved income statement accounts.

Pacific Printers Mart		
Income Statement		
For the month ending April 30, 1997		
Revenue:		
Commissions		$6,400
Expenses:		
Rent Expense	$400	
Telephone Expense	35	
Utilities Expense	70	
Office Supplies Expense	30	
Advertising and Promotion Expense	250	
Salaries Expense	600	1,385
Net Income:		$5,015

Exhibit 2-21: Income statement for April.

BALANCE SHEET

We must always prepare an income statement before we can prepare a balance sheet. This is because the amount of net income, obtained from the income statement, must be included in the owner's equity section of the balance sheet. This component of owner's equity arising from profitable operation of the business is added to the balance in the owner's equity account.

If the business has experienced an operating loss, the amount of the loss is subtracted from the balance in the owner's equity account. Also, any withdrawals of capital by the owner must be subtracted from the balance in the owner's equity account. The new balance in the owner's equity account of Pacific Printers Mart can be computed as follows:

Owner's equity at the beginning of April	$10,000
Add: Net Income for April	5,015
	$15,015
Subtract: Drawings during April	1,500
Owner's Equity at the end of April	$13,515

That is how the resulting net balance in owner's equity is computed at the end of the month by using logic and simple arithmetic. However, we cannot simply add the amount of net increase to the owner's equity account *Jack Fraser, Capital* because all entries in the ledger must be posted from entries in the journal. In the next chapter we will learn how to make these entries which will result in our automatically arriving at the correct net balance in the owner's equity account. In the meantime, a balance sheet may be produced, with the aid of our arithmetic computation to arrive at the proper amount of owner's equity, as illustrated in Exhibit 2-22.

Pacific Printers Mart
Balance Sheet
April 30, 1997

Assets:		*Liabilities and Owner's Equity*		
Cash	$3,070	*Liabilities:*		
Accounts Receivable	700	Accounts Payable		$1,655
Office Equipment	1,800	*Owner's Equity:*		
Furniture and Fixtures	2,400	J.F., Capital, April 1st		10,000
Automobile	7,200	Net Income	$5,015	
		Less: Drawings	1,500	3,515
	$15,170			$15,170

Exhibit 2-22: Balance sheet at the end of April.

SUMMARY

In this chapter we learned how to make entries to the journal and we posted these entries to the ledger to produce a set of financial statements—the balance sheet and income statement. We assigned account numbers to individual ledger accounts and made up a list of accounts to form a ledger index. And, at this stage; we now know the rules of debit and credit for all five types of accounts. We learned how to prepare an income statement and saw how the income statement ties into the balance sheet through the owner's equity section. Although it may appear that with the increasing number of accounts employed, accounting is quite complicated, we will see, in the chapters ahead, that with the use of a few more tools the process is really quite simple.

Exercises

1. How many columns does a page in a journal contain? State the purpose of each column.
2. What advantages are there to using a journal in accounting?
3. Explain what is meant by *posting.*
4. Is it necessary to post entries to ledger accounts immediately after entry to the journal? Explain.
5. Describe a quick way of checking journal entries to ensure that they appear to be correct.
6. What factor determines whether or not an account is listed in the trial balance?
7. What is the purpose of an income statement?
8. Name the two categories of accounts found on an income statement.
9. State the income statement equation.
10. What is revenue? Elaborate on the definition of revenue and give examples.
11. What are expenses? Elaborate and give examples.
12. Formulate the rules of debit and credit for revenue and expense accounts by considering the impact of revenue and expenses on owner's equity.
13. List the five different kinds of accounts. Indicate which of the financial statements each kind of account belongs to.
14. List and describe a logical sequence of steps that one may employ in analyzing a transaction.
15. Explain how the end result of operations, as determined in the income statement, ties into the balance sheet.
16. The owner of a small business withdraws $1,000 for her own use. Is this transaction an expense? Explain. This owner also withdraws $500 worth of office equipment from the business for her personal use. How do we account for this transaction? Explain.
17. A retailer of office equipment takes a computer from a customer in exchange for a collator. No further payment is involved. Did a transaction take place? Explain.

Problems

1. For the transactions listed below for Image Maker Beauty Salon:

   a. Make entries into the journal.
   b. Post entries to ledger accounts. Use the account numbers given in this book in numbering the accounts.
   c. Prepare a trial balance at the end of the month.
   d. Prepare a balance sheet.

July 1 John Brite deposits $100,000 in a bank account in the name of the business, Image Maker Beauty Salon.
5 Purchases a lot for $50,000. A down payment of $15,000 was made leaving the balance to be paid in equal monthly installments of $1,000 each, beginning with the month of August.
7 A suitable building was purchased for $20,000 and paid for in cash. The price included installing the building on the site.
12 Shop equipment, costing $8,000 was purchased and paid for in cash.
14 Office furniture costing $3,000 was purchased from ABC Suppliers Inc. Payment is to be made at the end of the month.
15 Easy chairs were purchased for $10,000. A down payment of $2,000 was made with the balance to be paid in equal monthly installments of $500 each beginning with the end of this month.
19 Additional shop equipment was purchased at a cost of $1,100 and paid for in cash.
22 Disposed of two easy chairs for $800. This was the same amount as Image Maker Beauty Salon had paid for them. Payment would be received at the end of August.
23 Hired a receptionist at a salary of $2,000 per month. She was to begin work on August 1st.
31 Remitted payment to ABC Suppliers Inc.
31 Remitted first installment payment in the amount of $500 for easy chairs purchased earlier.
31 John Brite withdrew $2,000 for his personal use.

2. For the transactions listed below for Fast Furniture Repair Service:

a. Journalize the transactions.
b. Post the entries to ledger accounts.
c. Prepare a trial balance.
d. Prepare a balance sheet.

May 1 Deposited $50,000 in a bank account in the name of the business. Proprietor, Mr. Dave Hardy.
3 Bought land with building. Land cost $50,000; building cost $10,000. A down payment of $15,000 was made with the balance to be paid in equal monthly installments of $800 per month, beginning with the end of this month. A note was signed for the unpaid balance.
12 Purchased office furniture from ACME Supply Company Inc. This furniture cost $1,600 and is to be paid for in four equal monthly installments. The first payment is to be made at the end of May.
14 Purchased a typewriter for $500. It was paid for in full at the time of purchase.

May 15 Shop equipment was acquired from Western Suppliers Inc. at a cost of $20,000. This equipment was paid for in full at the time of purchase.

19 A prefabricated building was purchased at a cost of $8,000 including delivery to the site. A down payment of $3,000 was made, with the balance to be paid in equal monthly installments of $1,000 each, beginning with the month of June.

20 Bought two office desks for $200 each, on credit. Payment to be made at the end of June.

25 Acquired shop equipment costing $2,000 with a down payment of $500. The balance is to be paid in three equal monthly installments of $500 each, beginning with the end of June.

31 The first installment payment was made on the land purchased at the beginning of the month.

3. Write out an analysis of each transaction given below and prepare appropriate journal entries.

March 1 Peter Brush opened a bank account in the name of the business, Qwik-Spray Student Painters, depositing $2,000 cash.

3 Deposited an additional $500 in the business bank account in an effort to increase his equity in the business.

5 Purchased a second-hand truck for $600 paying cash.

7 Bought insurance for the truck. Automobile insurance cost $40 per month and was paid for immediately.

9 Subscribed for telephone service. A contract was signed and the telephone was installed that very day.

11 Placed an advertisement in the classified section of the daily newspaper. This advertisement cost $25 and was paid for in cash.

12 Purchased aluminum ladders costing $300 in total. Paid for in cash at the time of purchase.

14 Signed a contract for his first job. Peter Brush agreed to paint a three bedroom bungalow for $2,700. The owner agreed to pay him for the work immediately upon completion of the job.

15 Purchased $200 worth of paint and painter's supplies on credit. Peter Brush agreed to pay the merchant at the end of the month.

20 Finished painting the house. The owner was delighted with the quality of the work and issued a check to Qwik-Spray Student Painters for $2,700. Peter Brush deposited the check in the business bank account the same day.

24 A home owner in the vicinity asked the manager of Qwik-Spray Student Painters to paint the steps of his hose a fiery red. A paint sprayer was rented for this job at a cost of $40 and was paid for in cash.

March 25 Received $120 in cash for painting the steps.
31 Received a bill for telephone service for the month of March in the amount of $15. This bill need not be paid until April 10th.
31 Filled the tank in the truck with gasoline costing $30. Paid for the gasoline with cash.
31 Paid for the paint and supplies which were purchased on credit earlier in the month.

4. Post the journal entries in problem 3 to appropriate ledger accounts. Prepare a trial balance, income statement, and balance sheet for the month of March.

5. For each transaction given below, make entries to a journal, post these entries to the ledger, prepare a trial balance and a set of financial statements at the end of June.

June 2 Deposited $3,000 in a bank account in the name of the business, Moonlight Brigade. Proprietor is Larry Swift.
3 Rented a minivan at a cost of $400 per month. Paid for the first month's rent in cash at the time of the rental.
4 Purchased a power sweeper on credit. It cost $900 and is to be paid for at the end of June.
7 Ordered 2,000 circulars from a printer. Paid the printer $120 in cash. Picked up the circulars this very same day.
9 Purchased $300 worth of cleaning supplies. Payment must be made by the end of the month.
10 Bought a tucker pole on credit, with a down payment of $200. The balance of $700 is to be paid in equal monthly installments of $100 each beginning with the end of June.
11 Signed four contracts for the provision of janitorial services. Payment would be on a semi-monthly basis. Work was to commence immediately.
14 Earned $350 for washing the windows of ten stores.
15 Received $900 in fees for work performed under contract.
16 Purchased additional supplies costing $80 and paid for with cash at the time of purchase.
19 Hired a helper on a casual basis. Paid him $240 for three days' work.
23 Earned $400 in fees for washing windows for a major department store. Payment for the work would be received at the end of July.
24 Larry Swift withdrew $1,000 from the business for his personal use.
28 Received the telephone bill for $20. Payment was to be made by July 10th.
29 Paid the landlord $300 in rent for shop space.
30 Paid for the power sweeper purchased earlier.
30 Paid for cleaning supplies that were purchased on credit at an earlier date.

June	30	Made a payment on the tucker pole purchased earlier.
	30	Received $2,000 for work performed under contract.

6. Spiro Handril, a dentist, opens a dental practice at the beginning of October. Journalize each transaction presented below, post the entries to ledger accounts, prepare a trial balance, income statement, and a balance sheet as at the end of October.

October	1	Opens a bank account for his dental practice. Deposits $10,000 in an account titled *Dr. Spiro Handril.*
	2	Signs a five year lease for premises suitable for his dental practice. The cost of the lease is $420 per month with payment to be made at the end of each month.
	3	Purchases a complete set of dental equipment from a retiring dentist, Dr. Howard Tamper. This equipment was thought to be worth at least $14,000 but was acquired for only $5,000. A down payment of $1,000 was made with the balance to be paid in equal monthly installments of $500 each beginning with the month of October.
	4	Purchases a power tooth extractor from Nuway Dental Equipment Inc. Issues a check for $1,247 in payment.
	4	Buys dental supplies costing $488 including all applicable taxes. Pays for these supplies in cash.
	5	Sells a spare dental chair to Dr. Harvey McFilman on credit for $800. Payment would be received in two equal installments, with the first installment expected at the end of October.
	5	Fees earned in the first week amounted to $3,517 with all patients paying for dental services in cash.
	8	Hires an attractive dental receptionist at a salary of $1,100 per month, with payment to be made on the 15th of each month and on the last day of each month.
	12	Dental work worth $1,418 is performed on a patient, on credit, with payment to be received in 60 days.
	12	Fees earned in the second week amount to $5,917 and are deposited in the bank account.
	15	Paid the dental receptionist her salary for one week's work. Check number 04 in the amount of $275 is issued in payment to Linda Brusher.
	19	Withdraws $3,000 for his personal use.
	22	Purchases office supplies costing $237, paying cash.
	23	Deposits fees amounting to $3,917 in the bank account.
	26	Purchases $36 worth of stamps.
	27	Donates $500 to the United Way Charity.
	28	Pays $1,900 to an accountant for advice on financial planning.
	29	Receives the telephone bill for the month of October. It amounts to $35 including a $6 charge for Yellow Pages

advertising. Payment is not due until November 10th.

October 31 Receives a bill for $102 for heat and electricity and remits payment immediately.

31 Pays Linda Brusher her salary for the second half of the month of October. Check number 07 in the amount of $550 is issued.

31 Remits $420 to the Ideal Realty Company in payment of the cost of leasing the premises during the month of October.

31 Makes a payment to Dr. Howard Tamper for dental equipment purchased earlier.

31 Receives a check for $400 from Dr. Harvey McFilman.

31 Deposits $6,221 in the bank account resulting from fees earned in the last week of October.

31 Withdraws an additional $2,000 for his personal use.

31 Remits $42 to City Hall as his share of property taxes on the premises.

CHAPTER THREE

Depreciation and Closing the Books

INTRODUCTION

At this stage we are acquainted with each of the five different kinds of accounts; we know how to analyze each of these kinds of accounts and we know how to record various transactions in the journal; we know how to post entries to the ledger; know how to produce a trial balance, and we know how to prepare a set of financial statements. In this chapter we will learn how to deal with certain transactions that span more than one accounting period and we will learn how to proceed from one accounting period to the next without confusing the results.

DEPRECIATION

Many assets have lives that extend over several accounting periods. These include office equipment, furniture and fixtures, automobiles, buildings, leasehold improvements, patent rights, etc. In accounting we attempt to spread the cost of an asset over its expected useful life. We do not charge off the entire cost of an automobile, for example, in the month in which it was purchased because this asset has an expected life of several years. To spread the cost of an asset over its expected useful life, we do so by recording entries for depreciation. Thus, when an automobile, for example, is purchased, the cost of this automobile is not recorded as an expense; it is recorded as an asset and this asset is converted to expense over its expected useful life as it wears out, or depreciates.

CALCULATING DEPRECIATION

Pacific Printers Mart owns three assets which are depreciable. These are office equipment, furniture and fixtures, and an automobile.

The office equipment cost $1,800 and has an expected life of six years. During each year we obtain an equal amount of use from this equipment. However, at the end of the sixth year its usefulness is ended and its salvage value is zero. We may compute depreciation as follows:

Depreciation = $1,800/6 = $300 per year

Yearly depreciation amounts to $300 each year. One-sixth of the value of this office equipment is used up or depreciated during each of the six years of its life. On a monthly basis depreciation works out to the following amount:

Depreciation = $300/12 = $25 per month

This equipment depreciates at the rate of $25 per month, based on straight line depreciation. We will consider various methods of depreciation after we learn how to record entries for depreciation.

RECORDING DEPRECIATION

In order to keep our example simple, we ignored depreciation for the month of April, when we were first introduced to the income statement in the previous chapter. We will now learn how to make these entries. No depreciation will be recorded for the month of March, even though the assets were purchased during March, because Pacific Printers Mart did not commence active operations until April. The journal entry recording depreciation of office equipment, during the month of April, is illustrated in Exhibit 3-1.

In analyzing the preceding transaction, the rules of debit and credit are applied to Depreciation Expense: Office Equipment in the usual manner. Expenses are recorded by debits so we debit Depreciation Expense: Office Equipment $25. What about the remaining item? We know that the remainder of the transaction must be a credit to some account, but which account should be credited? Logically, we might reason that the asset Office Equipment is being used up, or is wearing out, and simply apply the rules of debit and credit tot he asset account, Office Equipment. Decreases in assets are recorded by credits. So by virtue of that logic we would credit the asset account,

Journal **Page 3**

1997				
April	30	Depreciation Expense: Office Equipment	25	
		Accumulated Depreciation: Office Equipment		25
		To record depreciation for April.		

Exhibit 3-1: Journal entry to record depreciation of office equipment during April.

Office Equipment, with the amount of our entry. That logic is correct. However, we do not follow that procedure in entering the credit item in this transaction. Instead, we introduce a new account, *Accumulated Depreciation: Office Equipment,* in which to record the credit item resulting from decreases in assets due to depreciation.

This new account, Accumulated Depreciation: Office Equipment, is analyzed in the same manner as the asset account, Office Equipment. Decreases in assets (due to wearing out or depreciation) are recorded by credits. We credit the asset account Accumulated Depreciation: Office Equipment $25. We use the accumulated depreciation account for only one purpose, which is to record the decrease in an asset due to depreciation. This account is not used, for example, to record decreases in assets due to sale or other disposals of assets. The reason that we record depreciation this way, rather than record the credit item directly to the asset account Office Equipment, is that we obtain a clearer picture of the current value of assets if we know how much they cost to begin with. Using this method, the balance sheet shows the original cost of each asset and the amount by which it has depreciated.

The results of our transaction are shown in Exhibit 3-2. Notice that the Office Equipment account remains unchanged from before, as no new items have been entered to it.

Office Equipment — 112

1997						
March 11	1	1,800				

Accumulated Depreciation: Office Equipment — 113

			1997			
			April	*30*	*3*	*25*

Depreciation Expense: Office Equipment — 592

1997				
April 30	*3*	*25*		

Exhibit 3-2: Depreciation entered to ledger accounts.

Part of an asset section of a balance sheet is illustrated in Exhibit 3-3. Notice how the balance from the accumulated depreciation account is positioned in this statement. By examining the balance sheet, we can determine at a glance that the Office Equipment cost $1,800; that it has depreciated by $25; and, that its remaining book value is $1,775.

Pacific Printers Mart
Balance Sheet
April 30, 1997

Assets:		
Cash	$3,070	
Accounts Receivable		700
Office Equipment	$1,800	
Less: Accum. Depreciation: Office Equipment	25	1,775

Exhibit 3-3: Balance sheet showing accumulated depreciation.

Notice that the same end result is obtained, that is, an undepreciated value, otherwise known as *book value* of $1,775 for Office Equipment account. In addition to Office Equipment, we must also depreciate Furniture and Fixtures, and the Automobile. Furniture and Fixtures has a life of ten years and Automobile has a useful life of four years.

The monthly depreciation for Furniture and Fixtures is:

Depreciation = $2,400/10 = $240 per year
Depreciation = $240/12 = $20 per month

The monthly depreciation for Automobile works out to:

Depreciation = $7,200/4 = $1,800 per year
Depreciation = $1,800/12 = $150 per month

The journal entries corresponding to the amounts of depreciation which we have just finished calculating are illustrated in Exhibit 3-4.

Journal **Page 3**

1997				
April	30	Depreciation Expense: Furniture and Fixtures	20	
		Accum. Depreciation: Furn. and Fixtures		20
		To record depreciation for April.		
	30	Depreciation Expense: Automobile	150	
		Accumulated Depreciation: Automobile		150
		To record depreciation for April.		

Exhibit 3-4: Journal entries for depreciation.

After the entries in Exhibit 3-4 have been posted to the ledger, the ledger appears as shown in Exhibit 3-5. Again, notice that the accounts in which the assets were originally recorded remain unaffected by our entries for depreciation. Rather, the amount of decrease in value of each asset is recorded in the accumulated depreciation account for that particular asset.

Exhibit 3-5: Ledger accounts after depreciation for April has been posted.

Furniture and Fixtures — 114

1997					
March 15	1	2,400			

Accumulated Depreciation: Furniture and Fixtures — 115

			1997		
			April 30	*3*	*20*

Depreciation Expense: Furniture and Fixtures — 593

1997					
April 30	*3*	*20*			

Automobile — 116

1997			1997		
March 5	1	7,700	March 20	1	500

Accumulated Depreciation: Automobile — 117

			1997		
			April 30	*3*	*150*

Depreciation Expense: Automobile — 594

1997					
April 30	*3*	*150*			

Pacific Printers Mart
Balance Sheet
April 30, 1997

Assets:		
Cash		$3,070
Accounts Receivable		700
Office Equipment	$1,800	
Less: Accumulated Depreciation: Office Equipment	25	1,775
Furniture and Fixtures	$2,400	
Less: Accumulated Depreciation: Furniture and Fixtures	20	2,380
Automobile	$7,200	
Less: Accumulated Depreciation: Automobile	150	7,050

Exhibit 3-6: Asset section of a balance sheet showing depreciation for the month of April.

Part of the asset section of a balance sheet is illustrated in Exhibit 3-6 which includes the balances from the accumulated depreciation accounts. Virtually the complete financial history of each of the three assets can be determined at a glance. This information includes the original cost of each asset, the amount by which it has depreciated, and its remaining undepreciated value.

METHODS OF DEPRECIATION

The kind of depreciation that was employed in our illustration is known as*straight line* depreciation. This name derives from the fact that if we were to plot a graph of the undepreciated cost of the asset at the end of each accounting period, over the life of the asset, we would end up with a representation of a straight line. This is the simplest method of calculating depreciation, however, it is not usually employed in practice. The problem inherent in straight line depreciation is that the lives of most assets cannot be determined with accuracy and the value of most assets is something more than zero at the end of their lives. However, some assets do behave in a manner predicted by the straight line method. An asset such as a patent right has a fixed life and at the end of that life its value is absolutely zero. The life of an automobile, however, cannot be predicted with the same degree of accuracy. It might last four, five, or even six years, or perhaps only six months, depending upon how carefully it is driven. And it is virtually certain to have some salvage value at the end of that time. Clearly, straight line depreciation is not the optimum method under these circumstances.

Declining balance depreciation does away with the problems inherent in straight line depreciation without introducing too many new problems of its own. By using declining balance depreciation we do not have to estimate the life of an asset and this method always leaves a salvage value. It is not suitable for use where the life of an asset does indeed have a definite ascertainable time period and where the asset has zero value at the end of that time period. Declining balance depreciation is most suitable for use in depreciating assets such as office furniture, automobiles, equipment, and buildings where the life of these kinds of assets is unknown and where there is, or may be, some possibility of salvage value remaining at the end of their useful lives.

COMPUTING DEPRECIATION

To compute straight line depreciation we simply divide the cost of the asset by the life of the asset, to obtain the amount of depreciation per accounting period. Suppose the business owns a machine that costs $1,000 and has a useful life of 5 years with no salvage value at the end of this time. This machine will depreciate at the rate of $200 per year, every year, right up to the end of its useful life.

To compute declining balance depreciation, we multiply the undepreciated cost of the asset at the end of each accounting period times a rate prescribed for that type of asset. Thus, to depreciate our machine which costs $1,000 we may compute the amount of depreciation at the end of the first year by multiplying the undepreciated cost, $1,000 times the rate, 20%. This of course yields $200 as the amount of depreciation in year one. The undepreciated cost of our asset is now $1,000 - $200 = $800. So at the end of year two we multiply $800 x 20% to obtain the amount of depreciation during year two. This yields $160 as the amount of depreciation in year two, leaving an undepreciated cost of $800 - $160 = $640. And so on. As mentioned earlier, undepreciated cost is also known as *book value.* A table of book values, comparing the two methods of depreciation, for our example, is illustrated in Exhibit 3-7.

From the data in Exhibit 3-7 we can plot graphs as shown in Exhibit 3-8. Straight line depreciation is represented by a straight line whereas declining balance depreciation is represented by a curved line. Notice that, over time, the book value of the machine under the declining balance method of depreciation may approach, but will never reach, zero.

USAGE OF EACH TYPE OF DEPRECIATION

In our illustration of Pacific Printers Mart we employed straight line depreciation even though declining balance depreciation is normally called for to depreciate the kind of assets that we have been dealing with. This also happens sometimes in practice. When it does the discrepancy must be computed for tax purposes. The taxation department of the country in which the business is operating provides information on the maximum amount of depreciation allowed for each class of asset.

For taxation purposes in the USA the *Internal Revenue Service* stipulates how depreciation is to be calculated under the *General Depreciation System,* the *Modified Accelerated Cost Recovery System,* and the *Alternative Depreciation System.* In Canada, on the other hand, depreciation for tax purposes is referred to as *Capital Cost Allowance.* Regardless of the terminology employed, depreciation derives from the two basic methods that we have already covered. In the table in Exhibit 3-9 are listed some of the more common kinds of assets and the lives over which their cost may be recovered under the general depreciation system. For example, automobiles, computers, photocopiers, and typewriters belong to the five-year property class while office furniture and fixtures belong to the seven-year property class.

TABLE OF BOOK VALUES

End of Year	Straight Line Depreciation	Declining Balance Depreciation
0	$1,000	$1,000
1	800	800
2	600	640
3	400	512
4	200	409.60
5	0	327.68
6		262.14
7		209.72
8		167.77
9		134.22

Exhibit 3-7: **Book values at the end of each year.**

Exhibit 3-8: **Graphs to illustrate depreciation.**

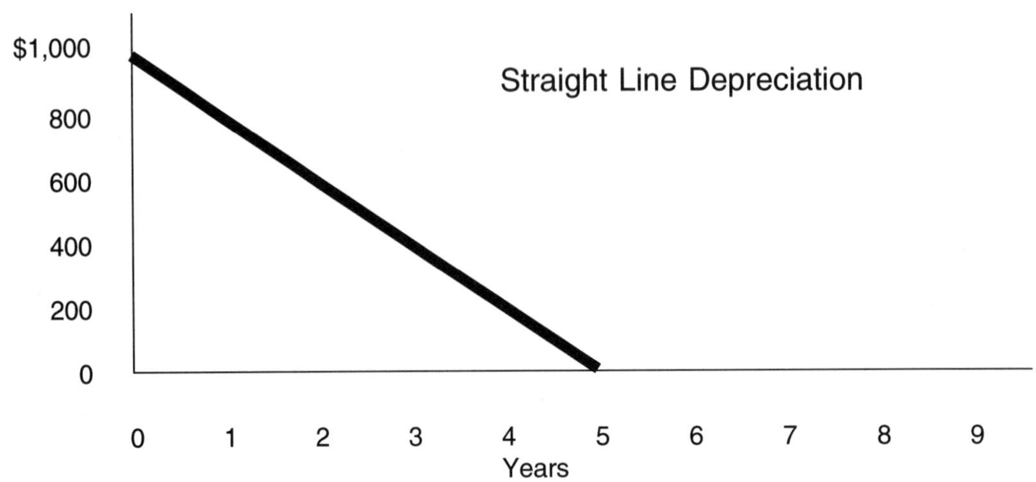

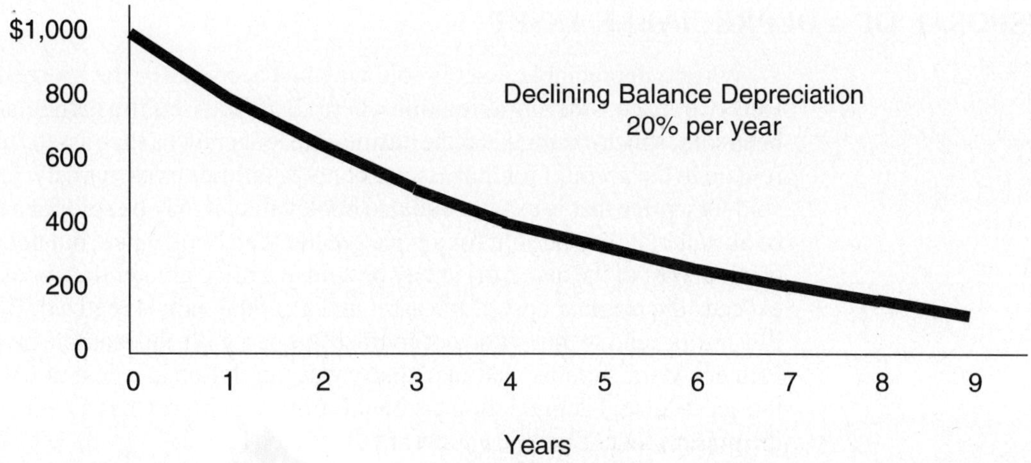

Exhibit 3-9: Cost recovery periods for various classes of assets.

GENERAL DEPRECIATION SYSTEM

3-year This class includes tractor units for over-the-road use and any race horse over two years old when placed in service.

5-year This class includes automobiles, taxis, buses, trucks, computers and peripheral equipment, office machinery (such as typewriters, calculators, copiers, etc.), and any property used in research and experimentation. It also includes breeding cattle and dairy cattle.

7-year This class includes office furniture and fixtures such as desks, files, safes, etc. Any property that does not have a class life and that has not been designated by law as being in any other class is also seven-year property.

10-year This class includes vessels, barges, tugs, similar water transportation equipment, any single purpose agricultural or horticultural structure, and any tree or vine bearing fruits or nuts.

15-year This class includes certain depreciable improvements made directly to land or added to it, such as shrubbery, fences, roads, and bridges.

20-year This class includes farm buildings (other than agricultural or horticultural structures).

Source: Internal Revenue Service, <u>How to Depreciate Property</u>, Publication 946, Cat. No. 13081F, Washington, DC: GPO, 1996.

DISPOSAL OF A DEPRECIABLE ASSET

When a depreciable asset is sold we must account for the proceeds of disposal. Here, we are considering a situation where all of the assets in a particular account have been sold, which means that if the business no longer owns such assets, no balance may remain in the account for that asset. Four possibilities exist, namely, an asset may be sold for a price that is exactly equal to book value; it may be sold for a price less than book value; it may be sold for a price greater than book value, but not exceeding the original cost of the asset; or, it may be sold at a price greater than book value, which exceeds the original cost of the asset and a capital gain is realized. For purposes of illustration, and so that we do not confuse this part with our example involving Pacific Printers Mart, suppose that machinery was purchased at a cost of $10,000 and that the accumulated depreciation account for this machinery has a balance of $8,000 at the present time. These accounts are illustrated below:

Machinery	
10,000	

Accumulated Depreciation: Machinery	
	8,000

ASSET DISPOSED OF AT BOOK VALUE

The book value of the machinery is $10,000 - $8,000 = $2,000. This amount is computed by subtracting the balance in the accumulated depreciation account from the balance in the asset account. In other words, book value is the remaining value of the asset, that is that fraction of its value, which has not yet been depreciated. The machinery is disposed of for $2,000. Before we make our journal entry we perform the arithmetic calculation below:

Cost of Machinery	$10,000
Less: Accumulated Depreciation	8,000
Book Value:	$2,000
Proceeds from Disposal:	$2,000

The journal entry corresponding to this situation is illustrated below:

Cash	2,000	
Accumulated Depreciation: Machinery	8,000	
Machinery		10,000
To record sale of machinery at book value.		

As all of the machinery has been disposed of, no balance may remain in either the machinery account or the accumulated depreciation account. The balances in these accounts have been reduced to zero as a result of our journal entry and we have properly accounted for the cash received from the sale of this machinery.

ASSET DISPOSED OF FOR LESS THAN BOOK VALUE

This time, let us suppose that the machinery was disposed of for only $1,500. As the book value of this machinery is $2,000 this means we have realized a loss on disposal. In order to know what to include in our journal entry let us perform the simple calculation shown below:

Cost of Machinery	$10,000
Less: Accumulated Depreciation	8,000
Book Value:	$2,000
Proceeds from Disposal	1,500
Loss on Disposal:	$500

The journal entry corresponding to a disposal of an asset at a price less than its book value is illustrated below:

Cash	1,500	
Accumulated Depreciation: Machinery	8,000	
Gain and Loss on Disposal	500	
Machinery		10,000
Machinery disposed of at a loss.		

As a terminal loss was incurred in the disposal of the machinery for a price less than book value, this loss is debited to an account titled *Gain and Loss on Disposal.* The same account is used for both capital gains and terminal losses. When this account has a net debit balance it means that a terminal loss was incurred; when it has a net credit balance a capital gain has been realized.

ASSET DISPOSED OF FOR MORE THAN BOOK VALUE, BUT LESS THAN COST

This time, let us suppose that the machinery was disposed of for $5,000. We may calculate the recapture of depreciation, as follows:

Cost of Machinery	$10,000
Less: Accumulated Depreciation	8,000
Book Value:	$2,000
Proceeds from Disposal	5,000
Recapture of Depreciation Expense	$(3,000)

Because we realized an amount on disposal that was greater than book value it means that we depreciated the machinery too quickly. We charged off more depreciation expense than we should have as attested to by the high price realized on disposal. Our books showed the machinery as having a net value of only $2,000 whereas we managed to dispose of it for $5,000. So now we must add this excess depreciation expense back to income. This is done by crediting the depreciation expense account as shown in our journal entry below:

Cash	5,000	
Accumulated Depreciation: Machinery	8,000	
Machinery		10,000
Depreciation Expense: Machinery		3,000
To record recapture of depreciation;machinery disposed of for more than book value.		

Expense accounts normally have debit balances and the usual procedure is to subtract expenses from revenue to arrive at net income. Because we have ended up with a credit balance in an expense account due to a recapture of depreciation this means that we must add this amount to revenue to arrive at net income. On the income statement we place brackets around the amount of depreciation expense *(3,000)* to denote that the account has a credit balance, rather than a debit balance which is the normal situation, and which means that we must add this amount to revenue, rather than subtract it from revenue, to arrive at the amount of net income.

ASSET DISPOSED OF FOR MORE THAN COST

It happens on occasion that an asset is disposed of for a price which is greater than the cost of the asset to begin with. With rising inflation this occurs more often than one would imagine. In the printing industry it is not unusual to sell paper cutters and certain kinds of offset presses for more on the second hand market than they cost originally. This is because these assets have long lives and the same equipment costs considerably more to buy new at current prices than they cost several years ago. So a second hand piece of equipment may be sold for twice its original price and still be only a fraction of the cost of new equipment.

This time, let us suppose that the machinery was disposed of for $11,000. We may calculate the amount of recapture of depreciation and the amount of capital gain, as shown below:

Cost of Machinery		$10,000
Less: Accumulated Depreciation		8,000
Book Value		$ 2,000
Proceeds from Disposal		11,000
Recapture of Depreciation	$8,000	
Gain on Disposal	1,000	
Recapture and Gain on Disposal		$(9,000)

Because we realized a price on disposal that was greater than the cost of the asset to begin with, this means that we should not have depreciated the machinery at all. Therefore, depreciation expense that was written off in previous periods must now be added back to income, which is done by crediting the depreciation expense account. In addition, we must also account for a capital gain of $1,000. This is illustrated in the journal entry that follows:

Cash	11,000	
Accumulated Depreciation: Machinery	8,000	
Machinery		10,000
Depreciation Expense: Machinery		8,000
Gain and Loss on Disposal		1,000
To record recapture of depreciation and capital gain; machinery disposed of at a price greater than cost.		

The credit entry to Depreciation Expense: Machinery is enclosed in brackets in the list of expenses in the income statement, meaning that this amount must be added, rather than subtracted, when arriving at a figure for net income. The capital gain is credited to an equity account called *Gain and Loss on Disposal.* We know that we have a capital gain because the account Gain and Loss on Disposal has a credit balance. On an income statement this capital gain is shown as an item of extraordinary income, as shown below:

Net Income:	$6,418
Extraordinary Income (capital gain)	1,000

It is important to note that capital gains are not included with revenue, in the revenue section of the income statement, nor are capital losses included with expenses, but are included as shown above.

TRIAL BALANCE AFTER ADJUSTMENTS FOR DEPRECIATION

We will now return to our example involving Pacific Printers Mart. Our ledger now includes accumulated depreciation and depreciation expense accounts for Office Equipment, Furniture and Fixtures, and Automobile, as shown in Exhibit 3-2 and Exhibit 3-5. These entries are adjusting entries for depreciation. The balances in the accumulated depreciation and depreciation expense accounts must be included in our financial statements. As the first step in preparing a new set of financial statements, which includes the results of depreciating these assets, let us first prepare a trial balance to be certain that the ledger as a whole is still in balance. The trial balance for Pacific Printers Mart, after adjusting entries for depreciation have been made at the end of April, is presented in Exhibit 3-10.

FINANCIAL STATEMENTS

Compare the trial balance in Exhibit 3-10 with the one in Exhibit 2-20. Our latest trial balance includes entries for depreciation. Even though no cash outlay is required at the time we record depreciation this does not mean that depreciation expense may be ignored. In fact, the recording of depreciation expense nevertheless results in the reduction of an asset, that is, the asset that is being depreciated. That asset was either paid for in cash at the time it was purchased or it was purchased on credit and is to be paid for at a later date. An income statement, including depreciation expense among its list of expenses, is presented in Exhibit 3-11. A balance sheet, including accumulated depreciation among its asset accounts, is presented in Exhibit 3-12.

Notice that the format of our balance sheet has changed. The format used previously was *account* form. The format of the balance sheet in Exhibit 3-12 is *report* form. This format makes it more convenient to print out the balance sheet on standard business sized letter paper.

Exhibit 3-10: Trial balance after adjustments for depreciation.

Pacific Printers Mart
Trial Balance Adjusted for Depreciation
April 30, 1997

Cash	$3,070	
Accounts Receivable	700	
Office Equipment	1,800	
Accumulated Depreciation: Office Equipment		$25
Furniture and Fixtures	2,400	
Accumulated Depreciation: Furniture and Fixtures		20
Automobile	7,200	
Accumulated Depreciation: Automobile		150
Accounts Payable		1,655
Jack Fraser, Capital		10,000
Jack Fraser, Drawings	1,500	
Commissions		6,400
Rent Expense	400	
Telephone Expense	35	
Utilities Expense	70	
Office Supplies Expense	30	
Advertising and Promotion Expense	250	
Salaries Expense	600	
Depreciation Expense: Office Equipment	25	
Depreciation Expense: Furniture and Fixtures	20	
Depreciation Expense: Automobile	150	
	$18,250	$18,250

Exhibit 3-11: Income statement for April after depreciation has been taken into consideration.

Pacific Printers Mart
Income Statement
For the month ending April 30, 1997

Revenue:		
Commissions		$6,400
Expenses:		
Rent Expense	$400	
Telephone Expense	35	
Utilities Expense	70	
Office Supplies Expense	30	
Advertising and Promotion Expense	250	
Salaries Expense	600	
Depreciation Expense: Office Equipment	25	
Depreciation Expense: Furniture and Fixtures	20	
Depreciation Expense: Automobile	150	1,580
Net Income:		$4,820

Exhibit 3-12: Balance sheet at the end of April after depreciation has been taken into consideration.

Pacific Printers Mart
Balance Sheet
April 30, 1997

Assets

Cash		$3,070
Accounts Receivable		700
Office Equipment	$1,800	
Less: Accumulated Depreciation: Office Equipment	25	1,775
Furniture and Fixtures	2,400	
Less: Accumulated Depreciation: Furniture and Fixtures	20	2,380
Automobile	7,200	
Less: Accumulated Depreciation: Automobile	150	7,050
		$14,975

Liabilities and Owner's Equity

Liabilities:			
Accounts Payable			$1,655
Owner's Equity:			
Jack Fraser, Capital, April 1, 1997		$10,000	
Net Income for April	$4,820		
Less: Drawings	1,500	3,320	
Jack Fraser, Capital, April 30, 1997			13,320
			$14,975

CLOSING THE BOOKS

An income statement gives us the results of operations over a period of time—an accounting period—such as a month or year. Income statements, of course, are prepared from the balances in those ledger accounts that pertain to the income statement, that is, all of the revenue and expense accounts. We saw how an income statement was produced for the month of April from the ledger account balances at the end of the month of April. Because we need to measure the results of operations each accounting period we cannot have any balance remaining from the previous accounting period in any of our ledger accounts for revenue and expenses. We achieve zero balances in these accounts through a procedure called *closing the books.*

The books are closed at the end of each accounting period by transferring the account balances of those accounts that appear in the income statement into a new account, that we have especially devised for this purpose, called the*Income Summary* account. Revenue accounts have credit balances so we transfer the balances in revenue accounts to the credit side of the Income Summary account. Expense accounts have debit balances so we transfer the debit balances in the expense accounts to the debit side of the Income Summary account. This is the first step in the process of closing the books. See the illustration in Exhibit 3-13.

Income Summary

Expenses	Revenue

Exhibit 3-13: Balances from the income statement accounts are transferred to the income summary account.

The books are closed at the end of the accounting period under consideration. Normally, this is at the end of the year, or if we wish we may close the books more often, say, at the end of each month, quarter, or semi-annually. We must, however, close the books at the end of every year. This may be the end of the calendar year which is December 31st or it may be the end of a fiscal year. A fiscal year is a twelve month period that a business has adopted as its operating year. A fiscal year, if desired, is initiated when the business files its first income tax return. A certain type of retail merchandising business, for example, might not find the December 31st date as a convenient year end but may instead adopt some other time, such as the end of April, when inventory is at its lowest and sales activity is slowest, and its fiscal year will then extend from May 1st of the current year to April 30th of the succeeding year, etc. Once established, the fiscal year is not normally changed.

In our example, Pacific Printers Mart, we will close the books at the end of April, the first operating month for this business, so that we can start fresh again in May with zero balances in all of the income statement accounts and measure results on a monthly basis. If we did not close the books at the end of April the results for the next accounting period, the month of May, would be mixed with the results for April. Therefore, if we wish to monitor the results of the business on a monthly basis, we must close the books at the end of each month. And, in any event, we must close the books at the end of each year for income tax purposes.

THE CLOSING PROCEDURE

To begin the closing procedure we turn to the ledger and examine the first account that belongs to the income statement, which is the revenue account *Commissions* and transfer its balance into the Income Summary account. The revenue account is reproduced in Exhibit 3-14.

Before we can make the transfer we must compute the balance in the revenue account, *Commissions,* if we have not already done so. The balance, of course, is a credit balance in the amount of $6,400. What we do is draw a line under the last entry that was posted from the journal and enter the total, $6,400.

Commissions 455

	1997			
	April	5	2	1,200
		12	2	700
		21	2	<u>4,500</u>
				6,400

Exhibit 3-14: Revenue account at the end of April.

We are allowed to perform arithmetic in a ledger account, such as computing the sum of entries, but all entries themselves must originate in the journal and be posted from the journal to the ledger. Our last operation is readily recognizable as the sum of the credit entries and is not likely to be confused with an entry posted from the journal. Having computed the credit balance in the revenue account we now make the appropriate entry in the journal, and post the two items resulting from this closing entry to ledger accounts. This leaves the revenue account, Commissions, with a net balance of zero, as its former balance has by this action been transferred to the credit side of the Income Summary account. The journal entry for this part of the closing procedure, that is closing the revenue account, is shown in Exhibit 3-15 and the ledger accounts, after posting our journal entry, are illustrated in Exhibit 3-16.

Journal — **Page 4**

1997					
April	30	Commissions	455	6,400	
		Income Summary	600		6,400
		To close the revenue account.			

Exhibit 3-15: Journal entry to close the revenue account.

Commissions — 455

1997				1997			
April	*30*	*4*	*6,400*	April	5	2	1,200
					12	2	700
					21	2	4,500
			6,400				6,400

Income Summary — 600

				1997			
				April	*30*	*4*	*6,400*

Exhibit 3-16: Ledger after closing revenue account.

Notice that the balance in the Commissions account is now zero as a result of posting the closing entry from the journal. Because the balance in this account is zero we may draw a dashed line through the account to signify the fact that we need not refer to the data above this dashed line. Entries for the next accounting period will be recorded below this dashed line, which in turn will also be closed out to Income Summary at the end of that period. The $6,400 credit balance that used to be in the Commissions account is now in the credit side of Income Summary.

At this stage you might ask if the rules of debit and credit apply in making closing entries. We do not apply them consciously. For closing entries, we simply make the entries necessary to accomplish the transfer, based on logic. Thus, to close a revenue account, which has a credit balance, we debit that account to reduce its balance to zero. We then credit Income Summary by the same amount. Closing entries are first recorded in the journal and then are posted to the ledger.

CLOSING EXPENSE ACCOUNTS

Closing expense accounts follows a procedure similar to that of closing revenue accounts. Expense accounts virtually always have debit balances. To close expense accounts, first we must compute the net (debit) balance in each expense account. Next, we make entries in the journal debiting Income Summary and crediting each expense account with the amount of its net debit balance. What results, of course, after these entries have been posted is a series of expense accounts, each with a net balance of zero. The sum of all the debit balances from all of the expense accounts now appears as a debit balance in the Income Summary account. A dashed line is drawn through each of the expense accounts and these accounts are now ready for the next month's entries. Closing the expense accounts is illustrated in the exhibits that follow. The first exhibit, Exhibit 3-17, is an illustration of the expense accounts as they appear in the ledger before any closing entries are made.

Exhibit 3-17: Expense accounts before closing the books.

Rent Expense 567

1997				
April	30	2	400	

Telephone Expense 568

1997				
April	30	2	35	

Utilities Expense 569

1997				
April	30	2	70	

Office Supplies Expense 572

1997				
April	7	2	30	

Advertising and Promotion Expense 574

1997				
April	1	2	100	
	14	2	150	
			250	

Salaries Expense 584

1997				
April	30	2	600	

Depreciation Expense: Office Equipment 592

1997				
April	30	3	25	

Depreciation Expense: Furniture and Fixtures 593

1997				
April	30	3	20	

Depreciation Expense: Automobile 594

1997				
April	30	3	150	

The journal entry to close the expense accounts is given in Exhibit 3-18. Notice that only one debit entry, in the amount of $1,580 is made to Income Summary. Rather than make a series of debit entries to Income Summary, that is, one to offset each expense account item, it is more convenient to simply make one debit entry to Income Summary equal to the sum of all the credit items. After this transaction to close expense accounts has been posted to the ledger, the ledger appears as shown in Exhibit 3-19.

Journal **Page 4**

1997					
April	30	Income Summary	600	1,580	
		Rent Expense	567		400
		Telephone Expense	568		35
		Utilities Expense	569		70
		Office Supplies Expense	572		30
		Advertising and Promotion Expense	574		250
		Salaries Expense	584		600
		Deprn. Expense: Office Equipment	592		25
		Deprn. Exp.: Furniture and Fixtures	593		20
		Depreciation Expense: Automobile	594		150
		To close the expense accounts.			

Exhibit 3-18: **Journal entry to close the expense accounts.**

Exhibit 3-19: **Ledger after closing expense accounts.**

Rent Expense 567

1997				1997			
April	30	2	400	*April*	*30*	*4*	*400*

Telephone Expense 568

1997				1997			
April	30	2	35	*April*	*30*	*4*	*35*

Utilities Expense 569

1997				1997			
April	30	2	70	*April*	*30*	*4*	*70*

Office Supplies Expense 572

1997				1997			
April	7	2	30	*April*	*30*	*4*	*30*

Advertising and Promotion Expense 574

1997				1997			
April	1	2	100	*April*	*30*	*4*	*250*
	14	2	150				
			250				250

Salaries Expense 584

1997				1997			
April	30	2	600	*April*	*30*	*4*	*600*

Depreciation Expense: Office Equipment 592

1997				1997			
April	30	3	25	*April*	*30*	*4*	*25*

Depreciation Expense: Furniture and Fixtures 593

1997				1997			
April	30	3	20	*April*	*30*	*4*	*20*

Depreciation Expense: Automobile 594

1997				1997			
April	30	3	150	*April*	*30*	*4*	*150*

CLOSING THE INCOME SUMMARY ACCOUNT

The debit side of the Income Summary account, Exhibit 3-20, contains the sum of all the expenses incurred during the month of April. The credit side of Income Summary contains the amount of revenue earned during April. By comparing our Income Summary account to our income statement for April, Exhibit 3-11, we see that the credit entry to Income Summary, which is $6,400 is the same as the amount of revenue on the income statement, as it must be if we have not made any errors. Total expenses in that income statement, which amount to $1,580 are equal to the debit entry to Income Summary. By computing the net balance in Income Summary, we obtain a credit balance of $4,820 which is the amount of net income for April (see Exhibit 3-11). This must be so because net income equals revenue minus expenses. What we have in Income Summary is revenue on the credit side and expenses on the debit side. Thus the net balance in Income Summary must be equal to revenue minus expenses which equals net income.

Recall that increases in owner's equity arise from two sources—investment of cash or other assets in the business by the owner and from profitable operation of the business. Any increase in equity arising from profitable operation of the business must be equal to the profit earned. In accounting terminology this is the amount of net income. The amount of net income for April, that is $4,820 is the amount by which the owner's equity in the business has grown. Extending this logic to our present example means that the amount of net income, represented by a net credit balance of $4,820 in Income Summary, must be transferred to the owner's equity account, *Jack Fraser, Capital.* We can accomplish this transfer through the journal entry in Exhibit 3-21 leaving the Income Summary account with a net balance of zero. The net credit balance that used to be in Income Summary has now been transferred to Jack Fraser, Capital. After these journal entries have been posted to the ledger, the Income Summary account and Jack Fraser, Capital account appear as shown in Exhibit 3-22.

Thus, the amount of net income, which is $4,820 and which was determined in our income statement, Exhibit 3-11, has been transferred to the owner's equity account, Jack Fraser, Capital, through the process of closing the books. This increase in owner's equity correctly reflects the amount by which the business has grown. As the owner made no additional investment of capital in the business the amount of net income is, at this stage, the only element causing an increase in owner's equity.

Income Summary 600

1997				1997			
April	*30*	*4*	*1,580*	*April*	*30*	*4*	*6,400*

Exhibit 3-20: Income Summary account after expense accounts have been closed.

Journal **Page 4**

1997					
April	30	Income Summary	600	4,820	
		Jack Fraser, Capital	343		4,820
		To close the Income Summary account.			

Exhibit 3-21: Journal entry to close the Income Summary account.

Once again, increases in owner's equity arise from only two sources—investment by the owner and profitable operation of the business. Decreases in owner's equity arise when the opposite happens, that is, if the business suffers an operating loss or if the owner withdraws assets, usually cash, from the business.

Jack Fraser, Capital — 343

				1997			
				March	1	1	10,000
				April	*30*	*4*	*4,820*

Income Summary — 600

1997				1997			
April	30	4	1,580	April	30	4	6,400
	30	*4*	*4,820*				
			6,400				6,400

Exhibit 3-22: Ledger after Income Summary account is closed.

CLOSING THE DRAWINGS ACCOUNT

By examining the drawings account*Jack Fraser, Drawings* we can determine the amount of cash or other assets that have been withdrawn from the business by the owner. A withdrawal of assets by the owner is a withdrawal of capital from the business. It is not a salary and no salary expense results when the owner withdraws cash for his or her own use. In our example, the drawings account is closed into the owner's equity account, Jack Fraser, Capital. In order to make our closing entry, we first examine the drawings account, Jack Fraser, Drawings, which is illustrated in Exhibit 3-23, and determine its balance. Next we make an entry to the journal to close out this account as shown in Exhibit 3-24. The ledger after closing entries have been posted is illustrated in Exhibit 3-25.

Jack Fraser, Drawings 344

1997							
April	30	2	1,500				

Exhibit 3-23: Owner's drawings account before closing.

Journal **Page 4**

1997					
April	30	Jack Fraser, Capital	343	1,500	
		Jack Fraser, Drawings	344		1,500
		To close the drawings account.			

Exhibit 3-24: Journal entry to close the drawings account.

Jack Fraser, Capital 343

1997				1997			
April	*30*	*4*	*1,500*	March	1	1	10,000
				April	30	4	4,820

Jack Fraser, Drawings 344

1997				1997			
April	30	2	1,500	*April*	*30*	*4*	*1,500*

Exhibit 3-25: Ledger after closing drawings account.

THE INCOME TAXES ACCOUNT

Like drawings, income taxes are not an expense, but rather are withdrawals of cash, to pay taxes, which serves to reduce owner's equity in the business. Income tax constitutes that fraction of net income that must be remitted to the government, and is computed as a percentage of net income. The income tax rate, of course, is prescribed by the income tax department, as determined from the budget passed by our elected representatives. Let us assume for the moment that the rate is 25%. At this rate, Pacific Printers Mart would have to pay the following amount of income taxes:

Income Taxes	=	Net Income	x	Tax Rate
Income Taxes	=	$4,820	x	25%
Income Taxes	=	$1,205		

This withdrawal of assets (cash) reduces owner's equity in the business inasmuch that it is a withdrawal of assets by the owner to pay income taxes. If we pay our income taxes immediately at the end of the month, the journal entry will appear as illustrated in Exhibit 3-26, with a credit entry to Cash.

Journal **Page 4**

1997					
April	30	Income Taxes	349	1,205	
		Cash	101		1,205
		To record income taxes for April.			

Exhibit 3-26: Journal entry to record income taxes.

In the event that these income taxes are not paid immediately at the end of the month then the credit entry must be made to Income Taxes Payable, a liability account. The entry to close the Income Taxes account is illustrated in Exhibit 3-27. The plural, income taxes, is employed because income taxes are paid to more than one level of government.

Journal **Page 4**

1997					
April	30	Jack Fraser, Capital	343	1,205	
		Income Taxes	349		1,205
		To close the Income Taxes account.			

Exhibit 3-27: Journal entry to close the Income Taxes account.

After the entries to record and close the Income Taxes account have been posted to the ledger, the ledger appears as illustrated in Exhibit 3-28.

Jack Fraser, Capital 343

1997					1997				
April	30		4	1,500	March	1		1	10,000
	30		*4*	*1,205*	April	30		4	4,820

Income Taxes 349

1997					1997				
April	30		4	1,205	*April*	*30*		*4*	*1,205*

Exhibit 3-28: **Ledger after the Income Taxes account has been closed.**

SUMMARY OF CLOSING PROCEDURE

It is desirable to clear out the accounts, that is, *close all of the income statement accounts and those accounts that affect owner's equity* on a monthly basis, if we wish to monitor progress closely. As the business grows larger the only means of objectively assessing business growth is through data generated by the accounting process. In any event, it is essential to close the accounts at the end of every year—calendar year or fiscal year—for income tax purposes. The closing procedure may be summarized by the following steps:

1. Close the revenue accounts by transferring their (credit) balances into the Income Summary account. A transfer is accomplished by making an entry in the journal and then posting this entry to the ledger.
2. Close the expense accounts by transferring their (debit) balances into the Income Summary account.
3. Compute the balance of the Income Summary account and close the Income Summary account by transferring its balance (credit balance if operations were profitable) into the owner's equity account (Jack Fraser, Capital, in our example).
4. Close the debit balance of the drawings account into the owner's equity account (Jack Fraser, Capital).
5. Compute, record, and post the amount of income taxes. Close the debit balance of the Income Taxes account into the owner's equity account (Jack Fraser, Capital).

This entire closing procedure may be more easily understood and visualized by referring to the diagram in Exhibit 3-29. Remember, all entries in the ledger, with the exception of arithmetic computations, must originate from journal entries and must be posted from the journal. Do not attempt to circumvent this procedure.

BALANCING BALANCE SHEET ACCOUNTS

As we have just learned, the closing procedure involves closing all of the accounts that affect the owner's equity account, Jack Fraser, Capital. Thus, it means that we must close all of the income statement accounts, the drawings account, and the income tax account into the owner's equity account, Jack Fraser, Capital. All of those accounts that must be closed at the end of each accounting period (or at the very least at the end of each year) serve to measure results over time. Revenue, for example, was so much in the period of time in question, expenses were so much during this period, the owner withdrew so much money during this period, and income taxes amounted to so much during this period.

Balance sheet accounts give us the financial position of a business *at a particular point in time,* normally at the end of the day on the last day in an accounting period. When we examine a balance sheet account we can determine the amount in the account of an asset, liability, or the amount of owner's equity at that point in time by simply computing the net balance of the account we are interested in. We do not close balance sheet accounts. So long as the business owns, for example, a particular asset, its cost must be reflected in the balance of the account for that asset.

Accounts that measure results over a period of time must be closed at the end of that period of time so that financial data for the next accounting period may be recorded in these same accounts without confusing this data with that of the succeeding accounting period, and so on. This is not the case with balance sheet accounts as they all serve to provide us with the financial position of the business at a point in time. The income tax and drawings accounts appear to be exceptions, but these accounts have an impact on the owner's equity account in the same manner as the income statement accounts do. In fact, had we wanted to, we could have taken every transaction involving revenue, expenses, drawings, and income taxes and recorded them in terms of their effect on owner's equity. But, had we done it this way we would have no details of operating results. We produce an income statement, and keep track of the amount of drawings and income taxes in separate accounts, so that we have detailed data with which to manage and control the operations of the business.

Although we do not close balance sheet accounts, we nevertheless perform an operation on these accounts so that their balances are readily apparent at the end of each accounting period. Some accounts, such as Cash, Accounts Receivable, and Accounts Payable, may have a large number of entries in them. This procedure which enables us to determine the balance of a balance sheet account at a glance is simply called *balancing the balance sheet accounts.* The first of the balance sheet accounts that we encounter in the ledger, the Cash account, is illustrated, after the balancing operation has been performed, in Exhibit 3-30. Basically, balancing a balance sheet account means computing its net balance and displaying this net balance, after the entries at the end of the period, so that the net balance at the end of the period stands out and is apparent at a glance without further computation.

By balancing the Cash account as shown in Exhibit 3-30 it is readily apparent that the balance in this account at the close of business on the last day of April is $1,865.

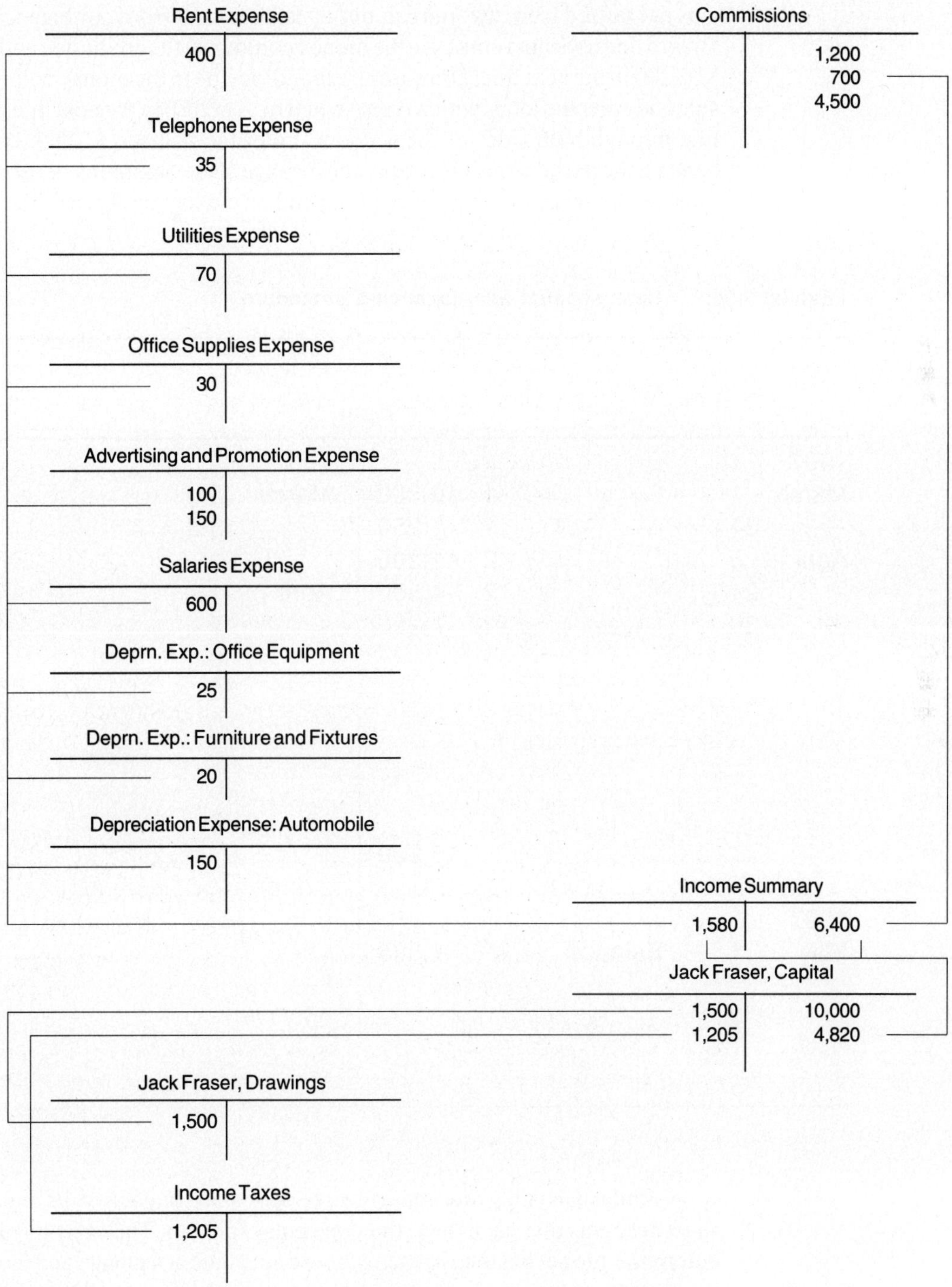

Exhibit 3-29: Diagram of closing procedure.

To balance the account simply compute the sum of the entries in both the debit and credit sides of the account. The sum on the debit side of the Cash account is larger than the sum of the entries on the credit side. Subtract the sum on the credit side from the sum on the debit side, $16,200 - $14,335 = $1,865. Next, enter this difference, $1,865 on the credit side of the Cash account. Use a ✓ (tick) mark to indicate that this entry was not posted from the journal, but instead, results from our balancing procedure. Draw a line under the entries in the money column on the credit side and enter the total, $16,200 in the next line. Draw a corresponding line in the money column on the debit side and enter the total (which is also equal to $16,200) in the next line. Draw a dashed line through both sides of the account. Enter the balance $1,865 on the debit side beneath the dashed line. Of course, the balance at the beginning of the day on May 1st must be the same as the balance at the end of the day on April 30th.

Exhibit 3-30: Cash account after balancing procedure.

Cash — 101

1997					1997				
March	1		1	10,000	March	5		1	7,700
	31		1	250		15		1	500
April	5		2	1,200		31		1	500
	21		2	4,500	April	1		2	100
	30	16,200	2	250		7		2	30
						30		2	600
						30		2	400
						30		2	1,500
						30	13,130	2	1,800
						30	14,335	4	1,205
						30	Balance	✓	1,865
				16,200					16,200
1997									
May	1	Balance	✓	1,865					

A similar balancing procedure must be performed on each of the remaining balance sheet accounts that have more than one entry in them. The objective is to be able to determine the net balance in each of these accounts at a glance and thereby facilitate preparation of the trial balance and balance sheet. The entire ledger is illustrated in Exhibit 3-31, after balancing the balance sheet accounts and closing the books.

Exhibit 3-31: Complete ledger after balancing and closing the accounts.

Cash 101

1997					1997				
March	1		1	10,000	March	5		1	7,700
	31		1	250		15		1	500
April	5		2	1,200		31		1	500
	21		2	4,500	April	1		2	100
	30	16,200	2	250		7		2	30
						30		2	600
						30		2	400
						30		2	1,500
						30	13,130	2	1,800
						30	14,335	4	1,205
						30	Balance	✓	1,865
				16,200					16,200
1997									
May	1	Balance	✓	1,865					

Accounts Receivable 103

1997					1997				
March	20		1	500	March	31		1	250
April	12	1,200	2	700	April	30	500	2	250
						30	Balance	✓	700
				1,200					1,200
1997									
May	1	Balance	✓	700					

Office Equipment 112

1997									
March	11		1	1,800					

Accumulated Depreciation: Office Equipment 113

					1997				
					April	30		3	25

Furniture and Fixtures 114

1997									
March	15		1	2,400					

Accumulated Depreciation: Furniture and Fixtures 115

					1997				
					April	30		3	20

Automobile 116

1997					1997				
March	5		1	7,700	March	20		1	500
					April	30	Balance	✓	7,200
				7,700					7,700
1997									
May	1	Balance	✓	7,200					

Accumulated Depreciation: Automobile 117

					1997				
					April	30		3	150

Accounts Payable 230

1997					1997				
March	31		1	500	March	11		1	1,800
April	30	2,300	2	1,800		15		1	1,900
	30	Balance	✓	1,655	April	14		2	150
						30		2	35
						30	3,955	2	70
				3,955					3,955
					1997				
					May	1	Balance	✓	1,655

Jack Fraser, Capital 343

1997					1997				
April	30		4	1,500	March	1		1	10,000
	30	2,705	4	1,205	April	30	14,820	4	4,820
	30	Balance	✓	12,115					
				14,820					14,820
					1997				
					May	1	Balance	✓	12,115

Jack Fraser, Drawings 344

1997					1997				
April	30		2	1,500	April	30		4	1,500

Income Taxes 349

1997					1997				
April	30		4	1,205	April	30		4	1,205

Commissions 455

1997					1997				
April	30		4	6,400	April	5		2	1,200
						12		2	700
						21		2	4,500
				6,400					6,400

Rent Expense 567

1997					1997				
April	30		2	400	April	30		4	400

Telephone Expense — 568

1997				1997			
April	30	2	35	April	30	4	35

Utilities Expense — 569

1997				1997			
April	30	2	70	April	30	4	70

Office Supplies Expense — 572

1997				1997			
April	7	2	30	April	30	4	30

Advertising and Promotion Expense — 574

1997				1997			
April	1	2	100	April	30	4	250
	14	2	150				
			250				250

Salaries Expense — 584

1997				1997			
April	30	2	600	April	30	4	600

Depreciation Expense: Office Equipment — 592

1997				1997			
April	30	3	25	April	30	4	25

Depreciation Expense: Furniture and Fixtures 593

1997				1997			
April	30	3	20	April	30	4	20

Depreciation Expense: Automobile 594

1997				1997			
April	30	3	150	April	30	4	150

Income Summary 600

1997				1997			
April	30	4	1,580	April	30	4	6,400
	30	4	4,820				
			6,400				6,400

FINAL FINANCIAL STATEMENTS

The set of financial statements presented in Exhibit 3-32 and Exhibit 3-33 is final in the sense that the income statement now includes a deduction of income taxes from net income and the equity section of the balance sheet takes income taxes into consideration in arriving at the amount of owner's equity. Thus we have gone a step beyond the financial statements presented in Exhibit 3-11 and Exhibit 3-12, to the final stage by taking income taxes into consideration.

Notice that in the owner's equity section of the balance sheet we have not detailed the changes in owner's equity as we did before in Exhibit 3-12. It is not necessary to compute owner's equity using the detailed arithmetic method as we did before when we employ the procedure of closing the books. Through the process of closing the books we automatically arrive at the final balance in Jack Fraser, Capital. For the sake of comparison let us work out owner's equity using the detailed arithmetic method.

Jack Fraser, Capital, April 1, 1997			$10,000
Net Income for April		$4,820	
Less: Withdrawals during April	$1,500		
Income Taxes	1,205	2,705	2,115
			$12,115

Thus, the balance in Jack Fraser, Capital, arrived at by arithmetic computation is the same as that arrived at automatically through the closing procedure. Even though the balance in owner's equity is arrived at automatically through the closing procedure it is still a good idea to detail the amount of drawings and income taxes in the owner's equity section of the balance sheet.

TRIAL BALANCE AFTER CLOSING THE BOOKS

After closing the books the only accounts that have balances remaining in them are balance sheet accounts. This is so because all of the income statement accounts, the drawings account, and the income taxes account have all been closed, that is, their balances have been transferred to the owner's equity account, Jack Fraser, Capital, in preparation for the next accounting period. Therefore a trial balance after closing the books will appear as shown in Exhibit 3-34. In practice an after-closing trial balance is not normally prepared, as it serves little or no useful purpose.

Pacific Printers Mart
Income Statement
For the month ending April 30, 1997

Revenue:		
Commissions		$6,400
Expenses:		
Rent Expense	$400	
Telephone Expense	35	
Utilities Expense	70	
Office Supplies Expense	30	
Advertising and Promotion Expense	250	
Salaries Expense	600	
Depreciation Expense: Office Equipment	25	
Depreciation Expense: Furniture and Fixtures	20	
Depreciation Expense: Automobile	150	1,580
Net Income:		$4,820
Less: Income Taxes		1,205
Net Income after Taxes:		$3,615

Exhibit 3-32: Income statement for April after computation of income taxes.

Exhibit 3-33: Balance sheet for April.

Pacific Printers Mart
Balance Sheet
April 30, 1997

Assets

Cash		$1,865
Accounts Receivable		700
Office Equipment	$1,800	
Less: Accumulated Depreciation: Office Equipment	25	1,775
Furniture and Fixtures	2,400	
Less: Accumulated Depreciation: Furniture and Fixtures	20	2,380
Automobile	7,200	
Less: Accumulated Depreciation: Automobile	150	7,050
		$13,770

Liabilities and Owner's Equity

Liabilities:	
Accounts Payable	$1,655
Owner's Equity:	
Jack Fraser, Capital	12,115
	$13,770

Pacific Printers Mart
Trial Balance
April 30, 1997

Cash	$ 1,865	
Accounts Receivable	700	
Office Equipment	1,800	
Accumulated Depreciation: Office Equipment		$ 25
Furniture and Fixtures	2,400	
Accumulated Depreciation: Furniture and Fixtures		20
Automobile	7,200	
Accumulated Depreciation: Automobile		150
Accounts Payable		1,655
Jack Fraser, Capital		12,115
	$13,965	$13,965

Exhibit 3-34: Trial balance after closing the books.

SUMMARY OF THE ACCOUNTING CYCLE

This procedure, which we have just gone through in our example involving Pacific Printers Mart, is known as the *accounting cycle.* Essentially it consists of all of the steps from analyzing and recording transactions to preparation of a set of financial statements. More specifically, a series of steps are involved, as indicated below:

1. Record all operating transactions during the period in question. First, these transactions are recorded in the journal and then, later, are posted to the ledger. Operating transactions are those that involve some active effort at the time of the transaction, such as purchasing assets, incurring expenses other than depreciation expense, etc.

2. Record adjusting entries for depreciation. Here, we do not have a transaction occurring in the same sense as when an operating transaction occurs. There is no bill of sale, cash register tape, or bill arriving in the mail to remind us to make entries for depreciation. Instead, we must simply be aware that entries for depreciation must be made at the end of each accounting period. The amount of the entry is arrived at by computation in each case. After all entries have been posted to the ledger a trial balance may be prepared, if desired. Balance the balance sheet accounts.

3. Close the books. This means closing all of the income statement accounts into the Income Summary account. Then, close the Income Summary account into the owner's equity account, Jack Fraser, Capital. Next, the drawings account is closed into the owner's equity account. Remember, in the closing procedure, as in all accounting, closing entries must first be recorded in the journal and then posted to the ledger. At this stage, a preliminary set of financial statements may be prepared to facilitate the computation of income taxes.

4. Compute and record the amount of income taxes. Post these entries to the ledger. Then record and post entries closing the Income Taxes account into the owner's equity account, Jack Fraser, Capital.

5. Prepare a set of financial statements, that is, an income statement and a balance sheet. Provided that no errors have been made, the balance sheet will balance and the amount of net income after taxes, from the income statement, will correctly correspond with the change in the owner's equity account on the balance sheet.

SUMMARY OF THIS CHAPTER

In this chapter we learned how to compute and make entries for depreciation. Because assets normally have lives that extend over several accounting periods we cannot simply charge off the costs of these assets as expenses in the period in which they were purchased. Rather, they are recorded as assets and converted to expense through the process of making entries for depreciation, over the course of their lives, which may span several accounting periods.

We also learned how to close the books. By closing the books the accounts may be used for recording information in the succeeding accounting period without confusing the information with entries from previous accounting periods. Through this procedure we automatically arrive at the new balance in the owner's equity account which serves to tie the income statement to the balance sheet. The entire procedure, from analyzing and recording transactions to preparation of financial statements, is known as the accounting cycle.

Exercises

1. What is meant by the term *depreciation?* What kinds of assets must be depreciated? Give examples.

2. A certain piece of equipment cost $3,000 and has an expected life of six years with no salvage value remaining at the end of that time. How much depreciation should be charged off each year?

3. What is the purpose of the accumulated depreciation account? Give an example of an asset and its corresponding accumulated depreciation account. Prepare a sample balance sheet which includes accumulated depreciation in the asset section.

4. Explain what is meant by straight line depreciation. Also, explain what is meant by declining balance depreciation.

5. A machine costs $600 and has an expected life of 5 years. Compute the amount of depreciation each year using the straight line method of depreciation and repeat the computation using the declining balance method of depreciation with a rate of 20%. Prepare a table of book values, using each of the two methods of depreciation, over a five year period.

6. Explain the difference between a recapture of depreciation and a capital gain on disposal of a depreciable asset.

7. What is the purpose of the Income Summary account? When may entries be made to this account?

8. Why must the books be closed at least once a year at the end of the accounting period? Describe the closing procedure.

9. What is the purpose of the balancing procedure? To what kind of accounts is it applied?

10. Briefly summarize the accounting cycle.

11. Can land be depreciated?

12. Into which account do we close the revenue and expense accounts? Into which account do we close the drawings and income taxes accounts?

13. How often should the books be closed?

14. Is the balancing procedure identical to the closing procedure?

Problems

1. Make journal entries to record the acquisition of each of the following assets. Calculate the amount of depreciation, if any, and make journal entries to record depreciation at the end of the year. Where less than a full 12 months has expired from the time of purchase of the asset to the end of the year, assume that income tax laws permit the business to charge off a full years worth of depreciation in any event.

   a. January 2 — Purchased an automobile, for $10,000 paying cash. Expected life is 5 years with no salvage value at the end of that time.

   b. January 11 — Office furniture costing $2,000 is purchased from Atlantic Furniture, on credit. Assume tax regulations permit furniture to be depreciated at any rate, so long as the rate does not exceed 20%, on a declining balance basis.

   c. March 19 — Arctic Airlines acquires a runway from an Eskimo village for $60,000 paying cash. No paved surface was visible and the runway markings were laid out on compacted snow. Assume that the income tax department allows airplane runways to be depreciated at a maximum rate of 8% on a declining balance basis. The president of Arctic Airlines asked his accountant to depreciate the runway in the shortest time possible, as he was concerned that the runway would disappear during the hot weeks of summer beginning and ending in July.

   d. June 30 — Rent-a-Rod Car Rentals acquired 10 automobiles with heavy duty bearings, springs, and axles at a cost of $100,000 with a down payment of $40,000 and a promissory note for the balance. It was anticipated that twice the normal amount of usage would be obtained from these vehicles. Because of rising profits, the president of the company asked her accountant to write off the cost of these vehicles to depreciation expense at the maximum rate. (Automobiles are considered to be five-year property by the income tax department).

   e. May 12 — Mystic Inventions acquires the patent rights on a secret formula to produce solid water at a cost of $5,100, paying cash. The patent rights give Mystic Inventions the exclusive right to manufacture and market this product for a period of 17 years. Nevertheless, the president orders the accountant to write off the cost of the patent, to depreciation expense, as soon as possible.

   f. October 10 — Houston Hauling Inc. purchases a tractor unit for

$90,000 on credit. The accountant could not recall the depreciation rate for this kind of asset. The trucker told him that they would have to replace the unit after three years.

g. December 8 Frontier Motors acquires land on which to construct a service station for $50,000. The owner of the business, Edward Bush, makes a down payment of $20,000 and signs a note for the balance on behalf of the company.

h. March 11 The manager of Bloominggale's Flower Shop purchases $5,000 worth of daffodils for resale to customers. Payment was made in cash. Because of the large sum involved the bookkeeper wondered whether or not the purchase qualified for depreciation. You explain the situation to the bookkeeper.

i. June 8 A taxi was purchased for $40,000 paying cash (5 year property).

j. May 17 Ample Department Stores buys ten delivery vehicles for $200,000 paying cash. The vice-president indicated to the accountant that their drivers were careful and the vehicles should last a long time.

k. February 3 Fabulous Designs buys $3,000 worth of office furniture for use in its reception area. The receptionist indicates that this furniture is subject to hard usage and points out cigarette burns on a leather chair.

l. April 28 ABC Enterprises pays $28,000 cash for certain patent rights which it does not want disclosed to the public. The accountant informs the president of ABC Enterprises that after seventeen years this asset will be entirely without any value whatsoever.

m. August 1 Jack Smith pays $10,000 for the inventory of a business and $9,800 for furnishings.

n. July 2 Able Farms purchases a frame granary for $10,000, paying cash. Farmer Jones mentioned that this structure was meant to replace the previous one which was acquired a decade ago.

o. May 22 The Hildon Hotel acquires additional land for future use at a cost of $31,000, paying cash.

p. January 19 Tacoma Transport buys a car for the use of its division manager, for $40,000, paying cash.

2. The Richmond Restaurant decides to terminate its delivery service. Accordingly, it no longer has any use for its delivery vehicles and disposes of these vehicles for $12,000 cash. The ledger includes the following accounts: Automobile—debit balance of $20,000. Accumulated Depreciation: Automobile—credit balance of $8,000. Prepare appropriate journal entries for the above transaction.

3. On March 9th, automobiles no longer required by a restaurant for use as

delivery vehicles are sold for $10,000 cash. These vehicles cost $20,000 and a total of $12,000 has already been written off as depreciation expense. Journalize this transaction.

4. Another restaurant discontinues its delivery service. Its vehicles, which originally cost $20,000 are sold for $15,000 cash. The accumulated depreciation account has a credit balance of $12,000 and a total of $12,000 has been written off as depreciation expense over the years. Prepare journal entries for this transaction, which occurred on June 11th.

5. Elite Restaurant disposes of its fabulous Mercedes delivery vehicle for $25,000. Payment was received on March 10th in cash. The manager chuckled when he noted that the car had only cost him $20,000 when he purchased it 6 years earlier. The accumulated depreciation account had a credit balance of $12,000 at the time of disposal. Journalize this transaction.

6. The North Shore Restaurant disposed of its delivery vehicle just one year after purchasing it for $10,000. Ten thousand dollars was realized from the sale. The accumulated depreciation account has a credit balance of $2,000. Journalize this transaction.

7. Ralph Gryndermann started a skate sharpening business on October 1st. The transactions for the first month of operations are listed below. Enter all operating transactions in a journal and post to the ledger (rule ordinary notebook paper with appropriate columns to make up the books). Prepare a trial balance. Compute and record adjusting entries for depreciation and post to the appropriate ledger accounts. Prepare a trial balance after adjusting entries have been posted. Close the books. Prepare a preliminary set of financial statements. Compute and record the amount of income taxes; post to the ledger; and close the income taxes account. Prepare a final set of financial statements, including the amount of income taxes. The tax rate is 20%.

October	1	Deposited $10,000 in a bank account in the name of the business, Ralph's Skate Sharpening Service.
	2	Rented suitable premises close to the skating rink. Paid $300 for rent for the month of October.
	3	Subscribed for telephone service.
	4	Purchased a skate sharpening machine. It cost $2,100 and was paid for in cash. Expected life is 7 years with no salvage value remaining at the end of that time.
	5	Purchased shop supplies costing $218 on credit. These must be paid for by the end of the month.
	8	Purchased benches, a desk, and a chair at a total cost of $756, paying cash. Estimated useful life is 7 years with no salvage value at the end of that time.
	12	Deposited fees earned for skate sharpening amounting to $642.

October 14 Hired an assistant who was to begin work the next day at a salary of $800 per month.
16 Purchased a second skate sharpening machine, identical to the one purchased earlier, paying cash.
20 Deposited fees for skate sharpening amounting to $798.
21 Purchased shop supplies costing $80, paying cash.
24 Deposited fees for skate sharpening amounting to $1,800.
27 Withdrew $500 for personal use.
31 Deposited fees for skate sharpening amounting to $1,200.
31 Received the telephone bill for October. Payment is due by November 10th. The amount of the bill is $37.
31 Remitted $218 in payment for shop supplies purchased earlier.
31 Paid assistant his salary for one half month's work.
31 Received bill for electricity in the amount of $66. Payment is due by November 15th.

8. For the transactions listed below:
   a. Prepare journal entries for all operating transactions.
   b. Post entries to the ledger.
   c. Prepare a trial balance.
   d. Compute and record adjusting entries for depreciation. Depreciate as required. Post entries for depreciation to the ledger.
   e. Prepare an adjusted trial balance.
   f. Prepare a preliminary set of financial statements (before income taxes have been taken into consideration).
   g. Compute the amount of income taxes. Income tax rate is 20%. Record entries for income taxes in the journal and post to the ledger.
   h. Close the books.
   i. Prepare a final set of financial statements.
   j. Prepare a trial balance after closing the books.

June 1 George Shilling deposits $30,000 in a bank account in the name of the business, Chicago Dollar Mart and Exchange. A commission is charged for cashing checks for customers and for providing other money related services.
2 Rents a suitable premises at a cost of $500 per month. Pays rent for the month of June at this time.
3 Leases a large neon sign at a cost of $150 per month. Pays the rental for June on this very day.
4 Purchases a fireproof safe costing $12,600. Makes a down payment of $3,000 with the balance to be paid in equal monthly installments of $1,000, with the first installment due at the end of June. Note signed. This is seven-year property.
5 Buys two bill changing machines at a cost of $1,800 each, paying cash. Depreciate over a 5-year period.
5 Buys office furnishings on credit. Total cost is $2,100, and is

		to be paid for by the end of July. Depreciate over seven years.
June	5	Commissions earned in the first week total $1,212.
	8	Buys office supplies costing $214, paying cash.
	12	Purchases lounge chairs for use in the reception area. Signed a note for $1,176. Full payment to be made at the end of the year.
	12	Deposits $2,914 in commissions earned during the second week.
	15	Remits $125 to City Hall for a business license.
	16	Hires an employee. Work to commence immediately. Salary of $1,200 per month to be paid semi-monthly.
	19	Commissions earned in the third week total $3,518.
	24	Pays an accountant $1,400 for advice on setting up a payroll book.
	25	Buys 20 spot commercials on radio station KIXI, at a cost of $1,000. Payment is due by the end of July.
	30	Commissions earned in the final week of June total $3,987.
	30	Paid employee her salary for the second half of June.
	30	Makes installment payment on safe purchased earlier.
	30	Telephone bill for June amounts to $33. Payment is due by July 10th.
	30	Withdraws $1,000 for his personal use.

CHAPTER FOUR

Adjusting Entries

INTRODUCTION

Consistent with the whole purpose of accounting is the objective of obtaining as complete and accurate a set of financial statements as possible. Thus, the balance sheet should show the amounts of assets, liabilities and owner's equity consistent with recognized accounting principles. For assets, we may recall, this consisted of recording them at cost and we did not later adjust these amounts to reflect changing market values. This same objective of accuracy requires that the income statement include all of the revenue and all of the expenses of a given period in the statement. And this same principle dictates that only revenue and expenses of a given period be included in the income statement and not revenue or expenses that belong to another accounting period. Therefore, the income statement for the month of April should include only revenue earned in April and only expenses incurred in the month of April. Expenses for the month of May, for example, should not be included in the income statement for April.

When a transaction benefits or affects more than one accounting period it must be recorded in the period in which it occurs even though the money connected with the transaction, for example, may not be received or paid out until a later period. Assets must be converted to expense over the period of their useful lives; revenue must be recorded in the period when it is earned, whether received in advance or at a later date, and expenses must be recorded in the period in which they are incurred. In order to apportion or record these transactions in the period in which they belong we must make *adjusting* entries. We have already been introduced to one kind of adjusting entry, depreciation. Adjusting entries may be required in each of four different situations.

These situations occur when the business buys assets that last several accounting periods, when revenue is received in advance, when expenses accrue but have not been recorded, and when revenue has been earned but not recorded.

RECORDED ASSETS

An insurance policy to cover fire, theft, and damage to property, is purchased on May 1st. It cost $360 for coverage extending twelve months. Because the business will derive the benefit of insurance protection over a twelve month period we cannot include the entire cost as an expense on the income statement for May. Rather, we record the cost of insurance as an asset, and convert this asset to expense over the twelve month period in which we derive benefits from this insurance policy. Therefore, only one-twelfth of $360 is to be included as an expense for insurance coverage for the month of May. The journal entry to record the purchase of insurance is illustrated in Exhibit 4-1.

Journal **Page 5**

1997					
May	1	Unexpired Insurance	106	360	
		Cash	101		360
		To record purchase of a 12-month insurance policy.			

Exhibit 4-1: Insurance policy recorded as an asset.

The purchase of the insurance policy is recorded as an asset because the benefits of insurance protection derived from this policy extend over a 12-month period, not just the month of May. So we cannot record the entire cost of that policy as an expense for the month of May, the month in which the policy was purchased. We must write off the cost of this insurance policy over the period during which insurance protection is provided.

Accordingly, at the end of May, one-twelfth of the cost of this insurance policy is written off as an expense. To do this, we make the adjusting entry in the journal as illustrated in Exhibit 4-2.

As is the case with all adjusting entries, this transaction is no exception in that it is not like an operating transaction where we have the immediate transaction itself accompanied by say, a bill, to remind us to make the entry. We must examine our records, or rely on memory, to make the entry. Usually we employ a combination of both processes, records and memory. After posting the journal entry, the Unexpired Insurance ledger account and Insurance Expense ledger account appear as shown in Exhibit 4-3.

Journal **Page 5**

1997					
May	31	Insurance Expense	571	30	
		Unexpired Insurance	106		30
		To record insurance expense for the month of May.			

Exhibit 4-2: **Adjusting entry to convert a fraction of an asset to expense.**

Unexpired Insurance 106

1997				1997			
May	1	5	360	*May*	*31*	*5*	*30*

Insurance Expense 571

1997							
May	*31*	*5*	*30*				

Exhibit 4-3: **Adjusting entry posted to ledger.**

In the balance sheet on May 31st, Unexpired Insurance will have a balance of $330 and the income statement for May will include Insurance Expense, in the amount of $30. This series of transactions gives us the correct financial situation at the end of May and was achieved through the use of an adjusting entry. At the end of each succeeding month we must also make adjusting entries for insurance expense until the balance in Unexpired Insurance is reduced to zero.

SECOND ASSET RECORDED

On May 6th, Jack Fraser purchases $800 worth of shop supplies for use in trying out some of the machines taken on consignment. Shop supplies such as ink, toner, and solvents are usually purchased in case lots so that there are sufficient supplies on hand to last several months. At the end of May, a glance at the shelves reveals that approximately $40 worth of supplies have been consumed during the month. When these supplies were purchased they were recorded as an asset as illustrated in Exhibit 4-4. The amount of shop supplies consumed during the month of May is recorded by means of an adjusting entry in the journal as illustrated in Exhibit 4-5.

		Journal			**Page 5**
1997					
May	6	Shop Supplies	111	800	
		Cash	101		800
		Purchased a large quantity of shop supplies.			

Exhibit 4-4: Shop supplies recorded as an asset.

Because these shop supplies are expected to last several months they cannot simply be recorded as an expense for the month of May, the month in which they were purchased. If we were to charge off the entire cost of shop supplies as an expense for the month of May this expense account would be overstated and the income statement would be inaccurate. Likewise, we would not have any shop supplies recorded as an asset on the balance sheet at the end of May, which would not be consistent with our actual situation. The fact of the matter is that we do have shop supplies on hand and this should be reflected in the balance sheet.

		Journal			**Page 5**
1997					
May	31	Shop Supplies Expense	573	40	
		Shop Supplies	111		40
		To record amount of shop supplies consumed during May.			

Exhibit 4-5: Adjusting entry at the end of May.

These shop supplies must be recorded as expense during the time they are consumed. This is accomplished by initially recording the purchase of shop supplies as an asset and then converting the asset to expense as these supplies are consumed, through the use of adjusting entries. When dealing with accounts such as shop supplies, be certain to employ the proper title of the account. Shop Supplies (account number 111) is an asset, while Shop Supplies Expense (account number 573) is an expense. If the term *Expense* is dropped from the account title, Shop Supplies Expense, then this account is likely to be confused with the asset account, Shop

Supplies. The Shop Supplies ledger account and the Shop Supplies Expense ledger account are illustrated in Exhibit 4-6 after the debit and credit items of the adjusting entry have been posted to these accounts.

Shop Supplies 111

1997				1997			
May	6	5	800	*May*	*31*	*5*	*40*

Shop Supplies Expense 573

1997							
May	*31*	*5*	*40*				

Exhibit 4-6: Ledger after posting adjusting entry.

DEPRECIABLE ASSETS RECORDED

Some depreciable assets were purchased in March and recorded in the journal at that time. These were Office Equipment, Furniture and Fixtures, and Automobile. Each month we must record the amount by which each of these assets has depreciated through the use of adjusting entries. Recall that we made entries for depreciation for each of these asset accounts, for the month of April, in the previous chapter. This process of recording depreciation is continued each month. Journal entries to record depreciation for the month of May are illustrated in Exhibit 4-7.

Exhibit 4-7: Adjusting entries for depreciation.

Journal **Page 5**

1997					
May	31	Depreciation Expense: Office Equipment	592	25	
		Accum. Deprn.: Office Equipment	113		25
		To record depreciation for May.			
	31	Deprn. Expense: Furniture and Fixtures	593	20	
		Accum. Deprn.: Furniture and Fixtures	115		20
		To record depreciation for May.			

May	31	Depreciation Expense: Automobile	594	150	
		Accumulated Depreciation: Automobile	117		150
		To record depreciation for May.			

After posting the adjusting entries for depreciation to the ledger the accounts appear as shown in Exhibit 4-8. As we learned earlier, the amount by which a depreciable asset has worn out is recorded in its accumulated depreciation account. We do not record the credit item for a decrease in assets, due to depreciation, in the account for the depreciable asset itself. Instead, the credit item is entered to a separate account, the accumulated depreciation account for the asset, and this accumulated depreciation account is analyzed in the same manner as the asset account is analyzed. Decreases in assets, due to depreciation, are recorded by credits so the accumulated depreciation account is credited.

Exhibit 4-8: Ledger accounts after adjusting entries have been posted.

Office Equipment — 112

Date		Ref.	Debit	Date		Ref.	Credit
1997							
March	11	1	1,800				

Accumulated Depreciation: Office Equipment — 113

Date		Ref.	Debit	Date		Ref.	Credit
				1997			
				April	30	3	25
				May	*31*	*5*	*25*

Depreciation Expense: Office Equipment — 592

Date		Ref.	Debit	Date		Ref.	Credit
1997				1997			
April	30	3	25	April	30	4	25
....				....			
1997							
May	*31*	*5*	*25*				

Furniture and Fixtures 114

1997									
March	15		1	2,400					

Accumulated Depreciation: Furniture and Fixtures 115

					1997				
					April	30		3	20
					May	*31*		*5*	*20*

Depreciation Expense: Furniture and Fixtures 593

1997					1997				
April	30		3	20	April	30		4	20
1997									
May	*31*		*5*	*20*					

Automobile 116

1997					1997				
March	5		1	7,700	March	20		1	500
					April	30	Balance	✓	7,200
				7,700					7,700
1997									
May	1	Balance	✓	7,200					

Accumulated Depreciation: Automobile 117

					1997				
					April	30		3	150
					May	*31*		*5*	*150*

Depreciation Expense: Automobile 594

1997					1997				
April	30		3	150	April	30		4	150
1997									
May	*31*		*5*	*150*					

REVENUE RECEIVED IN ADVANCE

On May 1st, the Compatible Darkroom Company installed a demonstration model darkroom at the Pacific Printers Mart premises with the objective of generating sales through referrals. For every referral and sale made as a result of the referral, Pacific Printers Mart would receive a $100 commission. It was anticipated that an average of one sale per month would be made. To demonstrate the sincerity of their promise of commission, the Compatible Darkroom Company forwarded $1,200 in advance to Pacific Printers Mart. On May 31st Pacific Printers Mart was advised that a sale was made by Compatible Darkroom Company as a result of a referral from Pacific Printers Mart. The journal entry to record the $1,200 revenue received in advance is illustrated in Exhibit 4-9, and the adjusting entry to record the commission is illustrated in Exhibit 4-10.

Journal — **Page 5**

1997					
May	1	Cash	101	1,200	
		Unearned Commissions	233		1,200
		To record commissions received in advance.			

Exhibit 4-9: **Journal entry to record a liability, Unearned Commissions.**

In order to analyze the transaction in Exhibit 4-9, you must recognize the nature of revenue received in advance. Despite the terminology employed, the true nature of unearned revenue is a *liability*. If the commission is not earned it will eventually have to be repaid. Increases in liabilities are recorded by credits, so Unearned Commissions is credited $1,200. This liability, Unearned Commissions, is converted to revenue, and placed in the Commissions account, by means of adjusting entries, as revenue is earned. Our first adjusting entry, to convert a liability to revenue, is recorded as illustrated in Exhibit 4-10. The ledger accounts, after posting the adjusting entry, are illustrated in Exhibit 4-11.

Journal — **Page 5**

1997					
May	31	Unearned Commissions	233	100	
		Commissions	455		100
		To record commissions earned in May.			

Exhibit 4-10: **Adjusting entry to record revenue.**

Unearned Commissions							233
1997				1997			
May	*31*	*5*	*100*	May	1	5	1,200

Commissions							455
1997				1997			
April	30	4	6,400	April	5	2	1,200
					12	2	700
					21	2	4,500
			6,400				6,400
				1997			
				May	*31*	*5*	*100*

Exhibit 4-11: Ledger accounts after posting adjusting entry.

ACCRUED EXPENSES

Accrued expenses are those expenses which belong to a particular accounting period, but for which no operating entries are required because payment need not be made until some subsequent period. These expenses, nevertheless, must be recorded in the period in which they were incurred and not in some later period in which they are paid.

An employee is hired by Pacific Printers Mart on May 1st. Terms of the employment agreement include a salary of $1,500 per month to be paid at the end of the first week in the month following the month in which the salary is earned. This means that the first payday will be on Friday, June 5th. The mere hiring of an employee does not result in any entry to the journal as no transaction has occurred from an accounting point of view. So no entry is required on May 1st. However, at the end of the month, an adjusting entry must be made to record the salary expense of this employee, even though this salary is not payable until June 5th. If we were to fail to make this adjusting entry for salary expense we would end up with an income statement at the end of May that was misleading in that it fails to include every item of expense incurred during the month of May. Therefore, at the end of May we must make the adjusting entry shown in Exhibit 4-12, to account for salary expense incurred during May, even though payday falls on June 5th in the next accounting period.

Journal					Page 5
1997					
May	31	Salaries Expense	584	1,500	
		Salaries Payable	231		1,500
		To record salary expense for May.			

Exhibit 4-12: Adjusting entry for salary expense.

The amount of salary expense accrued to the end of May is properly recorded by means of our adjusting entry. Thus, the income statement for the month of May will properly include this item of salary expense and the balance sheet prepared on May 31st will properly include the amount of accrued liability, salaries payable, in the amount of $1,500. The ledger after the adjusting entry has been posted is illustrated in Exhibit 4-13.

Salaries Payable — 231

				1997			
				May	*31*	*5*	*1,500*

Salaries Expense — 584

1997				1997			
April	30	2	600	April	30	4	600
1997							
May	*31*	*5*	*1,500*				

Exhibit 4-13: Ledger after adjusting entry has been posted.

On June 5th, when the employee is paid his salary, we make the entry shown in Exhibit 4-14. The effect of making payment is to eliminate the liability, Salaries Payable, and care must be taken not to record Salaries Expense a second time when the employee is actually paid his salary.

		Journal			Page 7
1997					
June	5	Salaries Payable	231	1,500	
		Cash	101		1,500
		To record payment of salary.			

Exhibit 4-14: Operating entry to record payment of salary.

ADDITIONAL ACCRUED EXPENSE

On May 1st, a five-year term loan for $10,000 was obtained from the New York Mutual Bank. The entire amount of principal was to be repaid at the end of the five year period in one lump sum. Interest was to be remitted, at the rate of 12%, on the anniversary date of the loan, each year. The journal entry to record this operating transaction is illustrated in Exhibit 4-15.

		Journal			Page 5
1997					
May	1	Cash	101	10,000	
		Notes Payable	240		10,000
		Obtained a 5-year, 12%, loan from the New York Mutual Bank.			

Exhibit 4-15: Operating entry to record loan.

Since interest, by the terms of the agreement, is payable annually on the anniversary date, no payment of interest will be made at the end of May. Interest expense, nevertheless, has accrued and must be recorded at the end of the month in order to end up with an accurate income statement. The income statement for May, as with any other accounting period, must include every expense incurred during the period. The amount of interest expense that has accrued up to the end of May may easily be calculated, as follows:

Amount of interest = $10,000 x 12% x 1/12 = $100

Therefore, our adjusting entry for accrued interest at the end of May will include the above amount as illustrated in Exhibit 4-16. The ledger, after the adjusting entry has been posted, is illustrated in Exhibit 4-17.

Journal **Page 5**

1997				
May 31	Interest and Service Charges Expense	575	100	
	Interest Payable	232		100
	To record accrued interest for May.			

Exhibit 4-16: Adjusting entry for accrued interest.

Interest Payable 232

		1997			
		May	*31*	*5*	*100*

Notes Payable 240

		1997			
		May	1	5	10,000

Interest and Service Charges Expense 575

1997					
May	*31*	*5*	*100*		

Exhibit 4-17: Ledger after adjusting entry is posted from the journal.

ACCRUED REVENUE

Revenue must be included in the income statement for the period in which it is earned and not in the period in which it is collected, if it is collected in a period later than the period in which it is earned. For example, commissions earned in May must be included in the income statement for May even though these commissions will not be collected until a later period, in June.

On May 5th, Rapid Photocopiers Inc. installs a photocopier on the premises of Pacific Printers Mart. As payment for this arrangement, Rapid Photocopiers Inc.

agrees to remit a commission of ten percent of revenue earned each month, from the photocopy machine, to Pacific Printers Mart, with payment to be made at the end of the second week in the month following the month in which the commission is earned. During the month of May, $2,000 worth of photocopying had been done by customers resulting in a commission of $200 to Pacific Printers Mart. This commission would not be received until the end of the second week in June. At the end of May, we make the adjusting entry illustrated in Exhibit 4-18. The ledger accounts appear as shown in Exhibit 4-19 after these items have been posted.

		Journal			**Page 5**
1997					
May	31	Accounts Receivable	103	200	
		Commissions	455		200
		To record commissions earned on photocopying during May.			

Exhibit 4-18: Entry to record accrued revenue.

Accounts Receivable — 103

1997					1997				
March	20		1	500	March	31		1	250
April	12	1,200	2	700	April	30	500	2	250
						30	Balance	✓	700
				1,200					1,200
1997									
May	1	Balance	✓	700					
	31		*5*	*200*					

Commissions — 455

1997					1997				
April	30		4	6,400	April	5		2	1,200
						12		2	700
						21		2	4,500
				6,400					6,400

1997				
May	31		5	100
	31		*5*	*200*

Exhibit 4-19: Ledger accounts after posting the adjusting entry.

On June 12th, when a check for $200 is received, no additional item is entered to the Commissions account. If we make an entry to Commissions at this time we would be double counting. The true nature of this transaction is the collection of an account receivable. To record this reduction in accounts receivable outstanding we make the journal entry crediting Accounts Receivable, illustrated in Exhibit 4-20.

Journal **Page 7**

1997				
June 12	Cash	101	200	
	Accounts Receivable	103		200
	Check received for commissions from Rapid Photocopiers Inc.			

Exhibit 4-20: Operating entry to record the collection of an account receivable.

OPERATING TRANSACTIONS FOR MAY

Journal entries for all of the operating transactions that occurred during the month of May are illustrated in Exhibit 4-21, below. This comprises the first step in the accounting cycle, which is to record all of the operating transactions for the period in question.

Exhibit 4-21: Journal entries for all of the operating transactions in May.

Journal **Page 5**

1997				
May 1	Unexpired Insurance	106	360	
	Cash	101		360
	To record the purchase of a 12-month insurance policy.			

May	1	Cash	101	1,200	
		Unearned Commissions	233		1,200
		To record commissions received in advance.			
	1	Cash	101	10,000	
		Notes Payable	240		10,000
		Obtained a 5-year, 12% loan from the New York Mutual Bank.			
	6	Shop Supplies	111	800	
		Cash	101		800
		Purchased a large quantity of shop supplies.			
	7	Accounts Payable	230	35	
		Cash	101		35
		Paid telephone bill for April.			
	10	Accounts Payable	230	70	
		Cash	101		70
		Paid bill for electricity for April.			
	15	Office Supplies Expense	572	70	
		Cash	101		70
		Purchased additional office supplies.			
	22	Advertising and Promotion Expense	574	150	
		Cash	101		150
		Placed an advertisement in the newspaper.			
	25	Advertising and Promotion Expense	574	60	
		Cash	101		60
		Placed another ad in the newspaper.			
	31	Cash	101	250	
		Accounts Receivable	103		250
		Received partial payment only of $700 commission due from client for sale made on April 12th.			
	31	Rent Expense	567	400	
		Cash	101		400
		Paid rent for May.			

May	31	Accounts Payable	230	150	
		Cash	101		150
		Paid for ad placed on April 14th.			
	31	Utilities Expense	569	80	
		Cash	101		80
		Paid bill for electricity and gas for May.			
	31	Accounts Payable	230	500	
		Cash	101		500
		Remitted payment for office furniture purchased in March.			
	31	Salaries Expense	584	600	
		Cash	101		600
		Paid the part-time secretary.			
	31	Telephone Expense	568	40	
		Cash	101		40
		Paid telephone bill for May.			
	31	Cash	101	7,100	
		Commissions	455		7,100
		To record commissions earned in May.			
	31	Jack Fraser, Drawings	344	2,000	
		Cash	101		2,000
		Withdrew cash for personal use.			

After the journal entries for the operating transactions for the month of May have been posted to the ledger, it is a good idea to prepare a trial balance to ensure that no errors in posting have been made up to this point of our procedure.

The trial balance prepared after all of the operating transactions for the month of May have been posted to the ledger is illustrated in Exhibit 4-22. The ledger, itself, is not shown at this stage, but do realize how the trial balance is prepared. We will illustrate the ledger after the adjusting entries for May have been posted.

Exhibit 4-22: Trial balance after operating transactions for May have been posted to the ledger.

Pacific Printers Mart
Trial Balance
May 31, 1997

Cash	$15,100	
Accounts Receivable	450	
Unexpired Insurance	360	
Shop Supplies	800	
Office Equipment	1,800	
Accumulated Depreciation: Office Equipment		$ 25
Furniture and Fixtures	2,400	
Accumulated Depreciation: Furniture and Fixtures		20
Automobile	7,200	
Accumulated Depreciation: Automobile		150
Accounts Payable		900
Unearned Commissions		1,200
Notes Payable		10,000
Jack Fraser, Capital		12,115
Jack Fraser, Drawings	2,000	
Commissions		7,100
Rent Expense	400	
Telephone Expense	40	
Utilities Expense	80	
Office Supplies Expense	70	
Advertising and Promotion Expense	210	
Salaries Expense	600	
	$31,510	$31,510

ADJUSTING ENTRIES FOR MAY

Because we worked carefully, no errors were made, and the trial balance balances. That was our only purpose in preparing a trial balance at this stage—to ensure that no errors had occurred, and had any errors occurred, to detect and correct them early in the accounting cycle. We may, therefore, go on to the next step in the accounting cycle, which is to enter all of the adjusting entries into the journal for the month of May. These adjusting entries are illustrated in Exhibit 4-23.

Exhibit 4-23: Adjusting entries for the month of May.

Journal — **Page 5**

1997					
May	31	Insurance Expense	571	30	
		Unexpired Insurance	106		30
		To record insurance expense for the month of May.			
	31	Shop Supplies Expense	573	40	
		Shop Supplies	111		40
		To record amount of shop supplies consumed during May.			
	31	Depreciation Expense: Office Equipment	592	25	
		Accum. Deprn.: Office Equipment	113		25
		To record depreciation for May.			
	31	Deprn. Expense: Furniture and Fixtures	593	20	
		Accum. Deprn.: Furniture and Fixtures	115		20
		To record depreciation for May.			
	31	Depreciation Expense: Automobile	594	150	
		Accumulated Depreciation: Automobile	117		150
		To record depreciation for May.			
	31	Unearned Commissions	233	100	
		Commissions	455		100
		To record commissions earned in May.			
	31	Salaries Expense	584	1,500	
		Salaries Payable	231		1,500
		To record salary expense for May.			
	31	Interest and Service Charges Expense	575	100	
		Interest Payable	232		100
		To record accrued interest for May.			
	31	Accounts Receivable	103	200	
		Commissions	455		200
		To record commissions earned on photocopying during May.			

LEDGER AFTER POSTING ADJUSTING ENTRIES

After the adjusting entries for the month of May have been posted to the ledger, the ledger appears as shown in Exhibit 4-24. Now that we have an opportunity to examine the ledger, we can see that the operating entries for May, although not shown by illustrating the ledger at that time, were posted after all.

Exhibit 4-24: Complete ledger after operating and adjusting entries have been posted.

				Cash					101
1997					1997				
March	1		1	10,000	March	5		1	7,700
	31		1	250		15		1	500
April	5		2	1,200		31		1	500
	21		2	4,500	April	1		2	100
	30	16,200	2	250		7		2	30
						30		2	600
						30		2	400
						30		2	1,500
						30	13,130	2	1,800
						30	14,335	4	1,205
						30	Balance	✓	1,865
				16,200					16,200
1997					1997				
May	1	Balance	✓	1,865	May	1		5	360
	1		5	1,200		6		5	800
	1		5	10,000		7		5	35
	31		5	250		10		5	70
	31		5	7,100		15		5	70
						22		5	150
						25		5	60
						31		5	400
						31		5	150
						31		5	80
						31		5	500
						31		5	600
						31		5	40
						31	5,315	5	2,000
						31	Balance	✓	15,100
				20,415					20,415

1997									
June	1	Balance	✓	15,100					

Accounts Receivable 103

1997					1997				
March	20		1	500	March	31		1	250
April	12	1,200	2	700	April	30	500	2	250
						30	Balance	✓	700
				1,200					1,200
1997					1997				
May	1	Balance	✓	700	May	31		5	250
	31		5	200		31	Balance	✓	650
				900					900
1997									
June	1	Balance	✓	650					

Unexpired Insurance 106

1997					1997				
May	1		5	360	May	31		5	30
						31	Balance	✓	330
				360					360
1997									
June	1	Balance	✓	330					

Shop Supplies 111

1997					1997				
May	6		5	800	May	31		5	40
						31	Balance	✓	760
				800					800
1997									
June	1	Balance	✓	760					

Office Equipment 112

1997								
March 11		1	1,800					

Accumulated Depreciation: Office Equipment 113

				1997				
				April	30		3	25
				May	31	50	5	25

Furniture and Fixtures 114

1997								
March 15		1	2,400					

Accumulated Depreciation: Furniture and Fixtures 115

				1997				
				April	30		3	20
				May	31	40	5	20

Automobile 116

1997				1997				
March 5		1	7,700	March	20		1	500
				April	30	Balance	✓	7,200
			7,700					7,700
1997								
May 1	Balance	✓	7,200					

Accumulated Depreciation: Automobile 117

				1997				
				April	30		3	150
				May	31	300	5	150

Accounts Payable 230

1997					1997				
March	31	1	500	March	11		1	1,800	
April	30	2,300	2	1,800		15		1	1,900
	30	Balance	✓	1,655	April	14		2	150
						30		2	35
						30	3,955	2	70
				3,955					3,955
1997					1997				
May	7		5	35	May	1	Balance	✓	1,655
	10		5	70					
	31		5	150					
	31		5	500					
	31	Balance	✓	900					
				1,655					1,655
					1997				
					June	1	Balance	✓	900

Salaries Payable 231

					1997				
					May	31		5	1,500

Interest Payable 232

					1997				
					May	31		5	100

Unearned Commissions 233

1997					1997				
May	31		5	100	May	1		5	1,200
	31	Balance	✓	1,100					
				1,200					1,200
					1997				
					June	1	Balance	✓	1,100

Notes Payable 240

					1997				
					May	1		5	10,000

Jack Fraser, Capital 343

1997					1997				
April	30		4	1,500	March	1		1	10,000
	30	2,705	4	1,205	April	30	14,820	4	4,820
	30	Balance	✓	12,115					
				14,820					14,820
					1997				
					May	1	Balance	✓	12,115

Jack Fraser, Drawings 344

1997					1997				
April	30		2	1,500	April	30		4	1,500
1997									
May	31		5	2,000					

Income Taxes 349

1997					1997				
April	30		4	1,205	April	30		4	1,205

Commissions 455

1997					1997				
April	30		4	6,400	April	5		2	1,200
						12		2	700
						21		2	4,500
				6,400					6,400
					1997				
					May	31		5	7,100
						31		5	100
						31		5	200

Rent Expense 567

Date		Ref.	Amount	Date		Ref.	Amount
1997				1997			
April	30	2	400	April	30	4	400
1997							
May	31	5	400				

Telephone Expense 568

Date		Ref.	Amount	Date		Ref.	Amount
1997				1997			
April	30	2	35	April	30	4	35
1997							
May	31	5	40				

Utilities Expense 569

Date		Ref.	Amount	Date		Ref.	Amount
1997				1997			
April	30	2	70	April	30	4	70
1997							
May	31	5	80				

Insurance Expense 571

Date		Ref.	Amount	Date		Ref.	Amount
1997							
May	31	5	30				

Office Supplies Expense 572

Date		Ref.	Amount	Date		Ref.	Amount
1997				1997			
April	7	2	30	April	30	4	30
1997							
May	31	5	70				

Shop Supplies Expense 573

Date		Ref.	Amount	Date		Ref.	Amount
1997							
May	31	5	40				

Advertising and Promotion Expense — 574

1997				1997			
April	1	2	100	April	30	4	250
	14	2	150				
			250				250
1997							
May	22	5	150				
	25	5	60				

Interest and Service Charges Expense — 575

1997							
May	31	5	100				

Salaries Expense — 584

1997				1997			
April	30	2	600	April	30	4	600
1997							
May	31	5	600				
	31	5	1,500				

Depreciation Expense: Office Equipment — 592

1997				1997			
April	30	3	25	April	30	4	25
1997							
May	31	5	25				

Depreciation Expense: Furniture and Fixtures — 593

1997				1997			
April	30	3	20	April	30	4	20
1997							
May	31	5	20				

Depreciation Expense: Automobile — 594

1997				1997			
April	30	3	150	April	30	4	150
1997							
May	31	5	150				

Income Summary — 600

1997				1997			
April	30	4	1,580	April	30	4	6,400
	30	4	4,820				
			6,400				6,400

TRIAL BALANCE

Once again, we may prepare a trial balance, now that the adjusting entries have been posted to the ledger, to ensure that the ledger is still in balance. Once we have proved that no errors have occurred, we may then proceed to prepare a preliminary set of financial statements with the objective of computing the amount of income taxes that are payable for the month of May. The trial balance for Pacific Printers Mart, prepared at the end of May after the adjusting entries have been posted to the ledger, is illustrated in Exhibit 4-25.

Pacific Printers Mart
Trial Balance
May 31, 1997

Cash	$15,100	
Accounts Receivable	650	
Unexpired Insurance	330	
Shop Supplies	760	
Office Equipment	1,800	
Accumulated Depreciation: Office Equipment		$ 50
Furniture and Fixtures	2,400	
Accumulated Depreciation: Furniture and Fixtures		40

Automobile	7,200	
Accumulated Depreciation: Automobile		300
Accounts Payable		900
Salaries Payable		1,500
Interest Payable		100
Unearned Commissions		1,100
Notes Payable		10,000
Jack Fraser, Capital		12,115
Jack Fraser, Drawings	2,000	
Commissions		7,400
Rent Expense	400	
Telephone Expense	40	
Utilities Expense	80	
Insurance Expense	30	
Office Supplies Expense	70	
Shop Supplies Expense	40	
Advertising and Promotion Expense	210	
Interest and Service Charges Expense	100	
Salaries Expense	2,100	
Depreciation Expense: Office Equipment	25	
Depreciation Expense: Furniture and Fixtures	20	
Depreciation Expense: Automobile	150	
	$33,505	$33,505

Exhibit 4-25: Trial balance after adjusting entries have been posted to the ledger.

PRELIMINARY FINANCIAL STATEMENTS

We may easily prepare a set of financial statements from the data in the trial balance in Exhibit 4-25. The purpose of this preliminary set of financial statements is to enable us to compute the amount of income taxes payable. Although only an income statement is required for this purpose, both statements are presented; the income statement is presented in Exhibit 4-26 and the balance sheet is presented in Exhibit 4-27.

The balance sheet in Exhibit 4-27 is presented in *classified report format.* All this means is that the accounts which make up the balance sheet have been separated into subgroups to make this statement more convenient to analyze. Assets have been divided into two groups—current assets, and plant and equipment. Liabilities have been divided into two groups as well—current liabilities and long-term liabilities. You will learn how to make use of these subgroups on the balance sheet when you study finance. At the moment, we are studying *small business accounting* and our objective is to learn how to properly analyze and record financial transactions and to learn how to properly prepare a set of financial statements from our accounting data.

Pacific Printers Mart
Income Statement
For the month ending May 31, 1997

Revenue:		
Commissions		$7,400
Expenses:		
Rent Expense	$400	
Telephone Expense	40	
Utilities Expense	80	
Insurance Expense	30	
Office Supplies Expense	70	
Shop Supplies Expense	40	
Advertising and Promotion Expense	210	
Interest and Service Charges Expense	100	
Salaries Expense	2,100	
Depreciation Expense: Office Equipment	25	
Depreciation Expense: Furniture and Fixtures	20	
Depreciation Expense: Automobile	150	3,265
Net Income:		$4,135

Exhibit 4-26: Income statement for May before computation of income taxes.

Exhibit 4-27: Balance sheet at the end of May, in classified report format, before computation of income taxes.

Pacific Printers Mart
Balance Sheet
May 31, 1997
Assets

Current Assets:		
Cash	$15,100	
Accounts Receivable	650	
Unexpired Insurance	330	
Total Current Assets:		$16,080

Plant and Equipment:			
Shop Supplies		$ 760	
Office Equipment	$1,800		
Less: Accumulated Depreciation: Office Equipment	50	1,750	
Furniture and Fixtures	2,400		
Less: Accumulated Depreciation: Furniture and Fixtures	40	2,360	
Automobile	7,200		
Less: Accumulated Depreciation: Automobile	300	6,900	
Total Plant and Equipment:			11,770
			$27,850

Liabilities and Owner's Equity

Current Liabilities:			
Accounts Payable		$ 900	
Salaries Payable		1,500	
Interest Payable		100	
Unearned Commissions		1,100	
Total Current Liabilities:			$3,600
Long-term Liabilities:			
Notes Payable			10,000
Owner's Equity:			
Jack Fraser, Capital, May 1, 1997		$12,115	
Net Income	$4,135		
Less: Jack Fraser, Drawings	2,000	2,135	
Jack Fraser, Capital, May 31, 1997			14,250
			$27,850

Notice that the amount of net income for May, which is $4,135 ties into the owner's equity section of the balance sheet. After adding the net income for the month to the balance in Jack Fraser, Capital, at the beginning of the month, and subtracting the amount of withdrawals, we arrive at the amount of owner's equity, in the account, Jack Fraser, Capital, at the end of May. We have not yet, however, calculated nor made any entries for income taxes.

INCOME TAXES

The only entry remaining before closing the books is the entry for income taxes. In order to compute the amount of income taxes we need to know the amount of net income. That is why we prepared a trial balance, and, in particular, an income statement—to arrive at a figure for the amount of net income. From Exhibit 4-26, the amount of net income is $4,135. Actually, it was not necessary to prepare an income statement to arrive at the amount of net income. We could just as well, have computed the amount of net income by examining the trial balance in Exhibit 4-25. All we need have done is taken the balance in the revenue account, Commissions, which is $7,400 and subtracted the sum of the debit entries of the accounts below the revenue account in the list of accounts in the trial balance, which amounts to $3,265, to arrive at the amount of net income. This way we obtain the very same figure for net income which is $4,135.

Let us assume that the income tax rate is 20%. The actual rate is prescribed by the tax department and may vary from year to year. But this figure will be sufficient for our purposes. The amount of income tax is calculated below:

Income taxes = $4,135 x 20% = $827

Now that we have computed the amount of income tax, we may make a journal entry for income tax as illustrated in Exhibit 4-28.

Journal **Page 5**

1997					
May	31	Income Taxes	349	827	
		Income Taxes Payable	236		827
		To record income taxes accrued to the end of May.			

Exhibit 4-28: Entry to record income taxes.

In our example, payment for income taxes need not be remitted to the tax department until July. Until that time the liability *Income Taxes Payable* will remain on the balance sheet. It is handled like any other liability. When these income taxes are paid, the Income Taxes Payable account will be debited and the Cash account will be credited.

As to the nature of the *Income Taxes* account, remember it is not an expense account, and does not appear among the list of expenses on the income statement. Rather, it appears as a deduction, on the income statement, from net income to arrive at the amount of *net income after taxes.* In the closing procedure, the Income Taxes account is closed directly into the owner's equity account, Jack Fraser, Capital. You might think of Income Taxes as a withdrawal of funds (and a corresponding decrease in owner's equity) to pay taxes. Closing the Income Taxes account employs the same logic as closing the drawings account. After posting our entry in Exhibit 4-28, the ledger appears as shown in Exhibit 4-29.

Income Taxes Payable							236
				1997			
				May	*31*	*5*	*827*

Income Taxes							349
1997				1997			
April	30	4	1,205	April	30	4	1,205
1997							
May	*31*	*5*	*827*				

Exhibit 4-29: Income taxes for May posted to ledger.

CLOSING ENTRIES AT THE END OF MAY

In closing the books, we begin by turning to the first income statement account in the ledger, which is the revenue account, Commissions. The credit balance in the revenue account is transferred to the credit side of the Income Summary account by means of making and posting an appropriate journal entry. We continue going through the ledger, and transfer the debit balances in the expense accounts to the debit side of Income Summary, by means of making and posting a journal entry. Next we compute the net balance in the Income Summary account, which has a credit balance when operations have been profitable. This credit balance in Income Summary is transferred to the credit side of Jack Fraser, Capital, closing the Income Summary account. (When an operating loss has occurred, the debit balance in Income Summary is transferred to the debit side of Jack Fraser, Capital). The transfer, of course, is accomplished by making an entry in the journal and then posting this entry to the ledger. Finally, the debit balances in Jack Fraser, Drawings, and Income Taxes are transferred to the debit side of Jack Fraser, Capital, by means of making and posting appropriate journal entries, closing out the drawings and income taxes accounts. The closing entries at the end of May are illustrated in Exhibit 4-30.

Exhibit 4-30: Closing entries at the end of May.

Journal **Page 6**

1997					
May	31	Commissions	455	7,400	
		Income Summary	600		7,400
		To close the revenue account.			
	31	Income Summary	600	3,265	
		Rent Expense	567		400
		Telephone Expense	568		40
		Utilities Expense	569		80
		Insurance Expense	571		30
		Office Supplies Expense	572		70
		Shop Supplies Expense	573		40
		Advertising and Promotion Expense	574		210
		Interest and Service Charges Expense	575		100
		Salaries Expense	584		2,100
		Depreciation Expense: Office Equipment	592		25
		Deprn. Expense: Furniture and Fixtures	593		20
		Depreciation Expense: Automobile	594		150
		To close the expense accounts.			
	31	Income Summary	600	4,135	
		Jack Fraser, Capital	343		4,135
		To close the Income Summary account.			
	31	Jack Fraser, Capital	343	2,000	
		Jack Fraser, Drawings	344		2,000
		To close the drawings account.			
	31	Jack Fraser, Capital	343	827	
		Income Taxes	349		827
		To close the Income Taxes account.			

There are no further entries of any kind to be made for the month of May. The balance sheet accounts have been ruled and balanced and the income statement accounts, the Income Summary account, the drawings account, and the Income Taxes account have all been closed in preparation for recording entries for the next month, the month of June. The complete ledger after posting the closing entries appears as shown in Exhibit 4-31. This complete ledger is followed by a set of financial statements; an income statement in Exhibit 4-32 and a balance sheet in Exhibit 4-33.

Exhibit 4-31: **Complete ledger after closing the books at the end of May.**

Cash 101

1997					1997				
March	1		1	10,000	March	5		1	7,700
	31		1	250		15		1	500
April	5		2	1,200		31		1	500
	21		2	4,500	April	1		2	100
	30	16,200	2	250		7		2	30
						30		2	600
						30		2	400
						30		2	1,500
						30	13,130	2	1,800
						30	14,335	4	1,205
						30	Balance	✓	1,865
				16,200					16,200
1997					1997				
May	1	Balance	✓	1,865	May	1		5	360
	1		5	1,200		6		5	800
	1		5	10,000		7		5	35
	31		5	250		10		5	70
	31		5	7,100		15		5	70
						22		5	150
						25		5	60
						31		5	400
						31		5	150
						31		5	80
						31		5	500
						31		5	600
						31		5	40
						31	5,315	5	2,000
						31	Balance	✓	15,100
				20,415					20,415
1997									
June	1	Balance	✓	15,100					

Accounts Receivable 103

1997					1997				
March	20		1	500	March	31		1	250
April	12	1,200	2	700	April	30	500	2	250
						30	Balance	✓	700
				1,200					1,200
1997					1997				
May	1	Balance	✓	700	May	31		5	250
	31		5	200		31	Balance	✓	650
				900					900
1997									
June	1	Balance	✓	650					

Unexpired Insurance 106

1997					1997				
May	1		5	360	May	31		5	30
						31	Balance	✓	330
				360					360
1997									
June	1	Balance	✓	330					

Shop Supplies 111

1997					1997				
May	6		5	800	May	31		5	40
						31	Balance	✓	760
				800					800
1997									
June	1	Balance	✓	760					

Office Equipment 112

1997									
March	11		1	1,800					

Accumulated Depreciation: Office Equipment — 113

					1997				
					April	30		3	25
					May	31	50	5	25

Furniture and Fixtures — 114

1997									
March	15		1	2,400					

Accumulated Depreciation: Furniture and Fixtures — 115

					1997				
					April	30		3	20
					May	31	40	5	20

Automobile — 116

1997					1997				
March	5		1	7,700	March	20		1	500
					April	30	Balance	✓	7,200
				7,700					7,700
1997									
May	1	Balance	✓	7,200					

Accumulated Depreciation: Automobile — 117

					1997				
					April	30		3	150
					May	31	300	5	150

Accounts Payable — 230

1997					1997				
March	31		1	500	March	11		1	1,800
April	30	2,300	2	1,800		15		1	1,900
	30	Balance	✓	1,655	April	14		2	150
						30		2	35
						30	3,955	2	70
				3,955					3,955

1997					1997				
May	7		5	35	May	1	Balance	✓	1,655
	10		5	70					
	31		5	150					
	31		5	500					
	31	Balance	✓	900					
				1,655					1,655
					1997				
					June	1	Balance	✓	900

Salaries Payable 231

					1997				
					May	31		5	1,500

Interest Payable 232

					1997				
					May	31		5	100

Unearned Commissions 233

1997					1997				
May	31		5	100	May	1		5	1,200
	31	Balance	✓	1,100					
				1,200					1,200
					1997				
					June	1	Balance	✓	1,100

Income Taxes Payable 236

					1997				
					May	*31*		*5*	*827*

Notes Payable 240

					1997				
					May	1		5	10,000

Jack Fraser, Capital 343

1997					1997				
April	30		4	1,500	March	1		1	10,000
	30	2,705	4	1,205	April	30	14,820	4	4,820
	30	Balance	✓	12,115					
				14,820					14,820
1997					1997				
May	31		6	2,000	May	1	Balance	✓	12,115
	31		6	827		31		6	4,135
	31	Balance	✓	13,423					
				16,250					16,250
					1997				
					June	1	Balance	✓	13,423

Jack Fraser, Drawings 344

1997					1997				
April	30		2	1,500	April	30		4	1,500
1997					1997				
May	31		5	2,000	May	31		6	2,000

Income Taxes 349

1997					1997				
April	30		4	1,205	April	30		4	1,205
1997					1997				
May	31		5	827	May	31		6	827

Commissions — 455

1997				1997			
April	30	4	6,400	April	5	2	1,200
					12	2	700
					21	2	4,500
			6,400				6,400
1997				1997			
May	31	6	7,400	May	31	5	7,100
					31	5	100
					31	5	200
			7,400				7,400

Rent Expense — 567

1997				1997			
April	30	2	400	April	30	4	400
1997				1997			
May	31	5	400	May	31	6	400

Telephone Expense — 568

1997				1997			
April	30	2	35	April	30	4	35
1997				1997			
May	31	5	40	May	31	6	40

Utilities Expense — 569

1997				1997			
April	30	2	70	April	30	4	70
1997				1997			
May	31	5	80	May	31	6	80

Insurance Expense 571

1997				1997			
May	31	5	30	May	31	6	30

Office Supplies Expense 572

1997				1997			
April	7	2	30	April	30	4	30
1997				1997			
May	31	5	70	May	31	6	70

Shop Supplies Expense 573

1997				1997			
May	31	5	40	May	31	6	40

Advertising and Promotion Expense 574

1997				1997			
April	1	2	100	April	30	4	250
	14	2	150				
			250				250
1997				1997			
May	22	5	150	May	31	6	210
	25	5	60				
			210				210

Interest and Service Charges Expense 575

1997				1997			
May	31	5	100	May	31	6	100

Salaries Expense — 584

1997				1997			
April	30	2	600	April	30	4	600
1997				1997			
May	31	5	600	May	31	6	2,100
	31	5	1,500				
			2,100				2,100

Depreciation Expense: Office Equipment — 592

1997				1997			
April	30	3	25	April	30	4	25
1997				1997			
May	31	5	25	May	31	6	25

Depreciation Expense: Furniture and Fixtures — 593

1997				1997			
April	30	3	20	April	30	4	20
1997				1997			
May	31	5	20	May	31	6	20

Depreciation Expense: Automobile — 594

1997				1997			
April	30	3	150	April	30	4	150
1997				1997			
May	31	5	150	May	31	6	150

Income Summary							600
1997				1997			
April	30	4	1,580	April	30	4	6,400
	30	4	4,820				
			6,400				6,400
1997				1997			
May	31	6	3,265	May	31	6	7,400
	31	6	4,135				
			7,400				7,400

Exhibit 4-32: Income statement for May.

Pacific Printers Mart
Income Statement
For the month ending May 31, 1997

Revenue:		
Commissions		$7,400
Expenses:		
Rent Expense	$400	
Telephone Expense	40	
Utilities Expense	80	
Insurance Expense	30	
Office Supplies Expense	70	
Shop Supplies Expense	40	
Advertising and Promotion Expense	210	
Interest and Service Charges Expense	100	
Salaries Expense	2,100	
Depreciation Expense: Office Equipment	25	
Depreciation Expense: Furniture and Fixtures	20	
Depreciation Expense: Automobile	150	3,265
Net Income:		$4,135
Less: Income Taxes		827
Net Income after Taxes:		$3,308

Exhibit 4-33: Balance sheet at the end of May.

Pacific Printers Mart
Balance Sheet
May 31, 1997

Assets

Current Assets:			
Cash		$15,100	
Accounts Receivable		650	
Unexpired Insurance		330	
Total Current Assets:			$16,080
Plant and Equipment:			
Shop Supplies		$ 760	
Office Equipment	$1,800		
Less: Accumulated Depreciation: Office Equipment	50	1,750	
Furniture and Fixtures	2,400		
Less: Accumulated Depreciation: Furniture and Fixtures	40	2,360	
Automobile	7,200		
Less: Accumulated Depreciation: Automobile	300	6,900	
Total Plant and Equipment:			11,770
			$27,850

Liabilities and Owner's Equity

Current Liabilities:		
Accounts Payable	$ 900	
Salaries Payable	1,500	
Interest Payable	100	
Unearned Commissions	1,100	
Income Taxes Payable	827	
Total Current Liabilities:		$4,427
Long-term Liabilities:		
Notes Payable		10,000
Owner's Equity:		
Jack Fraser, Capital, May 31, 1997		13,423
		$27,850

REVIEW OF THE ACCOUNTING CYCLE

The complete accounting cycle for a proprietorship engaged in the sale of services, but not the sale of merchandise, may be summarized as follows:

1. Record all operating transactions in the journal and post these entries to the ledger. Prepare a trial balance, if desired.
2. Determine the amount of all adjusting entries and record these entries in the journal. Post these adjusting entries to the ledger. Balance and rule the balance sheet accounts. It is advisable to prepare a trial balance.
3. Determine the amount of net income by inspecting the trial balance after the adjusting entries have been posted to the ledger or by preparing a preliminary income statement. Compute the amount of income taxes, record the entry for income taxes in the journal and post to the ledger.
4. Close the books. This means record entries in the journal, transferring the credit balance in the revenue account and the debit balances in the expense accounts to the Income Summary account. Post these entries to the ledger. Compute the balance in the Income Summary account. Make a journal entry to transfer the credit balance (if operations were profitable the balance will be a credit balance; otherwise it will be a debit balance if the business has suffered an operating loss) in Income Summary to the owner's equity account, Jack Fraser, Capital. Post this entry to the ledger. Make entries in the journal to transfer the debit balances in the drawings account, Jack Fraser, Drawings, and the Income Taxes account, to the owner's equity account, Jack Fraser, Capital. Draw a dashed line under the last entry in each account as it is closed.
5. Prepare an income statement and a balance sheet.

Exercises

1. Explain the difference between operating entries and adjusting entries. Are adjusting entries really necessary? What would be the likely consequence, in terms of impact on the financial statements, if adjusting entries were not made?

2. List four situations where adjusting entries are required.

3. How does a classified balance sheet differ from one that is in simple report form?

4. In proper sequence, list the steps of the accounting cycle.

Problems

1. Prepare journal entries for the transactions listed below. Also, prepare adjusting entries, where required, at the end of the month. Treat a substantial portion of a month as if it was a full month.

a.	March	1	A 12-month insurance policy costing $240 is purchased, paying cash.
b.	January	2	A quantity of office supplies, sufficient to last 10 months is purchased for $600, paying cash. At the end of the month it was estimated that $540 worth of office supplies remained unused.
c.	June	3	An automobile costing $14,000 was purchased with a down payment of $8,000 and the remainder is to be paid in equal monthly installments under the interest free plan. Five-year depreciation is to be employed.
d.	May	2	Advance car rental purchases 10 cars for a total cost of $100,000, paying cash. Use 5-year depreciation.
e.	May	3	Allied Wholesalers purchases warehouse equipment costing $60,000.
f.	April	2	A farm building was purchased for $25,000 cash (20-year property).
g.	May	2	The goodwill of a business was purchased for $6,000, paying cash.

h. January 2 — James Fitzbarman, Esq., an attorney, receives $10,000 cash in advance as a retainer fee from a client. During the month of January $2,400 was earned.

i. January 2 — Barry McAddman, an accountant, accepts $6,000 cash in advance payment for work to be done during the year. At the end of January his records reveal that $1,946 was earned during the month.

j. June 10 — Joe Clincher, a salesman, receives $4,000 in commissions in advance. During the month of June his earnings amounted to $1,944.

k. June 30 — The telephone bill for the month of June was received. Total amount of the bill is $46.82 with payment required by July 10th.

l. April 30 — Salaries expense for April is $1,800. Last day of the month falls on Thursday, April 30th. Payday is Friday, May 1st.

m. March 31 — Interest on a loan amounts to $47.18 but need not be paid until December 31st.

n. October 9 — Bob Clincher (no relation to Joe Clincher), a salesman, earns $900 in commissions which will not be received until November 15th.

o. July 31 — George Dazzler, a car salesman, earned $3,610 in commissions during the month of July. Payday is on August 10th.

p. May 1 — Automobile insurance costing $600 is purchased, paying cash.

q. June 28 — A maple boardroom table is purchased for $7,000 and paid for in cash.

r. July 2 — A quantity of shop supplies, sufficient to last several months, is purchased for $1,200, paying cash. During July $190 worth of supplies was consumed.

2. For the business listed below:
   a. Prepare journal entries for all operating transactions.
   b. Post all operating transactions to the ledger.
   c. Prepare a trial balance.
   d. Compute and record adjusting entries and post to the ledger.
   e. Prepare an adjusted trial balance.

f. Prepare a preliminary set of financial statements.
g. Compute the amount of income taxes. Rate is 20%. Record entry for income taxes in the journal and post to the ledger.
h. Close the books and prepare an after closing trial balance.
i. Prepare a final set of financial statements, taking income taxes into consideration.

October	1	Fred Fender deposits $90,000 in a bank account in the name of the business, Pacific Auto Body Shop.
	2	Buys land for $45,000, paying cash.
	3	Erects a building at a total cost of $18,720. The contractor is paid $10,000 immediately with the remaining balance to be paid by the end of the year. A promissory note was signed. Depreciate over 39 years.
	4	Sufficient supplies to paint a sign were purchased at a cost of $150, paying cash.
	5	Sold a strip of land to the neighboring business for $5,000. Payment would be received at the end of November.
	8	Purchased shop equipment costing $12,000, paying cash (5-year property).
	8	Purchased office furniture costing $1,764 on credit. To be paid for in three monthly installments with the first installment in the amount of $600 due at the end of October.
	8	Paid $120 for a business license (cost does not vary with time of year).
	8	A 24-month insurance policy is purchased for $720, paying cash. Coverage is retroactive to the beginning of the month.
	11	A quantity of shop supplies, sufficient to last several months, is purchased at a cost of $2,000, paying cash.
	14	A tow truck was purchased for $18,000. A down payment of $5,000 was made with the balance to be paid in equal monthly installments of $1,000 each beginning with the present month. Depreciate over 5 years.
	14	A loan for $30,000 was negotiated with the bank. A promissory note was signed, agreeing to pay back principal and interest at a rate of 10% per annum at the end of a five-year period.
	15	Receipts for the first half of the month totaling $8,941 were deposited in the bank account.
	16	An employee was hired at a salary of $2,000 per month. The first payday is on Friday, November 2nd.
	17	Ralph Speedster advances $3,000 to Pacific Auto Body Shop for auto body repairs to his Mercedes. By the end of the month only half of the work was completed.
	19	Fred Fender, proprietor, withdraws $2,000 from the business for his personal use.
	24	Advertisements are placed in the local newspaper, costing $2,418, and to be paid for by the end of November.

October 25	Office supplies costing $230 are purchased and paid for in cash. These supplies were used up within 5 days time.
31	Auto body repairs were made to three cars but are all only half completed. Firm quotes totaling $7,700 were given to the owners. Payment in full was received in advance.
31	Receipts for the second half of the month totaling $12,898 were deposited in the bank account.
31	The first installment payment was remitted on the tow truck.
31	Approximately $600 worth of shop supplies were used up during the month, based on a quick count of supplies in the storeroom.
31	Remitted payment on office furniture.

3. The net income for Eastern Timber Brokers is $147,060. Calculate the amount of income taxes at a rate of 20%.

4. Record the amount of income taxes from problem 3, in the journal.

5. Shop supplies costing $4,718 are purchased on January 2nd and paid for with cash. These supplies are expected to last six months. Record this event in the journal.

6. Record the adjusting entry at the end of January for supplies consumed during the month, from problem 5 above.

CHAPTER FIVE

Merchandising Transactions

RECORDING PURCHASES OF MERCHANDISE

In our Pacific Printers Mart example, so far, we have not considered the purchase of merchandise for resale. All revenue was earned by performing services for a fee or commission. Printing equipment, for example, that was owned by a client would be sold for the client and a commission collected on the sale. At this point in time, the beginning of June, Pacific Printers Mart owns no merchandise whatsoever, that was acquired for resale to customers.

On June 2nd, Pacific Printers Mart begins to acquire stock for resale to its customers. The first purchase consists of a variety of inks, solvents, plates, blankets, and other material used by printers. On June 2nd, the transaction in Exhibit 5-1 is entered in the journal to record the acquisition of stock for resale.

	Journal			**Page 7**
1997				
June 2	Purchases	463	8,000	
	Cash	101		8,000
	To record purchase of merchandise for resale from ACME Wholesale Inc.			

Exhibit 5-1: Journal entry to record purchase of merchandise for resale.

In analyzing this transaction, think of Purchases as an asset account and analyze it as an asset account, even though it appears after the revenue section of the small business ledger accounts index (see Appendix). Strictly speaking, the Purchases account is part of the *Cost of Goods Sold* section of the income statement, which is used to collect data to arrive at a figure on the cost of merchandise sold during a period. Merchandise that remains unsold is called Inventory. The Inventory account *is* located among the asset accounts on the balance sheet. Thus, we may apply the rules of debit and credit to Purchases and the remaining accounts in the Cost of Goods Sold section of the income statement in the same manner as if they were asset accounts. This explanation is easier to visualize than considering the impact of cost of goods transactions on owner's equity. None of the "asset" accounts in the Cost of Goods Sold section of the income statement, with the exception of ending inventory, ever appears in the asset section of the balance sheet, because this is not necessary. The reason this is so will become clear when we complete the merchandising cycle.

Only goods acquired for resale are debited to the Purchases account. Although goods such as shop supplies or office supplies, and other assets are undoubtedly purchased, these items are not purchases in the sense of having been acquired for resale.

In accounting, we must always consider the purpose of a transaction to determine its true nature. An automobile acquired for resale by a car dealer is a purchase; that same automobile acquired by a pizza parlor for use in delivering pizzas is an asset. In the first instance that automobile must be recorded in the Purchases account; in the second instance it must be recorded in the Automobile account.

Again, only goods acquired for resale are debited to the Purchases account. And, they must be debited to the Purchases account and not to the Inventory account. Each of these accounts has a specific meaning and purpose. (Remember, in accounting, absolutely every transaction is expressed in terms of money—dollars and cents—but money does not mean cash, unless we are referring to the Cash account, as Cash, itself, is a specific asset account).

Likewise with Purchases and Inventory. Inventory, specifically refers to those goods acquired for resale that remain unsold at the end of the accounting period and which will be available for resale at the beginning of the succeeding accounting period. The meaning of purchases and inventory will become clearer when we complete the merchandising cycle in our illustration.

COST OF FREIGHT ADDED TO PURCHASES

On June 3rd, additional merchandise is acquired for resale from XYZ Wholesale Inc.; this time on credit with payment to be made in 90 days. A separate trucking firm delivers the goods to the premises of Pacific Printers Mart and demands payment for delivery, in cash. A journal entry to record this transaction is shown in Exhibit 5-2.

Notice the new account, Transportation-in. This is one of the *Cost of Goods Sold* accounts and is analyzed as an asset account. It is not an expense account and does not appear in the expense section of the income statement. In fact, delivery charges must be added to the cost of merchandise to arrive at the true cost of that merchandise. So, freight charges, incurred in connection with the delivery of goods acquired for resale, are added to the cost of merchandise on the income statement.

1997		Journal			Page 7
June	3	Purchases	463	900	
		Transportation-in	464	50	
		Accounts Payable	230		900
		Cash	101		50
		Purchased merchandise from XYZ Wholesale Inc., payment due in 90 days; paid delivery charges.			

Exhibit 5-2: Entry to record purchase of merchandise and cost of delivery.

PURCHASE RETURNS AND ALLOWANCES

When the goods received from the wholesaler are inspected, it is discovered that some of the merchandise has been damaged. XYZ Wholesale Inc. is notified of the damage and agrees to deduct $100 from their invoice. This transaction is recorded in the books of Pacific Printers Mart as illustrated in Exhibit 5-3, below.

1997		Journal			Page 7
June	4	Accounts Payable	230	100	
		Purchase Returns and Allowances	465		100
		To record allowance from XYZ Wholesale Inc. for damaged merchandise.			

Exhibit 5-3: Entry to record allowance for damaged goods.

Whether the goods are returned to the supplier, or whether the supplier simply gives us an allowance for the damage, the entry is made to the same account, Purchase Returns and Allowances. The Purchase Returns and Allowances account is analyzed in the same way as the Purchases account itself. Decreases in purchases, i.e. assets, are recorded by credits. If we want to we could simply credit the Purchases account directly, but by crediting a separate account, Purchase Returns and Allowances, we can keep track of the amount of returns and allowances in a given year. Should the amount of returns and allowances continue to increase to higher and higher levels, this information alerts the managers of a business to re-evaluate their sources of supply and take action. This information would have been lost if returns and allowances were credited directly to the Purchases account. The credit balance in the Purchase Returns and Allowances account is deducted from the debit balance in the Purchases account, in the Cost of Goods Sold section of the income statement, to arrive at the net amount of purchases.

As a business continues to grow, the managers will be forced to rely more and more on information contained in the financial statements, as direct contact with many of the functions in the business will have been lost. Purchasing, for example, will likely be carried out by specific personnel assigned to this task, with management rarely, if ever, having direct contact with suppliers. The same principle applies as the business expands to include additional outlets. Thus, financial statements must include information essential to the management and control of a business. That is why anyone managing a business should have a knowledge of accounting. Accounting involves collecting financial data and using this data to manage the financial aspects of a business.

PURCHASE DISCOUNTS

On June 11th, $1,000 worth of merchandise was purchased for resale from Speedy Distributors Inc. On the bottom of the invoice, the terms *2/10, net 30* appeared, meaning that if Pacific Printers Mart paid Speedy Distributors Inc. within ten days it could deduct 2% from the amount of the bill. If the bill was not paid within the time of the discount period the full amount of the invoice was due within 30 days. Suppliers often include discount terms on their invoices to induce prompt payment. This way the wholesaler, who sells on credit, does not itself have to borrow as much money to maintain a given size of operations, as the cash it requires is raised by collecting sooner on its credit sales.

For the retailer who does not take advantage of such discounts offered by suppliers the cost may be quite high. Consider the terms offered by the supplier in our example, 2/10, net 30. If the bill is not paid within the ten day discount period, we have use of the money that otherwise would have gone towards paying the bill for an extra 20 days, as payment is due within 30 days from the time of purchase. The cost of using this money an extra 20 days is the amount of the discount that has been lost; in percentage terms it is 2%. The annual cost of not taking advantage of discounts may be calculated as follows:

Annual cost of lost discounts = 365/20 x 2% = 36.5%

The annual cost of not taking advantage of discounts works out to 36.5%. Most businesses are able to borrow money at a much lower rate of interest. Therefore, it pays to borrow money from a bank or other lender, at a lower rate of interest, in order to take advantage of purchase discounts, or any other similar discounts. Some suppliers, in an effort to increase their cash flow, offer an additional discount if actual cash, as opposed to a check, is offered immediately at the time of purchase.

Not taking advantage of purchase discounts, or similar discounts, offered when goods or services are purchased on credit, known as trade credit, can be expensive. But sometimes this is the only source of credit available to a small business, and trade credit, with its high cost, simply reflects the higher degree of risk that suppliers are taking in extending credit to firms which may not be financially stable. Trade credit has traditionally been an important source of funding for small businesses mainly because it is relatively easy to obtain and is tied to the purchase of goods or services which the supplying firm is selling. Generally speaking, no lengthy or complicated application form need be submitted in order to qualify for and obtain trade credit and, in many instances, extensive credit checks are not made.

The journal entry to record the latest purchase of merchandise for resale, by Pacific Printers Mart, is illustrated in Exhibit 5-4.

Journal **Page 7**

1997				
June 11	Purchases	463	1,000	
	Accounts Payable	230		1,000
	Purchased merchandise from Speedy Distributors Inc. Terms 2/10, net 30.			

Exhibit 5-4: Entry for merchandise purchased on credit with terms.

Pacific Printers Mart pays its bill within the time of the discount period and is entitled to deduct the amount of the discount from the amount stated on the bill. This transaction, entered in the journal on June 20th, is illustrated in Exhibit 5-5.

Journal **Page 7**

1997				
June 20	Accounts Payable	230	1,000	
	Cash	101		980
	Purchase Discounts	466		20
	Paid Speedy Distributors Inc.			

Exhibit 5-5: Journal entry to record purchase discounts.

Because the bill was paid within the time of the discount period, $20 may be deducted from the amount due stated on the bill, and $980 is remitted in full settlement of this bill.

In analyzing this transaction consider what has happened. Because the bill was paid in full the entire amount in Accounts Payable must be eliminated, so we debit Accounts Payable $1,000. To offset this amount, we credit Cash $980 which is equal to the amount of payment made, and credit Purchase Discounts $20 which is equal to the amount of the discount ($1,000 x 2% = $20).

As was the case with Purchase Returns and Allowances discussed in the previous section, the same principle applies to the Purchase Discounts account. That is, if we wish, we may credit the amount of the discount to Purchases instead of to a separate account.

But that is poor accounting practice. Information on the amount of purchase discounts is required by the managers of a business in order to determine whether bills are being paid within the time of the discount period. If not, and if there is sufficient cash in the firm to do so, remedial action must be taken. The credit balance in the Purchase Discounts account is deducted from the debit balance in the Purchases account, in the Cost of Good Sold section of the income statement. In this manner we end up with the same result as if the Purchases account had been credited directly with the amount of the discount, but by employing a Purchase Discounts account we collect information that is useful in managing the business.

COST OF GOODS SOLD

To accommodate merchandising accounts, an income statement for a business engaged in the purchase and resale of goods, must include a Cost of Goods Sold section. This section appears just below the revenue section in the income statement. Accounts in the Cost of Goods Sold section should not be confused with expenses, although their impact on owner's equity is similar to that of expenses. All of the accounts in the Cost of Goods Sold section of the income statement may be analyzed as asset accounts, because in reality, purchases are nothing more than assets acquired for resale at a price which is higher than was paid for, in order to earn a profit. Because these goods have been marked-up in price for resale with the objective of earning a profit it makes sense to include these accounts on the income statement. The income statement, after all, was formulated to determine the amount of "profit" or net income earned during a period of time. Only the Inventory account appears among the asset accounts in the balance sheet. The remaining merchandising accounts appear in the Cost of Goods Sold section of the income statement. The arrangement of merchandising accounts on an income statement is illustrated in a sample income statement which was made up for this purpose (not the actual statement) in Exhibit 5-6.

The objective of the Cost of Goods Sold section is, like the name sounds, to arrive at the cost of goods sold during the period in question. To do this, we start by determining beginning inventory. Because Pacific Printers Mart has not previously engaged in merchandising, the beginning inventory on June 1st will be zero. Remember, inventory consists of those goods that were acquired for resale that remain unsold at the end of one accounting period and which, of course, are available for sale at the beginning of the next accounting period. To beginning inventory we add the delivered cost of purchases and subtract the amount of returns, allowances, and discounts to arrive at the Cost of Goods Available for Sale. At the close of business on June 30th, the merchandise that remains unsold is counted and priced at cost to arrive at the amount of ending inventory. This amount, $3,000 is also the beginning inventory in the succeeding accounting period, that is, the month of July. By subtracting the ending inventory from the cost of goods available for sale we arrive at the Cost of Goods Sold. This entire procedure follows a simple arithmetic logic.

Pacific Printers Mart
Income Statement
For the month ending June 30,1997

Revenue:				
Sales				$12,000
Cost of Goods Sold:				
Inventory, June 1st			$ 000	
Purchases		$9,900		
Add: Transportation-in		50		
Delivered Cost of Purchases		9,950		
Less: Purchase Returns and Allowances	$100			
Purchase Discounts	20	120		
Net Purchases			9,830	
Cost of Goods Available for Sale			9,830	
Less: Inventory, June 30th			3,000	
Cost of Goods Sold:				6,830
Gross Profit:				$ 5,170
Expenses:				
Etc.				

Exhibit 5-6: Illustration of the Cost of Goods Sold section in an income statement.

In our illustration, the cost of goods sold amounts to $6,830. This figure is subtracted from the amount of sales, $12,000 to obtain the amount of Gross Profit, which works out to $5,170. What does all of this mean? It means that the goods sold during the month of June cost $6,830. A mark-up of $5,170 was added to the cost of these goods and they were sold for $12,000. By converting these dollar figures to percentages we have a tool whereby we can compare and evaluate the average percentage mark-up from period to period. Thus, if the percentage mark-up continues to decline from period to period that is an indication that we are not raising prices in line with inflation. The percentage mark-up may be calculated as follows:

Mark-up = [Gross Profit on Sales]/Sales x 100%
Mark-up = $5,170/$12,000 x 100% = 43.08%

On average, our goods have been marked up by 43% (the nearest whole number is close enough). Notice that mark-up is added to cost to arrive at selling price (for each individual item) but the percentage mark-up is computed as a percentage of sales; it is not computed as a percentage of cost. Consider an individual item:

Cost	+	Mark-up	=	Selling Price
$10	+	$5	=	$15
Mark-up	=	$5/$15 x 100%	=	33.3%

Thus, the Gross Profit figure in the income statement represents the amount by which the goods that have been sold have been marked up, in terms of dollars and cents, which hopefully is sufficient to cover operating expenses and leave the small business with a net income.

REVENUE ACCOUNTS IN MERCHANDISING

In a merchandising business, revenue is earned by selling goods, so the revenue account is called *Sales.* In a service business the revenue account is called Fees or Commissions depending upon the nature and source of income.

On June 2nd, the cash register tape indicates total sales of $400 at the end of the day. All of the sales were cash sales to customers in the printing trade and therefore exempt from sales tax. The journal entry to record revenue earned on June 2nd is illustrated in Exhibit 5-7.

Journal **Page 7**

1997					
June	2	Cash	101	400	
		Sales	460		400
		To record sales of merchandise on June 2nd.			

Exhibit 5-7: Entry to record revenue earned by selling goods.

Journal					Page 7
1997					
June	3	Accounts Receivable	103	700	
		Sales	460		700
		To record sales of merchandise on credit.			

Exhibit 5-8: Entry to record sale of merchandise on credit.

On June 3rd, sales in the amount of $700 were made on credit. The journal entry for these sales, made on credit, is illustrated in Exhibit 5-8.

SALES RETURNS AND ALLOWANCES

On June 4th, a customer to whom some merchandise was sold on June 2nd returns a few items and asks for a refund. A refund is given to the customer and the journal entry, illustrated in Exhibit 5-9, is made.

Journal					Page 7
1997					
June	4	Sales Returns and Allowances	461	100	
		Cash	101		100
		Gave customer a refund for goods returned.			

Exhibit 5-9: Entry to record refund.

When a customer returns goods and requests a refund, or when a customer only asks for an allowance on the price if some items have suffered minor damage, we do not debit the Sales account. Instead, we debit a separate account, *Sales Returns and Allowances,* which is analyzed in the same manner as the Sales account. Decreases in revenue are recorded by debits. The debit balance in the Sales Returns and Allowances account is subtracted from the credit balance in the Sales account on the income statement to arrive at the amount of net sales.

SALES DISCOUNTS

On June 25th, credit sales totalling $6,000 were made which carried terms of 2/10, net 30. No further credit sales were made during the month of June. The journal entry to record these credit sales is illustrated in Exhibit 5-10.

Journal				Page 7
1997				
June 25	Accounts Receivable	103	6,000	
	Sales	460		6,000
	To record sales made on credit during June. Terms: 2/10, net 30.			

Exhibit 5-10: To record sales made on credit in June.

As all of the customers were anxious to obtain the discount, they all paid their bills within the time of the discount period. This transaction is illustrated in Exhibit 5-11.

Journal				Page 7
1997				
June 30	Cash	101	5,880	
	Sales Discounts	462	120	
	Accounts Receivable	103		6,000
	To record collection of receivables, less discounts.			

Exhibit 5-11: Journal entry to record sales discounts.

In actual fact, credit sales were made throughout the month and accounts receivable were collected throughout the month, but we have simplified this series of transactions to two transactions for the purpose of illustration. The important point is that all receivables (i.e. Accounts Receivable) were collected within the time of the discount period, even though this may not appear to be the case by looking at the dates of the two journal entries in Exhibit 5-10 and Exhibit 5-11, respectively.

REVENUE FOR REMAINDER OF JUNE

The remaining revenue for the month of June consisted of $5,120 in cash sales. The journal entry for the remaining sales in June is illustrated in Exhibit 5-12.

Journal **Page 7**

1997				
June 30	Cash	101	5,120	
	Sales	460		5,120
	To record sales of merchandise.			

Exhibit 5-12: Entry to record the remainder of cash sales in June.

REVENUE SECTION OF INCOME STATEMENT

In Exhibit 5-13 is shown the revenue section of the income statement for the month of June. Notice how the Sales Returns and Allowances account and the Sales Discounts account balances are set out in the income statement. The balances in these two accounts are subtracted from the balance in the Sales account in order to arrive at the amount of net sales.

Pacific Printers Mart
Income Statement
For the month ending June 30, 1997

Revenue:			
Sales:		$12,220	
Less: Sales Returns and Allowances	$100		
Sales Discounts	120	220	
Net Sales:			$12,000
Cost of Goods Sold:			
Etc.			

Exhibit 5-13: Revenue section of an income statement for a merchandising business.

OPERATING ENTRIES FOR THE MONTH OF JUNE

To place the merchandising entries into context, let us journalize all of the operating entries for the month of June. These are presented in Exhibit 5-14.

Exhibit 5-14: Operating entries for the month of June.

Journal **Page 7**

1997					
June	2	Purchases	463	8,000	
		Cash	101		8,000
		To record purchase of merchandise for resale from ACME Wholesale Inc.			
	2	Cash	101	400	
		Sales	460		400
		To record sales of merchandise on June 2nd.			
	3	Purchases	463	900	
		Transportation-in	464	50	
		Accounts Payable	230		900
		Cash	101		50
		Purchased merchandise from XYZ Wholesale Inc., payment due in 90 days; paid delivery charges.			
	3	Accounts Receivable	103	700	
		Sales	460		700
		To record sales of merchandise on credit.			
	3	Accounts Payable	230	100	
		Purchase Returns and Allowances	465		100
		To record allowance from XYZ Wholesale Inc. for damaged merchandise.			
	4	Sales Returns and Allowances	461	100	
		Cash	101		100
		Gave customer a refund for goods returned.			
	5	Salaries Payable	231	1,500	
		Cash	101		1,500
		To record payment of salary.			
	11	Purchases	463	1,000	
		Accounts Payable	230		1,000
		Purchased merchandise from Speedy Distributors Inc. Terms 2/10, net 30.			

June	12	Cash	101	200	
		Accounts Receivable	103		200
		Check for commissions received from Rapid Photocopiers Inc.			
	17	Cash	101	700	
		Accounts Receivable	103		700
		Collected amount due from customer for sales made on June 3rd.			
	18	Office Supplies Expense	572	35	
		Cash	101		35
		Purchased office supplies.			
	20	Accounts Payable	230	1,000	
		Cash	101		980
		Purchase Discounts	466		20
		Paid Speedy Distributors Inc. and received discount.			
	21	Advertising and Promotion Expense	574	250	
		Cash	101		250
		Placed ads in the newspaper.			
	25	Accounts Receivable	103	6,000	
		Sales	460		6,000
		To record sales made on credit during June. Terms: 2/10, net 30.			
	30	Cash	101	5,880	
		Sales Discounts	462	120	
		Accounts Receivable	103		6,000
		To record collection of receivables, less discounts.			
	30	Cash	101	5,120	
		Sales	460		5,120
		To record sales of merchandise.			
	30	Cash	101	450	
		Accounts Receivable	103		450
		Received remainder of commission on platemaker sold on April 12th.			

June 30	Salaries Expense	584	600	
	Cash	101		600
	Paid the part-time secretary.			
30	Rent Expense	567	400	
	Cash	101		400
	Paid rent for June.			
30	Telephone Expense	568	50	
	Cash	101		50
	Paid telephone bill for June.			
30	Utilities Expense	569	90	
	Cash	101		90
	Paid bill for electricity and gas consumed during June.			
30	Jack Fraser, Drawings	344	1,500	
	Cash	101		1,500
	Cash withdrawn for personal use.			

ADJUSTING ENTRIES FOR JUNE

After all of the operating transactions have been recorded in the journal for the month of June, the next step in the accounting cycle is to record the adjusting entries. The adjusting entries are illustrated in Exhibit 5-15.

Exhibit 5-15: Adjusting entries for the month of June.

Journal **Page 7**

1997				
June 30	Insurance Expense	571	30	
	Unexpired Insurance	106		30
	To record insurance expense for the month of June.			

June	30	Shop Supplies Expense	573	50	
		Shop Supplies	111		50
		To record amount of shop supplies consumed during June.			
	30	Depreciation Expense: Office Equipment	592	25	
		Accum. Deprn.: Office Equipment	113		25
		To record depreciation for June.			
	30	Deprn. Expense: Furniture and Fixtures	593	20	
		Accum. Deprn.: Furniture and Fixtures	115		20
		To record depreciation for June.			
	30	Depreciation Expense: Automobile	594	150	
		Accumulated Depreciation: Automobile	117		150
		To record depreciation for June.			
	30	Unearned Commissions	233	100	
		Commissions	455		100
		To record commissions earned in June.			
	30	Salaries Expense	584	1,500	
		Salaries Payable	231		1,500
		To record salary expense for June; to be paid on July 10th.			
	30	Interest and Service Charges Expense	575	100	
		Interest Payable	232		100
		To record accrued interest for June.			
	30	Accounts Receivable	103	150	
		Commissions	455		150
		To record commissions earned on photocopying in June; to be collected in July.			

LEDGER AFTER POSTING ADJUSTING ENTRIES

The ledger after all of the operating and adjusting entries have been posted is shown in Exhibit 5-16. These entries must be posted to enable us to carry on with the succeeding steps in the accounting cycle.

Exhibit 5-16: **Complete ledger after operating and adjusting entries have been posted for the month of June.**

Cash 101

1997					1997				
March	1		1	10,000	March	5		1	7,700
	31		1	250		15		1	500
April	5		2	1,200		31		1	500
	21		2	4,500	April	1		2	100
	30	16,200	2	250		7		2	30
						30		2	600
						30		2	400
						30		2	1,500
						30	13,130	2	1,800
						30	14,335	4	1,205
						30	Balance	✓	1,865
				16,200					16,200
1997					1997				
May	1	Balance	✓	1,865	May	1		5	360
	1		5	1,200		6		5	800
	1		5	10,000		7		5	35
	31		5	250		10		5	70
	31		5	7,100		15		5	70
						22		5	150
						25		5	60
						31		5	400
						31		5	150
						31		5	80
						31		5	500
						31		5	600
						31		5	40
						31	5,315	5	2,000
						31	Balance	✓	15,100
				20,415					20,415
1997					1997				
June	1	Balance	✓	15,100	June	2		7	8,000
	2		7	400		3		7	50
	12		7	200		4		7	100
	17		7	700		5		7	1,500

	30		7	5,880		18		7	35
	30		7	5,120		20		7	980
	30		7	450		21		7	250
						30		7	600
						30		7	400
						30		7	50
						30		7	90
						30	13,555	7	1,500
						30	Balance	✓	14,295
				27,850					27,850
1997									
July	1	Balance	✓	14,295					

Accounts Receivable 103

1997					1997				
March	20		1	500	March	31		1	250
April	12		2	700	April	30	500	2	250
						30	Balance	✓	700
				1,200					1,200
1997					1997				
May	1	Balance	✓	700	May	31		5	250
	31		5	200		31	Balance	✓	650
				900					900
1997					1997				
June	1	Balance	✓	650	June	12		7	200
	3		7	700		17		7	700
	25		7	6,000		30		7	6,000
	30		7	150		30	7,350	7	450
						30	Balance	✓	150
				7,500					7,500
1997									
July	1	Balance	✓	150					

Unexpired Insurance — 106

1997					1997				
May	1		5	360	May	31		5	30
						31	Balance	✓	330
				360					360
1997					1997				
June	1	Balance	✓	330	June	30		7	30
						30	Balance	✓	300
				330					330
1997									
July	1	Balance	✓	300					

Shop Supplies — 111

1997					1997				
May	6		5	800	May	31		5	40
						31	Balance	✓	760
				800					800
1997					1997				
June	1	Balance	✓	760	June	30		7	50
						30	Balance	✓	710
				760					760
1997									
July	1	Balance	✓	710					

Office Equipment — 112

1997									
March	11		1	1,800					

Accumulated Depreciation: Office Equipment — 113

					1997				
					April	30		3	25
					May	31	50	5	25
					June	30	75	7	25

Furniture and Fixtures 114

1997									
March	15		1	2,400					

Accumulated Depreciation: Furniture and Fixtures 115

					1997				
					April	30		3	20
					May	31	40	5	20
					June	30	60	7	20

Automobile 116

1997					1997				
March	5		1	7,700	March	20		1	500
					April	30	Balance	✓	7,200
				7,700					7,700
1997									
May	1	Balance	✓	7,200					

Accumulated Depreciation: Automobile 117

					1997				
					April	30		3	150
					May	31	300	5	150
					June	30	450	7	150

Accounts Payable 230

1997					1997				
March	31		1	500	March	11		1	1,800
April	30	2,300	2	1,800		15		1	1.900
	30	Balance	✓	1,655	April	14		2	150
						30		2	35
						30	3,955	2	70
				3,955					3,955
1997					1997				
May	7		5	35	May	1	Balance	✓	1,655
	10		5	70					

	31		5	150					
	31	755	5	500					
	31	Balance	✓	900					
				1,655					1,655
1997					1997				
June	4		7	100	June	1	Balance	✓	900
	20	1,100	7	1,000		3		7	900
	30	Balance	✓	1,700		11		7	1,000
				2,800					2,800
					1997				
					July	1	Balance	✓	1,700

Salaries Payable 231

1997					1997				
June	5		7	1,500	May	31		5	1,500
	30	Balance	✓	1,500	June	30		7	1,500
				3,000					3,000
					1997				
					July	1	Balance	✓	1,500

Interest Payable 232

					1997				
					May	31		5	100
					June	30	200	7	100

Unearned Commissions 233

1997					1997				
May	31		5	100	May	1		5	1,200
	31	Balance	✓	1,100					
				1,200					1,200

1997					1997				
June	30		7	100	June	1	Balance	✓	1,100
	30	Balance	✓	1,000					
				1,100					1,100
					1997				
					July	1	Balance	✓	1,000

Income Taxes Payable 236

					1997				
					May	31		5	827

Notes Payable 240

					1997				
					May	1		5	10,000

Jack Fraser, Capital 343

1997					1997				
April	30		4	1,500	March	1		1	10,000
	30		4	1,205	April	30		4	4,820
	30	Balance	✓	12,115					
				14,820					14,820
1997					1997				
May	31		6	2,000	May	1	Balance	✓	12,115
	31		6	827		31		6	4,135
	31	Balance	✓	13,423					
				16,250					16,250
					1997				
					June	1	Balance	✓	13,423

Jack Fraser, Drawings — 344

1997				1997			
April	30	2	1,500	April	30	4	1,500
1997				1997			
May	31	5	2,000	May	31	6	2,000
1997							
June	30	7	1,500				

Income Taxes — 349

1997				1997			
April	30	4	1,205	April	30	4	1,205
1997				1997			
May	31	5	827	May	31	6	827

Commissions — 455

1997				1997			
April	30	4	6,400	April	5	2	1,200
					12	2	700
					21	2	4,500
			6,400				6,400
1997				1997			
May	31	6	7,400	May	31	5	7,100
					31	5	100
					31	5	200
			7,400				7,400
				1997			
				June	30	7	100
					30	7	150

Sales 460

				1997			
				June	2	7	400
					3	7	700
					25	7	6,000
					30	7	5,120

Sales Returns and Allowances 461

1997							
June	4	7	100				

Sales Discounts 462

1997							
June	30	7	120				

Purchases 463

1997							
June	2	7	8,000				
	3	7	900				
	11	7	1,000				

Transportation-in 464

1997							
June	3	7	50				

Purchase Returns and Allowances 465

				1997			
				June	4	7	100

Purchase Discounts 466

				1997			
				June	20	7	20

Rent Expense 567

1997				1997			
April	30	2	400	April	30	4	400
1997				1997			
May	31	5	400	May	31	6	400
1997							
June	30	7	400				

Telephone Expense 568

1997				1997			
April	30	2	35	April	30	4	35
1997				1997			
May	31	5	40	May	31	6	40
1997							
June	30	7	50				

Utilities Expense 569

1997				1997			
April	30	2	70	April	30	4	70
1997				1997			
May	31	5	80	May	31	6	80
1997							
June	30	7	90				

Insurance Expense 571

1997				1997			
May	31	5	30	May	31	6	30
1997							
June	30	7	30				

Office Supplies Expense 572

1997				1997			
April	7	2	30	April	30	4	30
1997				1997			
May	15	5	70	May	31	6	70
1997							
June	18	7	35				

Shop Supplies Expense 573

1997				1997			
May	31	5	40	May	31	6	40
1997							
June	30	7	50				

Advertising and Promotion Expense 574

1997				1997			
April	1	2	100	April	30	4	250
	14	2	150				
			250				250
1997				1997			
May	22	5	150	May	31	6	210
	25	5	60				
			210				210
1997							
June	21	7	250				

Interest and Service Charges Expense 575

1997				1997			
May	31	5	100	May	31	6	100
1997							
June	30	7	100				

Salaries Expense 584

1997				1997			
April	30	2	600	April	30	4	600
1997				1997			
May	31	5	600	May	31	6	2,100
	31	5	1,500				
			2,100				2,100
1997							
June	30	7	600				
	30	7	1,500				

Depreciation Expense: Office Equipment 592

1997				1997			
April	30	3	25	April	30	4	25
1997				1997			
May	31	5	25	May	31	6	25
1997							
June	30	7	25				

Depreciation Expense: Furniture and Fixtures 593

1997				1997			
April	30	3	20	April	30	4	20
1997				1997			
May	31	5	20	May	31	6	20
1997							
June	30	7	20				

Depreciation Expense: Automobile 594

1997				1997			
April	30	3	150	April	30	4	150

1997				1997			
May	31	5	150	May	31	6	150
1997							
June	30	7	150				

Income Summary							600
1997				1997			
April	30	4	1,580	April	30	4	6,400
	30	4	4,820				
			6,400				6,400
1997				1997			
May	31	6	3,265	May	31	6	7,400
	31	6	4,135				
			7,400				7,400

TRIAL BALANCE

After the operating and adjusting entries have been posted to the ledger it is a good idea to prepare a trial balance to be certain that the books still balance. A trial balance prepared at this time is illustrated in Exhibit 5-17.

Exhibit 5-17: Trial balance.

Pacific Printers Mart
Trial Balance
June 30, 1997

Cash	$14,295	
Accounts Receivable	150	
Unexpired Insurance	300	
Shop Supplies	710	
Office Equipment	1,800	
Accumulated Depreciation: Office Equipment		$ 75
Furniture and Fixtures	2,400	
Accumulated Depreciation: Furniture and Fixtures		60

Automobile	7,200	
Accumulated Depreciation: Automobile		450
Accounts Payable		1,700
Salaries Payable		1,500
Interest Payable		200
Unearned Commissions		1,000
Income Taxes Payable		827
Notes Payable		10,000
Jack Fraser, Capital		13,423
Jack Fraser, Drawings	1,500	
Commissions		250
Sales		12,220
Sales Returns and Allowances	100	
Sales Discounts	120	
Purchases	9,900	
Transportation-in	50	
Purchase Returns and Allowances		100
Purchase Discounts		20
Rent Expense	400	
Telephone Expense	50	
Utilities Expense	90	
Insurance Expense	30	
Office Supplies Expense	35	
Shop Supplies Expense	50	
Advertising and Promotion Expense	250	
Interest and Service Charges Expense	100	
Salaries Expense	2,100	
Depreciation Expense: Office Equipment	25	
Depreciation Expense: Furniture and Fixtures	20	
Depreciation Expense: Automobile	150	
	$41,825	$41,825

THE INVENTORY ACCOUNT

At the end of June, the merchandise that remained unsold was counted and priced at cost, on a first-in, first-out, basis (in accordance with stock rotation) to determine the ending inventory. No inventory is taken at any other time, other than at the close of business on the last day of the accounting period. This method of determining inventory is called the periodic inventory method. That is because inventory is only taken periodically; it is not kept track of on a daily basis. This method is especially suitable where numerous, low-priced items are offered for sale. Unless computerized electronic cash registers have been installed, it is virtually impossible to keep track of inventory on an item-by-item or on a daily basis.

Where relatively few, high-priced items are offered for sale, such as cars in an automobile dealership, a perpetual inventory is kept. This means that a list of the, perhaps, 80 cars is made, listing the wholesale price of each car, and as each car is sold it is struck off the list. As additional cars are bought for resale they are added to the list. In this manner, inventory may be kept perpetual. The total cost of all unsold cars is entered at the bottom of the list. When a car is sold, its cost is subtracted from the total; when a car is purchased for resale, its cost is added to this total. That is all there is to it.

Whichever method of keeping track of inventory is used, the end result is the same. Inventory is the sum of the cost of all the goods that remain unsold at the time the inventory is taken. When goods are purchased for resale, the cost of these goods is debited to the Purchases account, and not the Inventory account. At the end of each accounting period, the cost of the purchases, that is, goods, that remain unsold is determined and an entry is made in the journal to record this inventory. The inventory at the end of one accounting period is also the inventory at the beginning of the succeeding accounting period. Inventory appears in both the balance sheet and the income statement.

INVENTORY AT THE END OF JUNE

A physical count of the goods that remain unsold and priced at cost reveals that Pacific Printers Mart has an ending inventory of $3,000. There was no beginning inventory because no goods were purchased for resale in May, and hence, there could not be any goods that remained unsold at the end of May. Ending inventory at the end of May is beginning inventory at the beginning of June. All of the goods offered for sale in June came from purchases made in June. The entry to record ending inventory at the end of June is illustrated in Exhibit 5-18.

Journal — **Page 8**

1997					
June	30	Income Summary	600	9,900	
		Purchases	463		9,900
		To close the purchases account.			
	30	Inventory	105	3,000	
		Income Summary	600		3,000
		To record the ending inventory.			

Exhibit 5-18: Entries to close the Purchases account and to record inventory.

In order to record ending inventory, the Purchases account must first be closed to Income Summary. If we did not do so, we would end up recording the same goods twice. Inventory consists of goods that remain unsold, and which have already been recorded in the journal as Purchases. First we make an entry transferring the entire debit balance of the Purchases account to Income Summary, closing out the Purchases account. Because a physical count of individual items, priced at cost on a first-in first-out basis, reveals that $3,000 worth of these purchases have been sold, these goods are brought back on the books. But instead of re-entering these unsold purchases back in the Purchases account they are entered into a new account devised for this specific purpose, the Inventory account. Therefore, Inventory is debited $3,000 and Income Summary is credited $3,000 transferring back the value of unsold goods to the Inventory account from Income Summary. This is the only time that entries are made to the Inventory account—at the end of each accounting period when an inventory of goods that remain unsold is taken.

INVENTORY AT THE END OF JULY

Let us leap ahead to the end of the next accounting period, the end of July. During the month of July, merchandise costing $11,000 is purchased for resale. Inventory on hand at the end of the day on July 31st is counted and invoices are consulted to determine the wholesale cost of these items that remain unsold. A total of $4,000 worth of goods, wholesale value on a first-in first-out stock rotation basis (that is, at cost to the retailer), remains unsold at the close of business on July 31st.

Before the ending inventory may be brought on the books at the end of July, we must clear the Inventory account of any balance that remains from the previous accounting period. To do so, first we must inspect the Inventory account in the ledger, which is reproduced in Exhibit 5-19, to determine the amount of beginning inventory that remains on the books.

Inventory — 105

1997				
June	30	8	3,000	

Exhibit 5-19: Inventory account at the end of July.

The inventory recorded at the end of June remains on the books throughout the month of July, until it is replaced with a new ending inventory taken at the end of July. A balance of $3,000 (our beginning inventory) remains in the Inventory account, which must be removed before the inventory at the end of July may be entered. The beginning inventory is taken off the books, and the ending inventory is placed on the books, on July 31st, by means of the entries shown in Exhibit 5-20.

By means of the journal entries in Exhibit 5-20, we have transferred the entire balance in Purchases to Income Summary, closing out the Purchases account. The beginning inventory is closed and the new ending inventory is brought on the books. The entire debit balances in Purchases and beginning inventory were transferred to the Income Summary account. An amount, $4,000 was transferred back from Income Summary to Inventory, which is our ending inventory. Thus, the balance in the Inventory account now agrees with the amount determined by a physical count of goods that remain unsold on July 31st. The Inventory account is reproduced in Exhibit 5-21.

Journal **Page 10**

1997					
July	31	Income Summary	600	11,000	
		Purchases	463		11,000
		To close the Purchases account.			
	31	Income Summary	600	3,000	
		Inventory	105		3,000
		To close the beginning inventory.			
	31	Inventory	105	4,000	
		Income Summary	600		4,000
		To record the ending inventory.			

Exhibit 5-20: Entries to close out beginning inventory and to bring ending inventory on the books.

Inventory 105

1997				1997			
June	30	8	3,000	July	31	10	3,000
1997							
July	31	10	4,000				

Exhibit 5-21: Inventory account at the end of July after the beginning inventory has been closed and the ending inventory has been placed on the books.

PRELIMINARY FINANCIAL STATEMENTS

The purpose of preparing a set of financial statements at this time is to enable us to compute the amount of income taxes, and in order to do this we need to determine the amount of net income. In fact only the income statement is required to achieve our objective, but since financial statements are always prepared as a set, we will prepare a balance sheet as well. This way, we can ensure that the amount of net income correctly ties into the owner's equity section of the balance sheet, at this stage.

The amount of net income may be determined by other means, such as by inspecting the trial balance, if you work carefully and include all of the accounts that must be included in an income statement. However, this method is prone to error, so it is recommended that a preliminary set of financial statements always be prepared in order to determine the amount of net income at this point of the accounting cycle.

The income statement for Pacific Printers Mart is illustrated in Exhibit 5-22 and the balance sheet is illustrated in Exhibit 5-23. An income statement must always be prepared before the balance sheet, otherwise you will not have the necessary financial data (i.e., the amount of net income), which comes from the income statement, to include in the owner's equity section of the balance sheet.

Pacific Printers Mart
Income Statement
For the month ending June 30, 1997

Revenue:				
Commissions				$ 250
Sales			$12,220	
Less: Sales Returns and Allowances		$100		
Sales Discounts		120	220	
Net Sales:				12,000
Cost of Goods Sold:				
Inventory, June 1st			000	
Purchases		9,900		
Add: Transportation-in		50		
Delivered Cost of Purchases		9,950		
Less: Purchase Ret. & Allowances	$100			
Purchase Discounts	20	120		
Net Purchases			9,830	
Cost of Goods Available for Sale			9,830	
Less: Inventory, June 30th			3,000	
Cost of Goods Sold:				6,830
Gross Profit:				$ 5,420

Expenses:		
Rent Expense	$ 400	
Telephone Expense	50	
Utilities Expense	90	
Insurance Expense	30	
Office Supplies Expense	35	
Shop Supplies Expense	50	
Advertising and Promotion Expense	250	
Interest and Service Charges Expense	100	
Salaries Expense	2,100	
Depreciation Expense: Office Equipment	25	
Depreciation Expense: Furniture and Fixtures	20	
Depreciation Expense: Automobile	150	3,300
Net Income:		$ 2,120

Exhibit 5-22: Income statement before income taxes have been computed.

Pacific Printers Mart
Balance Sheet
June 30, 1997

Assets

Current Assets:			
Cash		$14,295	
Accounts Receivable		150	
Inventory		3,000	
Unexpired Insurance		300	
Total current assets:			$17,745
Plant and Equipment:			
Shop Supplies		$ 710	
Office Equipment	$1,800		
Less: Accumulated Depreciation: Office Equipment	75	1,725	
Furniture and Fixtures	$2,400		
Less: Accumulated Depreciation: Furniture and Fixtures	60	2,340	
Automobile	$7,200		
Less: Accumulated Depreciation: Automobile	450	6,750	
Total plant and equipment:			11,525
			$29,270

Liabilities and Owner's Equity			
Current Liabilities:			
Accounts Payable		$1,700	
Salaries Payable		1,500	
Interest Payable		200	
Unearned Commissions		1,000	
Income Taxes Payable		827	
Total current liabilities:			$ 5,227
Long-term Liabilities:			
Notes Payable:			10,000
Owner's Equity:			
Jack Fraser, Capital, June 1, 1997		$13,423	
Net Income	$2,120		
Less: Jack Fraser, Drawings	1,500	620	
Jack Fraser, Capital, June 30, 1997			14,043
			$29,270

Exhibit 5-23: Balance sheet before income taxes for the month of June have been computed.

INCOME TAXES

Now that we know the amount of net income for the month of June we may proceed to compute the amount of income taxes and record this amount in the journal. From Exhibit 5-22, net income for June is $2,120. Let us assume that the tax rate is 20%. The calculation of income taxes follows:

Income taxes = $2,120 x 20% = $424

The journal entry for income taxes for the month of June is presented in Exhibit 5-24.

Journal — **Page 8**

1997				
June 30	Income Taxes	349	424	
	Income Taxes Payable	236		424
	To record income taxes for the month of June.			

Exhibit 5-24: Entry to record income taxes.

That is the amount of income taxes that have accrued on net income for the month of June. Let us suppose that these income taxes are not due and payable until July when they must be remitted to the income tax department. A liability, Income Taxes Payable, in the amount of $827 in the balance sheet prepared on June 30, 1997 (see Exhibit 5-23) remains from the month of May, as it is not due and payable until July.

To this amount is added our current entry, $424 as illustrated in the ledger account for Income Taxes Payable, in Exhibit 5-25.

Income Taxes Payable						236
	1997					
	May	31			5	827
	June	30		1,251	8	424

Exhibit 5-25: **Income Taxes Payable ledger account after income taxes for June have been posted.**

CLOSING THE BOOKS

Our next step is to close the books. To do this we systematically go through the ledger and close all of the income statement accounts, the Income Summary account, the drawings account, and the Income Taxes account as shown in Exhibit 5-26.

Journal **Page 8**

1997				
June 30	Income Summary	600	13,470	
	Sales Returns and Allowances	461		100
	Sales Discounts	462		120
	Purchases	463		9,900
	Transportation-in	464		50
	Rent Expense	567		400
	Telephone Expense	568		50
	Utilities Expense	569		90
	Insurance Expense	571		30
	Office Supplies Expense	572		35
	Shop Supplies Expense	573		50
	Advertising and Promotion Expense	574		250
	Interest and Service Charges Expense	575		100
	Salaries Expense	584		2,100
	Depreciation Expense: Office Equipment	592		25
	Depreciation Expense: Furn. and Fixtures	593		20
	Depreciation Expense: Automobile	594		150
	To close all of the income statement accounts that have debit balances.			

June	30	Inventory	105	3,000	
		Commissions	455	250	
		Sales	460	12,220	
		Purchase Returns and Allowances	465	100	
		Purchase Discounts	466	20	
		Income Summary	600		15,590
		To record ending inventory and to close all of the income statement accounts that have credit balances.			
	30	Income Summary	600	2,120	
		Jack Fraser, Capital	343		2,120
		To close the Income Summary account.			
	30	Jack Fraser, Capital	343	1,500	
		Jack Fraser, Drawings	344		1,500
		To close the drawings account.			
	30	Jack Fraser, Capital	343	424	
		Income Taxes	349		424
		To close the income taxes account.			

Exhibit 5-26: Closing entries at the end of June.

LEDGER AFTER POSTING CLOSING ENTRIES

In Exhibit 5-27 the complete ledger is illustrated after all of the closing entries for the month of June have been posted, and the ending inventory has been counted and placed on the books.

Exhibit 5-27: Ledger after closing the books.

Cash 101

1997					1997				
March	1		1	10,000	March	5		1	7,700
	31		1	250		15		1	500
April	5		2	1,200		31		1	500
	21		2	4,500	April	1		2	100
	30	16,200	2	250		7		2	30
						30		2	600
						30		2	400

						30		2	1,500
						30	13,130	2	1,800
						30	14,335	4	1,205
						30	Balance	✓	1,865
				16,200					16,200

1997					1997				
May	1	Balance	✓	1,865	May	1		5	360
	1		5	1,200		6		5	800
	1		5	10,000		7		5	35
	31		5	250		10		5	70
	31		5	7,100		15		5	70
						22		5	150
						25		5	60
						31		5	400
						31		5	150
						31		5	80
						31		5	500
						31		5	600
						31		5	40
						31	5,315	5	2,000
						31	Balance	✓	15,100
				20,415					20,415

1997					1997				
June	1	Balance	✓	15,100	June	2		7	8,000
	2		7	400		3		7	50
	12		7	200		4		7	100
	17		7	700		5		7	1,500
	30		7	5,880		18		7	35
	30		7	5,120		20		7	980
	30		7	450		21		7	250
						30		7	600
						30		7	400
						30		7	50
						30		7	90
						30	13,555	7	1,500
						30	Balance	✓	14,295
				27,850					27,850

1997									
July	1	Balance	✓	14,295					

Accounts Receivable — 103

1997					1997				
March	20		1	500	March	31		1	250
April	12		2	700	April	30	500	2	250
						30	Balance	✓	700
				1,200					1,200
1997					1997				
May	1	Balance	✓	700	May	31		5	250
	31		5	200		31	Balance	✓	650
				900					900
1997					1997				
June	1	Balance	✓	650	June	12		7	200
	3		7	700		17		7	700
	25		7	6,000		30		7	6,000
	30		7	150		30	7,350	7	450
						30	Balance	✓	150
				7,500					7,500
1997									
July	1	Balance	✓	150					

Inventory — 105

1997									
June	30		8	3,000					

Unexpired Insurance — 106

1997					1997				
May	1		5	360	May	31		5	30
						31	Balance	✓	330
				360					360
1997					1997				
June	1	Balance	✓	330	June	30		7	30

						30	Balance	✓	300
				330					330
1997									
July	1	Balance	✓	300					

Shop Supplies 111

1997					1997				
May	6		5	800	May	31		5	40
						31	Balance	✓	760
				800					800
1997					1997				
June	1	Balance	✓	760	June	30		7	50
						30	Balance	✓	710
				760					760
1997									
July	1	Balance	✓	710					

Office Equipment 112

1997									
March	11		1	1,800					

Accumulated Depreciation: Office Equipment 113

					1997				
					April	30		3	25
					May	31	50	5	25
					June	30	75	7	25

Furniture and Fixtures 114

1997									
March	15		1	2,400					

Accumulated Depreciation: Furniture and Fixtures — 115

					1997				
					April	30		3	20
					May	31	40	5	20
					June	30	60	7	20

Automobile — 116

1997					1997				
March	5		1	7,700	March	20		1	500
					April	30	Balance	✓	7,200
				7,700					7,700
1997									
May	1	Balance	✓	7,200					

Accumulated Depreciation: Automobile — 117

					1997				
					April	30		3	150
					May	31	300	5	150
					June	30	450	7	150

Accounts Payable — 230

1997					1997				
March	31		1	500	March	11		1	1,800
April	30	2,300	2	1,800		15		1	1,900
	30	Balance	✓	1,655	April	14		2	150
						30		2	35
						30	3,955	2	70
				3,955					3,955
1997					1997				
May	7		5	35	May	1	Balance	✓	1,655
	10		5	70					
	31		5	150					
	31	755	5	500					
	31	Balance	✓	900					

				1,655					1,655
1997					1997				
June	4		7	100	June	1	Balance	✓	900
	20	1,100	7	1,000		3		7	900
	30	Balance	✓	1,700		11		7	1,000
				2,800					2,800
					1997				
					July	1	Balance	✓	1,700

Salaries Payable 231

1997					1997				
June	5		7	1,500	May	31		5	1,500
	30	Balance	✓	1,500	June	30		7	1,500
				3,000					3,000
					1997				
					July	1	Balance	✓	1,500

Interest Payable 232

					1997				
					May	31		5	100
					June	30	200	7	100

Unearned Commissions 233

1997					1997				
May	31		5	100	May	1		5	1,200
	31	Balance	✓	1,100					
				1,200					1,200
1997					1997				
June	30		7	100	June	1	Balance	✓	1,100
	30	Balance	✓	1,000					
				1,100					1,100
					1997				
					July	1	Balance	✓	1,000

Income Taxes Payable — 236

					1997				
					May	31		5	827
					June	30	1,251	8	424

Notes Payable — 240

					1997				
					May	1		5	10,000

Jack Fraser, Capital — 343

1997					1997				
April	30		4	1,500	March	1		1	10,000
	30		4	1,205	April	30		4	4,820
	30	Balance	✓	12,115					
				14,820					14,820
1997					1997				
May	31		6	2,000	May	1	Balance	✓	12,115
	31		6	827		31		6	4,135
	31	Balance	✓	13,423					
				16,250					16,250
1997					1997				
June	30		8	1,500	June	5	Balance	✓	13,423
	30	1,924	8	424		30	15,543	8	2,120
	30	Balance	✓	13,619					
				15,543					15,543
					1997				
					July	1	Balance	✓	13,619

Jack Fraser, Drawings — 344

1997					1997				
April	30		2	1,500	April	30		4	1,500
1997					1997				
May	31		5	2,000	May	31		6	2,000

1997				1997			
June	30	7	1,500	June	30	8	1,500

Income Taxes 349

1997				1997			
April	30	4	1,205	April	30	4	1,205
1997				1997			
May	31	5	827	May	31	6	827
1997				1997			
June	30	8	424	June	30	8	424

Commissions 455

1997				1997			
April	30	4	6,400	April	5	2	1,200
					12	2	700
					21	2	4,500
			6,400				6,400
1997				1997			
May	31	6	7,400	May	31	5	7,100
					31	5	100
					31	5	200
			7,400				7,400
1997				1997			
June	30	8	250	June	30	7	100
					30	7	150
			250				250

Sales — 460

1997				1997			
June	30	8	12,220	June	2	7	400
					3	7	700
					25	7	6,000
					30	7	5,120
			12,220				12,220

Sales Returns and Allowances — 461

1997				1997			
June	4	7	100	June	30	8	100

Sales Discounts — 462

1997				1997			
June	30	7	120	June	30	8	120

Purchases — 463

1997				1997			
June	2	7	8,000	June	30	8	9,900
	3	7	900				
	11	7	1,000				
			9,900				9,900

Transportation-in — 464

1997				1997			
June	3	7	50	June	30	8	50

Purchase Returns and Allowances — 465

1997				1997			
June	30	8	100	June	4	7	100

Purchase Discounts 466

1997				1997			
June	30	8	20	June	20	7	20

Rent Expense 567

1997				1997			
April	30	2	400	April	30	4	400
1997				1997			
May	31	5	400	May	31	6	400
1997				1997			
June	30	7	400	June	30	8	400

Telephone Expense 568

1997				1997			
April	30	2	35	April	30	4	35
1997				1997			
May	31	5	40	May	31	6	40
1997				1997			
June	30	7	50	June	30	8	50

Utilities Expense 569

1997				1997			
April	30	2	70	April	30	4	70
1997				1997			
May	31	5	80	May	31	6	80
1997				1997			
June	30	7	90	June	30	8	90

Insurance Expense 571

1997				1997			
May	31	5	30	May	31	6	30
1997				1997			
June	30	7	30	June	30	8	30

Office Supplies Expense 572

1997				1997			
April	7	2	30	April	30	4	30
1997				1997			
May	15	5	70	May	31	6	70
1997				1997			
June	18	7	35	June	30	8	35

Shop Supplies Expense 573

1997				1997			
May	31	5	40	May	31	6	40
1997				1997			
June	30	7	50	June	30	8	50

Advertising and Promotion Expense 574

1997				1997			
April	1	2	100	April	30	4	250
	14	2	150				
			250				250
1997				1997			
May	22	5	150	May	31	6	210
	25	5	60				
			210				210

1997				1997			
June	21	7	250	June	30	8	250

Interest and Service Charges Expense 575

1997				1997			
May	31	5	100	May	31	6	100
1997				1997			
June	30	7	100	June	30	8	100

Salaries Expense 584

1997				1997			
April	30	2	600	April	30	4	600
1997				1997			
May	31	5	600	May	31	6	2,100
	31	5	1,500				
			2,100				2,100
1997				1997			
June	30	7	600	June	30	8	2,100
	30	7	1,500				
			2,100				2,100

Depreciation Expense: Office Equipment 592

1997				1997			
April	30	3	25	April	30	4	25
1997				1997			
May	31	5	25	May	31	6	25
1997				1997			
June	30	7	25	June	30	8	25

Depreciation Expense: Furniture and Fixtures — 593

1997				1997			
April	30	3	20	April	30	4	20
1997				1997			
May	31	5	20	May	31	6	20
1997				1997			
June	30	7	20	June	30	8	20

Depreciation Expense: Automobile — 594

1997				1997			
April	30	3	150	April	30	4	150
1997				1997			
May	31	5	150	May	31	6	150
1997				1997			
June	30	7	150	June	30	8	150

Income Summary — 600

1997				1997			
April	30	4	1,580	April	30	4	6,400
	30	4	4,820				
			6,400				6,400
1997				1997			
May	31	6	3,265	May	31	6	7,400
	31	6	4,135				
			7,400				7,400
1997				1997			
June	30	8	13,470	June	30	8	15,590
	30	8	2,120				
			15,590				15,590

TRIAL BALANCE AFTER CLOSING THE BOOKS

If we wish we may produce a trial balance to ensure that the books are still in balance after closing the books. At this point in time only balance sheet accounts have balances remaining in them as all of the income statement accounts, the drawings account, and the income taxes account have been closed. The trial balance at the end of June after closing the books is illustrated in Exhibit 5-28.

Pacific Printers Mart
Trial Balance
June 30, 1997

Cash	$14,295	
Accounts Receivable	150	
Inventory	3,000	
Unexpired Insurance	300	
Shop Supplies	710	
Office Equipment	1,800	
Accumulated Depreciation: Office Equipment		$ 75
Furniture and Fixtures	2,400	
Accumulated Depreciation: Furniture and Fixtures		60
Automobile	7,200	
Accumulated Depreciation: Automobile		450
Accounts Payable		1,700
Salaries Payable		1,500
Interest Payable		200
Unearned Commissions		1,000
Income Taxes Payable		1,251
Notes Payable		10,000
Jack Fraser, Capital		13,619
	$29,855	$29,855

Exhibit 5-28: Trial balance after closing the books.

FINANCIAL STATEMENTS

The final set of financial statements, after income taxes have been calculated and taken into consideration, may now be prepared. The income statement is presented in Exhibit 5-29 and the balance sheet is presented in Exhibit 5-30.

Pacific Printers Mart
Income Statement
For the month ending June 30, 1997

Revenue:				
Commissions				$ 250
Sales			$12,220	
Less: Sales Returns and Allowances		$100		
Sales Discounts		120	220	
Net Sales:				12,000
Cost of Goods Sold:				
Inventory, June 1st			000	
Purchases		9,900		
Add: Transportation-in		50		
Delivered Cost of Purchases		9,950		
Less: Purchase Ret. & Allowances	$100			
Purchase Discounts	20	120		
Net Purchases			9,830	
Cost of Goods Available for Sale			9,830	
Less: Inventory, June 30th			3,000	
Cost of Goods Sold:				6,830
Gross Profit:				$ 5,420
Expenses:				
Rent Expense			$ 400	
Telephone Expense			50	
Utilities Expense			90	
Insurance Expense			30	
Office Supplies Expense			35	
Shop Supplies Expense			50	
Advertising and Promotion Expense			250	
Interest and Service Charges Expense			100	
Salaries Expense			2,100	
Depreciation Expense: Office Equipment			25	
Depreciation Expense: Furniture and Fixtures			20	
Depreciation Expense: Automobile			150	3,300
Net Income:				$ 2,120
Less: Income Taxes				424
Net Income after Taxes:				$ 1,696

Exhibit 5-29: Income statement for the month of June.

Pacific Printers Mart
Balance Sheet
June 30, 1997

Assets

Current Assets:				
Cash			$14,295	
Accounts Receivable			150	
Inventory			3,000	
Unexpired Insurance			300	
Total current assets:				$17,745
Plant and Equipment:				
Shop Supplies			$ 710	
Office Equipment		$1,800		
Less: Accumulated Depreciation: Office Equipment		75	1,725	
Furniture and Fixtures		$2,400		
Less: Accumulated Depreciation: Furniture and Fixtures		60	2,340	
Automobile		$7,200		
Less: Accumulated Depreciation: Automobile		450	6,750	
Total plant and equipment:				11,525
				$29,270

Liabilities and Owner's Equity

Current Liabilities:				
Accounts Payable			$1,700	
Salaries Payable			1,500	
Interest Payable			200	
Unearned Commissions			1,000	
Income Taxes Payable			1,251	
Total current liabilities:				$ 5,651
Long-term Liabilities:				
Notes Payable:				10,000
Owner's Equity:				
Jack Fraser, Capital, June 1, 1997			$13,423	
Net Income		$2,120		
Less: Jack Fraser, Drawings	$1,500			
Income Taxes	424	1,924	196	
Jack Fraser, Capital, June 30, 1997				13,619
				$29,270

Exhibit 5-30: Balance sheet at the end of June.

FURTHER REVIEW OF THE ACCOUNTING CYCLE

The complete accounting cycle for a proprietorship engaged in merchandising may be summarized as follows:

1. Record all operating transactions in the journal and post these entries to the ledger.
2. Determine the amount of each adjusting entry. Record the adjusting entries in the journal and post these entries to the ledger. Prepare a trial balance, if desired.
3. Determine the amount of ending inventory by physical count, priced at cost on a first-in first-out stock rotation basis.
4. a. Close all of the income statement accounts that have debit balances, and the beginning inventory, into the Income Summary account.
   b. Record ending inventory and close all of the income statement accounts that have credit balances into the Income Summary account.
   c. Compute the net balance of the Income Summary account. Close the Income Summary account into Jack Fraser, Capital.
5. Determine the amount of net income by preparing preliminary financial statements on scratch paper. Compute the amount of income taxes, record the entry for income taxes in the journal and post to the ledger.
6. a. Close the drawings account, Jack Fraser, Drawings, into the owner's equity account, Jack Fraser, Capital.
   b. Close the Income Taxes account into the owner's equity account, Jack Fraser, Capital.
   c. Balance and rule the balance sheet accounts. (This may be done in step two above, prior to preparing a trial balance).

Of course, closing each of these accounts means making appropriate entries in the journal and then posting these entries to the ledger, and placing a dashed line under the last entry in each account as it is closed.

7. Prepare an income statement and a balance sheet.

Exercises

1. What is meant by *Purchases* in accounting terminology? Are not all goods purchased and therefore purchases? Explain.

2. Should the cost of hiring a truck to transport merchandise purchased for resale, from the wholesaler to the retailer, be added to the cost of the merchandise or charged off as an expense in the income statement?

3. Is there any advantage to recording purchase returns and allowances in a separate account instead of crediting the Purchases account directly?

4. Why do suppliers include terms on their invoices for goods sold on credit when payment is usually due in 30 days in any event? Does it pay to take advantage of the discount offered by suppliers by paying the bill early?

5. What is the equivalent annual rate of interest if the terms on an invoice are 2/5, net 10?

6. Which accounts are included in the Cost of Goods Sold section of an income statement?

7. Explain the distinction between *Purchases* and *Inventory*.

8. What is gross profit? What is mark-up? How is percentage mark-up calculated?

9. What is the title of the account for revenue earned by selling merchandise?

10. At what point in time is inventory taken using the periodic inventory method? What must be done with beginning inventory, as recorded in the books, before ending inventory may be brought on the books?

11. What is the purpose of preparing a preliminary set of financial statements? How does the final set of financial statements differ from the preliminary set of financial statements?

12. Summarize the accounting cycle for a business engaged in merchandising.

Problems

1. Prepare journal entries for each of the following transactions:

   a. April 28: Purchased $5,000 worth of merchandise for resale from

Gamma Distributors Inc. Paid for in cash at the time of purchase.

b. April 29: Paid Speedy Delivery Company $600 for hauling merchandise to the premises.

c. March 8: Acquired $8,000 worth of goods, on credit, from Consolidated Suppliers Inc. Payment is due in 90 days time.

d. March 11: Damaged merchandise costing $500 is returned to Consolidated Suppliers Inc.

e. June 21: Purchased $2,000 worth of merchandise from Allied Distributors Inc. on credit. Terms: 2/10, net 30.

f. June 30: Paid Allied Distributors Inc.

g. March 19: Acquired $2,418.99 worth of merchandise from Supreme Wholesalers (1987) Inc. Issued a check for the full amount.

2. Merchandise costing ninety dollars is sold for one hundred and thirty dollars. Calculate the percentage mark-up.

3. Company policy is to mark-up all merchandise acquired for resale by fifty percent. Calculate the selling price of each item listed below:

	Item	*Cost*	*Selling Price*
a.	Washing machine	$300	
b.	Garbage cans	$4	
c.	Fertilizer	$3.40	
d.	Lawn mower	$208	
e.	Alarm clock	$9.45	

4. During the month of February, a retailer realized $15,418 in cash sales. The cost of goods sold amounted to $8,000. Calculate the percentage mark-up.

5. What level of sales is necessary to enable a retailer to earn a gross profit of seven thousand dollars if the cost of goods sold equals five thousand dollars?

6. Prepare journal entries for each of the following transactions:

a. April 15: Cash sales of merchandise for the first half of the month amounted to $8,419.

b. June 10: Sold a lawn mower, priced at $459.95 to a customer, on credit.

c. March 9: Sold several items to a customer; total amount of sale $624. Payment made by check.
March 10: The customer returns an item costing $86 and asks for a refund.

d. July 19: Sales totaling $4,018 were made on credit. Terms: 2/10, net thirty days.
July 29: Payment received for credit sales made on July 19th.

7. For the business described below, do the following:
   a. Record all operating transactions in a journal and post to the ledger (draw appropriate column rulings on ordinary notebook paper).
   b. Prepare a trial balance.
   c. Compute and record all adjusting entries. Post to the ledger. Prepare an adjusted trial balance.
   d. Record ending inventory and close the books.
   e. Prepare a preliminary set of financial statements.
   f. Compute the amount of income taxes at a rate of 20%. Record in the journal and post to the ledger and close the Income Taxes account.
   g. Prepare an after closing trial balance.
   h. Prepare a final set of financial statements.

May 1 Sandra Brite opens a bank account in the name of the business, the Granville Toy Shoppe. Fifty thousand dollars in cash is deposited into the account.

2 Leases a premises at a cost of $500 per month. Pays the rent for the month of May at this time. Lease is for a five-year term.

3 Buys an electronic cash register at a cost of $1,980. Pays for it in cash at this time. Depreciate over 5 years.

4 Buys office furniture on credit. A bill for $924 is to be paid by the end of the month. Seven-year property.

7 Purchases merchandise costing $3,000 from Philadelphia Toyhouse Inc. Paid for by check.

8 Paid National Freight Company $400 in delivery charges.

10 Sales for the first ten days of business amounted to $4,040.

12 Purchases merchandise costing $2,000 from Pacific Toy Wholesalers Inc., on credit. Terms: 2/10, net 30.

May	13	Purchases office supplies costing $150 for use during the current month. Check number 106 is issued in payment.
	14	Discovers damaged goods in the shipment from Pacific Toy Wholesalers Inc. The wholesaler agrees to an allowance in the amount of $120.
	15	A customer returns a toy laser gun and asks for a refund. A cash refund of $65 is given to the customer.
	16	Sells $1,400 worth of toys to Burrard Girls' Club, on credit. Terms are 2/10, net 30.
	17	Purchases merchandise costing $2,000 from Ace Toy Wholesalers Inc. Terms are 1/5, net 15.
	20	Cash sales for the second ten days in May amount to $9,045.
	21	Withdraws $1,000 from the business for her own personal use.
	22	Pays Ace Toy Wholesalers Inc.
	25	Receives a check from the Burrard Girls' Club.
	25	Purchases $1,000 worth of merchandise from Outer Space Distributors (1966) Inc. Paid for at the time of purchase. Pays Speedy Delivery Inc. $80 for delivering the merchandise.
	26	Obtains insurance coverage on the contents of the premises retroactive to the beginning of the month. A 12-month policy costing $240 was paid for at this time.
	27	Hires an assistant to help with a one-day promotional sale. Pays her $90 in cash at the end of the day.
	28	Pays radio station KNX to run several spot commercials on the air. Check number 119 in the amount of $340 is issued.
	31	Sales for the remainder of the month amounted to $8,111.
	31	The telephone bill for $34 was received. Payment is due by June 10th.
	31	Pays for office furniture purchased earlier.
	31	Sent Pacific Toy Wholesalers Inc. a check for $1,880.

May 31 A count of inventory reveals $3,000 in unsold merchandise.

8. Examine the following journal entry for Joan Vera's Vitamin Shop and calculate the amount of net income for the month of May.

1997					
May	30	Income Summary	600	17,728	
		Inventory	105		4,000
		Sales Returns and Allowances	461		80
		Sales Discounts	462		100
		Purchases	463		8,047
		Rent Expense	567		2,000
		Telephone Expense	568		44
		Utilities Expense	569		129
		Insurance Expense	571		41
		Office Supplies Expense	572		25
		Advertising and Promotion Expense	574		1,022
		Salaries Expense	584		2,200
		Depreciation Expense: Furn. and Fixtures	593		40
		To close beginning inventory and all of the income statement accounts that have debit balances.			
May	30	Inventory	105	5,000	
		Sales	460	27,880	
		Purchase Returns and Allowances	465	220	
		Purchase Discounts	466	44	
		Income Summary	600		33,144
		To bring ending inventory on the books and to close all of the income statement accounts that have credit balances.			

9. Make an entry in the journal to close Income Summary in problem 8. The name of the owner's equity account is Joan Vera, Capital.

CHAPTER SIX

Miscellaneous Transactions

RECORDING SALES TAX

Up to the end of June, all sales were made directly to firms in the trade, and accordingly no sales tax was collected from customers. Now beginning with the month of July, the marketing strategy of Pacific Printers Mart is altered so that all sales will be made directly to the end user. It is the customer, who is the end user of a product, who must pay the sales tax. Pacific Printers Mart must collect this tax from its customers and remit it to the government in the month following the month in which it is collected. For the services performed in collecting sales tax on behalf of the government, Pacific Printers Mart is entitled to retain a commission based and calculated on the amount of sales tax collected. The tax rate is 6% and the amount of commission allowed is 3% of the amount of sales tax collected. Both of these rates are set by the government and vary from time to time. A record of sales made during the month of July, and sales tax collected, is shown in Exhibit 6-1.

Rather than make entries to the journal every day, a sales book is kept in which daily sales are recorded. At the end of the month total sales are computed, the amount of sales tax collectible is calculated, and any cash shortage or overage is accounted for. The sum of the individual entries in the sales book is recorded by means of an entry in the journal as illustrated in Exhibit 6-2.

RECORD OF DAILY SALES

Date	Credit Sales	Sales Tax	Cash Sales	Sales Tax	Cash Overage	Cash Shortage
July 2			$ 500	$ 30	$ 2	
3			1,200	72	9	
6			900	54	7	
7			1,100	66		$ 14
8			1,500	90		10
9			1,000	60	20	
10			700	42		3
13	$ 500	$ 30	300	18	5	
14	200	12	900	54		2
15			1,400	84		7
16			1,200	72		15
17			1,000	60	1	
20	800	48				
21	700	42				
22	1,000	60				
23			800	48	3	
24	400	24				
27	900	54				
28	600	36				
29			1,000	60		15
30			800	48	10	
31	600	36	—	—	—	—
	$5,700	$342	$14,300	$858	$57	$66

Exhibit 6-1: Entries in sales book for the month of July.

Journal					Page 9
1997					
July	31	Cash	101	15,149	
		Cash Shortage	589	9	
		Sales	460		14,300
		Sales Tax Payable	235		858
		To record taxable cash sales for the month of July.			
	31	Accounts Receivable	103	6,042	
		Sales	460		5,700
		Sales Tax Payable	235		342
		To record taxable sales made on credit during the month of July.			

Exhibit 6-2: Journal entries to record taxable sales.

REMITTING SALES TAX

Sales tax collectible on sales made in July need not be remitted until August. A total of $1,200 in sales tax is collectible on sales made during July and this amount is remitted to the government on August 15th. Pacific Printers Mart is entitled to retain 3% of the amount of sales tax collectible as a commission for collecting the tax. The journal entry to record this transaction is illustrated in Exhibit 6-3.

Journal					Page 11
1997					
August	15	Sales Tax Payable	235	1,200	
		Cash	101		1,164
		Commissions	435		36
		Remitted sales tax collectible for the month of July.			

Exhibit 6-3: Journal entry to record remittance of sales tax and commission earned for collecting the tax.

CASH OVERAGES AND SHORTAGES

When numerous cash sales, particularly in small amounts, are made throughout the day, errors in making change resulting in cash overages or shortages will inevitably occur. This means that total sales as indicated on the cash register tape will differ from the total amount of cash in the till. When this happens we do not dip into our wallets to make up the shortage nor do we pocket the cash overage. Instead, we handle such errors through accounting entries.

From Exhibit 6-1, we can determine that the sum of cash overages for the month of July is $57; the sum of cash shortages is $66; leaving a net cash shortage of $9. This net cash shortage was recorded in our journal entry in Exhibit 6-2. A cash shortage is an item of expense and is found among the other expenses on the income statement.

An analysis of the record of daily cash sales for the month of August reveals that a net cash overage of $10 remains at the end of the month. The journal entry to record this cash overage is illustrated in Exhibit 6-4.

Journal — **Page 11**

1997				
August 31	Cash	101	10,610	
	Sales	460		10,000
	Sales Tax Payable	235		600
	Cash Overage	457		10
	To record taxable cash sales for the month of August.			

Exhibit 6-4: Journal entry to record taxable cash sales.

A cash overage is treated as an item of revenue and is found among the revenue accounts in the income statement. Both the Cash Overage and Cash Shortage accounts, as appropriate, are closed into the Income Summary account when the books are closed at the end of the accounting period.

The terms cash overage and cash shortage often cause unwarranted controversy when they appear on an income statement, when the income statement is studied by someone who does not appreciate the true significance of these accounts. For this reason cash overages are often recorded in an account titled *Miscellaneous Revenue* and cash shortages are recorded in an account titled *Miscellaneous Expense*. The term miscellaneous expense does not have the same negative connotation as cash shortage and is not likely to provoke controversy.

BAD DEBTS

Every business ends up with accounts receivable that have to be written off because they prove impossible to collect. This happens even when the policy of the business is cash sales only. Businesses that sell merchandise or services on credit end up with even greater losses. Bad debt losses are an inevitable part of doing business and some losses due to uncollectible accounts is evidence of basically sound management. To not incur any bad debt losses whatsoever probably means that the business owners have decided not to take any chances with anyone and will suffer reduced sales as a result. Such a policy, for example, means that a manager would not take a check from a customer known to have ample funds in the unlikely event that the check may turn out to be a bad check.

Sales on credit and non-sufficient fund checks are the usual sources of bad debts. If it turns out that these accounts cannot be collected then they must be written off. There is no point in keeping uncollectible accounts receivable on the books unless you expect to collect them eventually. If accounts receivable that have been written off are later unexpectedly collected, they may be reinstated on the books.

NON-SUFFICIENT FUND CHECKS

A policy of cash sales only means that sales are not made on credit, but the business does take checks. However, a policy formulated in that manner may result in unexpected credit sales. This happens when the bank returns checks stamped N.S.F., meaning non-sufficient funds. Simply stated, the person who wrote the check does not have sufficient funds in his or her account to cover the amount of the check and the bank will not honor it.

On July 20th, the bank returns two checks to Pacific Printers Mart, stamped N.S.F. The first one bore the date July 13th and was for $212 while the second check bore the date July 14th and was for $106. Attempts to contact the customers who wrote these checks failed. The bank advises that these two accounts have been inactive for some time. Our first step is to convert the cash sales to credit sales by means of the journal entries in Exhibit 6-5.

Journal **Page 9**

1997					
July	20	Accounts Receivable	103	212	
		Cash	101		212
		N.S.F. check returned by the bank.			
	20	Accounts Receivable	103	106	
		Cash	101		106
		N.S.F. check returned by the bank.			

Exhibit 6-5: Entries to convert cash sales to credit sales.

Further inquiries reveal that there appears to be little likelihood that we can collect on these two accounts. The first customer purchased a one-way ticket to the Bahamas and the second customer is insolvent. A decision is made to write off both accounts receivable as uncollectible. This is accomplished by means of the two journal entries illustrated in Exhibit 6-6.

		Journal			Page 9
1997					
July	22	Bad Debts Expense	578	212	
		Accounts Receivable	103		212
		To write off an uncollectible account.			
	23	Bad Debts Expense	578	106	
		Accounts Receivable	103		106
		To write off an uncollectible account.			

Exhibit 6-6: Journal entries to write off uncollectible accounts.

This method of writing off uncollectible accounts receivable is known as the direct write off method of accounting for bad debts. It is the usual method employed by most small businesses whose sales are mainly cash sales. However, this method cannot always be employed and a second method will be considered shortly (after the next section).

REINSTATING AN ACCOUNT RECEIVABLE

On July 27th Pacific Printers Mart is notified that the second customer will be paying for his merchandise after all. Accordingly, his account is reinstated by means of the journal entry in Exhibit 6-7.

		Journal			Page 9
1997					
July	27	Accounts Receivable	103	106	
		Bad Debts Expense	578		106
		To reinstate an account previously written off.			

Exhibit 6-7: Journal entry to reinstate the account written off on July 23rd.

When the account receivable, in Exhibit 6-7, is collected on July 28th, the journal entry in Exhibit 6-8 is made.

		Journal			Page 9
1997					
July	28	Cash	101	106	
		Accounts Receivable	103		106
		Collected from the customer.			

Exhibit 6-8: Entry to record collection of reinstated account.

PROVISION FOR LOSSES FROM UNCOLLECTIBLE ACCOUNTS RECEIVABLE

The direct write off method of accounting for bad debt expense may only be employed when an account receivable is written off in the same period as when it was placed on the books. At least that is the theory. Using the direct write off method to write off an account receivable in a subsequent accounting period results in a distorted income statement, as bad debt expense which should have been included in the income statement of one period is not included until a later period. Even in spite of this resulting distortion many small businesses employ only the direct write off method as it is convenient to use.

At the end of July, of the $5,700 in credit sales made during the month, plus sales tax amounting to $342 resulting in Accounts Receivable of $6,042, only $2,042 in accounts receivable was collected, leaving a balance of $4,000 outstanding to be collected in subsequent months. Of this balance of $4,000 in accounts receivable outstanding, it is believed that 5% will ultimately prove to be uncollectible and will have to be written off as bad debt expense. At the moment we do not know which specific accounts will prove uncollectible. The specific accounts that prove to be bad will not be determined until a later date, in some subsequent accounting period. In the meantime, we must include as bad debt expense in our income statement for July expected credit losses resulting from sales made on credit in July and not in a later month when anticipated losses materialize. We provide for these expected losses by means of an estimate as illustrated in Exhibit 6-9.

		Journal			Page 9
1997					
July	31	Bad Debts Expense	578	200	
		Allowance for Bad Debts	104		200
		To record bad debt expense estimated at 5% of outstanding accounts receivable.			

Exhibit 6-9: Journal entry to provide for expected losses from uncollectible accounts.

Notice that the credit item is entered to Allowance for Bad Debts instead of to Accounts Receivable. This is because at this point in time we are simply basing our losses on an estimate and are not yet actually writing off specific Accounts Receivable. The credit balance in the Allowance for Bad Debts account is subtracted from the debit balance in Accounts Receivable, on the balance sheet, to arrive at the net value of Accounts Receivable. In August, when a specific account receivable turns out to be worthless, the journal entry in Exhibit 6-10 is made to write off the account.

	Journal			**Page 11**
1997				
August 25	Allowance for Bad Debts	104	180	
	Accounts Receivable	103		180
	To write off an account receivable as uncollectible.			

Exhibit 6-10: Journal entry to write off an account receivable.

In the event that an account previously written off proves to be collectible, it is necessary to enter a reversing entry in the journal, with a debit to Accounts Receivable and a credit to Allowance for Bad Debts.

As it turns out we overestimated the amount of bad debt loss for the month of July and a credit balance of $20 remains in the Allowance for Bad Debts account at the end of August. At the end of August $5,000 in Accounts Receivable remains outstanding. The amount of bad debt loss expected from the outstanding Accounts Receivable for credit sales made in August is $5,000 x 5% = $250. Because we overestimated bad debt losses in July and a balance of $20 remains in the account, we need only add $250 - $20 = $230 to the Allowance for Bad Debts account. This is done as illustrated in the journal entry in Exhibit 6-11.

	Journal			**Page 11**
1997				
August 31	Bad Debts Expense	578	230	
	Allowance for Bad Debts	104		230
	To record estimated bad debts expense for the month of August.			

Exhibit 6-11: Journal entry to provide for expected losses from uncollectible accounts.

MERCHANDISE CONSUMED BY RETAILER

When a retailer consumes some of the goods purchased for resale, the retailer must account for these goods. The advantage is that the retailer obtains these goods at the wholesale price. In concept, the withdrawal of merchandise from the business for personal consumption by a proprietor is no different than the withdrawal of cash by the owner of a business for his or her own use.

On July 15th, Pacific Printers Mart acquires some merchandise for resale, as illustrated by the journal entry in Exhibit 6-12.

Journal **Page 9**

1997					
July	15	Purchases	463	2,000	
		Cash	101		2,000
		To record purchase of merchandise for resale.			

Exhibit 6-12: Journal entry to record merchandise acquired for resale.

On July 18th, Jack Fraser removes some of the merchandise for his personal consumption. The journal entry to record this transaction is illustrated in the following exhibit, Exhibit 6-13.

Journal **Page 9**

1997					
July	18	Jack Fraser, Drawings	344	300	
		Purchases	463		300
		To record withdrawal of goods for personal consumption.			

Exhibit 6-13: Journal entry to record withdrawal of merchandise by the owner for his own use.

As this merchandise was withdrawn for personal consumption, Jack Fraser must remit the amount of sales tax on the merchandise withdrawn as he is the final user. The cash to pay the sales tax must come out of his own pocket. If it does not, then the cash taken from the business to pay the sales tax on merchandise withdrawn for personal consumption must be recorded as drawings.

The journal entry to record sales tax on merchandise withdrawn by the owner of the business for his personal consumption is illustrated in Exhibit 6-14.

Journal				Page 9
1997				
July 18	Cash	101	18	
	Sales Tax Payable	235		18
	To record collection of sales tax on merchandise removed for personal use.			

Exhibit 6-14: Journal entry to record sales tax collected on goods removed for personal consumption.

The $18 in cash, of course, is taken from the pocket of Jack Fraser and handed over to Pacific Printers Mart. It is essential that the business actually receive this amount of cash. An alternative way of handling this situation, is to debit Jack Fraser, Drawings, instead of debiting Cash, in which case the owner does not reach into his wallet and hand the sales tax money over to the business. Sales tax paid by the business on behalf of the owner becomes drawings by the owner. Think of it this way—the owner withdraws cash from the business in order to pay sales tax on goods withdrawn for personal consumption. In paying this tax the owner gives the money back to the business and the business remits the money to the government in due course. When the sales tax is remitted to the government, the journal entry which is illustrated in Exhibit 6-15 must be made.

Journal				Page 11
1997				
August 15	Sales Tax Payable	235	18	
	Cash	101		18
	Remitted sales tax on goods removed for personal consumption in July.			

Exhibit 6-15: Journal entry to record payment of sales tax on goods removed for personal consumption.

Notice how the entry in Exhibit 6-15 differs from the entry in Exhibit 6-3. No commission is earned by the vendor on sales tax collected on merchandise removed from the business for the vendor's personal consumption.

PETTY CASH

A petty cash account is usually employed in a large organization where the bureaucratic procedure involved in buying two dollars worth of pencils, stamps, or paying taxi fare, would otherwise be quite complicated. Most small businesses have a straightforward procedure regarding such matters and, hence, the need for a petty cash account does not arise. A petty cash account is required where certain employees may need to make small expenditures from time to time, but where it may not be convenient to bother the owner to ask for this cash when it is needed. Thus, the owner or manager of a small business does not require a petty cash account for his or her own use, but may set up a petty cash fund for the use of certain employees.

On July 15th, a petty cash fund is set up for use by the part-time secretary to enable her to buy office supplies, where the need to buy these supplies arises between regular purchases of office supplies. An entry in the journal to establish a petty cash fund is made as shown in Exhibit 6-16.

Journal **Page 9**

1997					
July	15	Petty Cash	102	50	
		Cash	101		50
		To establish a petty cash fund.			

Exhibit 6-16: Journal entry to establish a petty cash fund.

A check is made out to *Petty Cash* and is cashed at the bank. This money is given to the part-time secretary who places it in a cookie jar or other suitable container which she keeps locked away in her desk. She spends the money as required on sundry items and keeps the receipts and a record of expenditures. During the month of July the entries in Exhibit 6-17 were made in the petty cash book.

PETTY CASH

1997			
July	16	Stamps	$ 3.00
	17	Pencils	2.30
	24	Fertilizer	4.70
	27	Sugar	1.40
	29	Taxi Fare	4.60
	31	Typewriter ribbon	6.00
			$22.00

Exhibit 6-17: Entries in petty cash book during July.

At the end of July, $28 remains in the petty cash fund. The fund is replenished by making the journal entry shown in Exhibit 6-18 and by making out a check for $22 to *Petty Cash* which is cashed and deposited in the cookie jar. The fund, once again, stands at $50.

Journal **Page 9**

1997					
July	31	Office Supplies Expense	572	22	
		Cash	101		22
		To record office supplies expense paid for with petty cash.			

Exhibit 6-18: Journal entry to replenish petty cash fund.

After the petty cash fund is established, no further journal entries are made debiting the Petty Cash account unless it is desired to increase the size of the fund. Notice that in our journal entry in Exhibit 6-18, the account Cash, and not, Petty Cash, is credited. The $22 taken from the Cash account is used to replenish the petty cash fund, bringing its balance back up to $50. When a balance sheet is prepared at the end of July, Petty Cash is not shown as a separate item. Its total is combined with the balance in the Cash account and the sum of the balances of these two accounts is simply represented as if they were one account, namely, Cash.

PREPARING FOR MONTH END

The books at the end of the month are illustrated in the next several exhibits. First of all, the operating entries for the month of July are illustrated in Exhibit 6-19; the adjusting entries are illustrated in Exhibit 6-20; a trial balance after adjusting entries have been posted to the ledger is illustrated in Exhibit 6-21; a preliminary income statement for the month of July is illustrated in Exhibit 6-22; and, a preliminary balance sheet (one that is prepared before income taxes have been taken into consideration) is presented in Exhibit 6-23. After this preliminary work has been done, income taxes for the month of July may be computed, the books may be closed, and a final set of financial statements may be prepared, completing the accounting cycle for the month of July.

Exhibit 6-19: Operating entries for the month of July.

Journal **Page 9**

1997					
July	2	Purchases	463	4,300	
		Accounts Payable	230		4,300
		To record purchase of merchandise from Alpha Wholesale Inc. Terms 2/10, net 30.			
	2	Transportation-in	464	200	
		Cash	101		200
		Paid Fastic Freight Corporation for delivery of merchandise.			
	3	Salaries Payable	231	1,500	
		Cash	101		1,500
		Paid employee his salary for work in June.			
	10	Office Supplies Expense	572	40	
		Cash	101		40
		Purchased office supplies.			
	10	Cash	101	150	
		Accounts Receivable	103		150
		Check for commissions earned on photocopying in June received from Rapid Photocopiers Inc.			
	10	Accounts Payable	230	4,300	
		Cash	101		4,214
		Purchase Discounts	466		86
		Paid Alpha Wholesale Inc. for merchandise purchased on July 2nd.			
	13	Advertising and Promotion Expense	574	220	
		Cash	101		220
		Placed ads in the newspaper.			
	14	Purchases	463	5,000	
		Accounts Payable	230		5,000
		Purchased merchandise from ACME Wholesale Inc. No terms. Payment due July 31st.			

July	15	Petty Cash	102	50	
		Cash	101		50
		To establish a petty cash fund.			
	15	Purchases	463	2,000	
		Cash	101		2,000
		To record purchase of merchandise for resale.			
	17	Accounts Payable	230	200	
		Purchase Returns and Allowances	465		200
		To record allowance from ACME Wholesale Inc. for damaged merchandise.			
	18	Jack Fraser, Drawings	344	300	
		Purchases	463		300
		To record withdrawal of goods for personal consumption.			
	18	Cash	101	18	
		Sales Tax Payable	235		18
		To record collection of sales tax on merchandise removed for personal use.			
	20	Accounts Receivable	103	212	
		Cash	101		212
		N.S.F. check returned by the bank.			
	20	Accounts Receivable	103	106	
		Cash	101		106
		N.S.F. check returned by the bank.			
	22	Bad Debts Expense	578	212	
		Accounts Receivable	103		212
		To write off an uncollectible account.			
	23	Bad Debts Expense	578	106	
		Accounts Receivable	103		106
		To write off an uncollectible account.			
	24	Automobile Maintenance Expense	570	60	
		Cash	101		60
		Purchased gasoline for truck.			
	27	Accounts Receivable	103	106	
		Bad Debts Expense	578		106
		To reinstate an account previously written off.			

July	28	Cash	101	106	
		Accounts Receivable	103		106
		Collected from the customer.			
	31	Accounts Payable	230	4,800	
		Cash	101		4,800
		Paid ACME Wholesale Inc. for merchandise purchased on July 14th.			
	31	Accounts Payable	230	500	
		Cash	101		500
		Made 3rd installment payment on office furniture purchased from Superior Office Products Inc. on March 15th.			
	31	Cash	101	15,149	
		Cash Shortage	589	9	
		Sales	460		14,300
		Sales Tax Payable	235		858
		To record taxable cash sales for the month of July.			
	31	Accounts Receivable	103	6,042	
		Sales	460		5,700
		Sales Tax Payable	235		342
		To record taxable sales made on credit during the month of July.			
	31	Cash	101	2,042	
		Accounts Receivable	103		2,042
		Collected on some credit sales, leaving $4,000 to be collected.			
	31	Office Supplies Expense	572	22	
		Cash	101		22
		To record office supplies paid for with petty cash.			
	31	Salaries Expense	584	600	
		Cash	101		600
		Paid the part-time secretary.			
	31	Rent Expense	567	400	
		Cash	101		400
		Paid rent for July.			

July	31	Telephone Expense	568	54	
		Cash	101		54
		Paid telephone bill for July.			
	31	Utilities Expense	569	80	
		Cash	101		80
		Paid bill for electricity and gas consumed during July.			
	31	Interest and Service Charges Expense	575	4	
		Cash	101		4
		To record bank service charges for the month of July.			
	31	Jack Fraser, Drawings	344	1,000	
		Cash	101		1,000
		Cash withdrawn for personal use.			

Exhibit 6-20: Adjusting entries for the month of July.

Journal **Page 9**

1997					
July	31	Unearned Commissions	233	100	
		Commissions	455		100
		To record commissions earned in July from arrangement with Compatible Darkroom Company.			
	31	Accounts Receivable	103	160	
		Commissions	455		160
		Commissions earned on photocopying in July; to be collected in August.			
	31	Salaries Expense	584	1,500	
		Salaries Expense	231		1,500
		To record salary expense for July.			
	31	Insurance Expense	571	30	
		Unexpired Insurance	106		30
		To record insurance expense for July.			

July	31	Shop Supplies Expense	573	20	
		Shop Supplies	111		20
		To record shop supplies used up during July.			
	31	Interest and Service Charges Expense	575	100	
		Interest Payable	232		100
		To record interest charges accrued during the month of July.			
	31	Bad Debts Expense	578	200	
		Allowance for Bad Debts	104		200
		To record bad debts expense estimated at 5% of outstanding accounts receivable.			
	31	Depreciation Expense: Office Equipment	592	25	
		Accum. Depreciation: Office Equipment	113		25
		To record depreciation for July.			
	31	Deprn. Expense: Furniture and Fixtures	593	20	
		Accum. Deprn.: Furniture and Fixtures	115		20
		To record depreciation for July.			
	31	Depreciation Expense: Automobile	594	150	
		Accumulated Depreciation: Automobile	117		150
		To record depreciation for July.			

TRIAL BALANCE

After these entries have been made in the journal they are posted to the ledger. We will not reproduce the ledger at this stage, but do realize that all of these entries have been posted. Because of the large number of entries that have been made it is useful to produce a trial balance to ensure that the books are still in balance. To determine the net balance in the balance sheet accounts we balance and rule the balance sheet accounts as required. Then we prepare a two column schedule by going through the ledger and listing each account that has a balance, together with its balance, and end up with a trial balance. This trial balance is illustrated in Exhibit 6-21. Because the sum of debits equals the sum of credits we know that we have not made any errors and can proceed to prepare a set of preliminary financial statements from the data in the trial balance, or from the net balances in the ledger, whichever we prefer. Either way the end result is the same and we end up with an income statement that correctly ties into the balance sheet and a balance sheet that balances. The whole system of accounting is designed to enable you to obtain absolutely accurate results despite a large number of entries.

Exhibit 6-21: Trial balance after operating and adjusting entries have been posted at the end of July.

Pacific Printers Mart
Trial Balance
July 31, 1997

Cash	$15,698	
Petty Cash	50	
Accounts Receivable	4,160	
Allowance for Bad Debts		$ 200
Inventory (June 30, 1997)	3,000	
Unexpired Insurance	270	
Shop Supplies	690	
Office Equipment	1,800	
Accumulated Depreciation: Office Equipment		100
Furniture and Fixtures	2,400	
Accumulated Depreciation: Furniture and Fixtures		80
Automobile	7,200	
Accumulated Depreciation: Automobile		600
Accounts Payable		1,200
Salaries Payable		1,500
Interest Payable		300
Unearned Commissions		900
Sales Tax Payable		1,218
Income Taxes Payable		1,251
Notes Payable		10,000
Jack Fraser, Capital		13,619
Jack Fraser, Drawings	1,300	
Commissions		260
Sales		20,000
Purchases	11,000	
Transportation-in	200	
Purchase Returns and Allowances		200
Purchase Discounts		86
Rent Expense	400	
Telephone Expense	54	
Utilities Expense	80	
Automobile Maintenance Expense	60	
Insurance Expense	30	
Office Supplies Expense	62	
Shop Supplies Expense	20	
Advertising and Promotion Expense	220	
Interest and Service Charges Expense	104	

Bad Debts Expense	412	
Salaries Expense	2,100	
Cash Shortage	9	
Depreciation Expense: Office Equipment	25	
Depreciation Expense: Furniture and Fixtures	20	
Depreciation Expense: Automobile	150	
	$51,514	$51,514

Exhibit 6-22: Income statement before income taxes for the month of July have been computed.

Pacific Printers Mart
Income Statement
For the month ending July 31, 1997

Revenue:				
Commissions				$ 260
Sales				20,000
Cost of Goods Sold:				
Inventory, July 1st			$ 3,000	
Purchases		11,000		
Add: Transportation-in		200		
Delivered Cost of Purchases		11,200		
Less: Purchase Ret. & Allowances	$200			
Purchase Discounts	86	286		
Net Purchases			10,914	
Cost of Goods Available for Sale			13,914	
Less: Inventory, June 30th			4,000	
Cost of Goods Sold:				9,914
Gross Profit:				$10,346
Expenses:				
Rent Expense			$ 400	
Telephone Expense			54	
Utilities Expense			80	
Automobile Maintenance Expense			60	
Insurance Expense			30	
Office Supplies Expense			62	
Shop Supplies Expense			20	
Advertising and Promotion Expense			220	

Interest and Service Charges Expense	104	
Bad Debts Expense	412	
Salaries Expense	2,100	
Cash Shortage	9	
Depreciation Expense: Office Equipment	25	
Depreciation Expense: Furniture and Fixtures	20	
Depreciation Expense: Automobile	150	3,746
Net Income:		$ 6,600

Exhibit 6-23: Balance sheet before income taxes for the month of July have been computed.

Pacific Printers Mart
Balance Sheet
July 31, 1997

Assets

Current Assets:			
Cash		$15,748	
Accounts Receivable	$4,160		
Less: Allowance for Bad Debts	200	3,960	
Inventory, July 31, 1997		4,000	
Unexpired Insurance		270	
Total current assets:			$23,978
Plant and Equipment:			
Shop Supplies		$ 690	
Office Equipment	$1,800		
Less: Accumulated Depreciation: Office Equipment	100	1,700	
Furniture and Fixtures	$2,400		
Less: Accumulated Depreciation: Furniture and Fixtures	80	2,320	
Automobile	$7,200		
Less: Accumulated Depreciation: Automobile	600	6,600	
Total plant and equipment:			11,310
			$35,288

Liabilities and Owner's Equity

Current Liabilities:		
Accounts Payable	$1,200	
Salaries Payable	1,500	
Interest Payable	300	
Unearned Commissions	900	
Sales Tax Payable	1,218	
Income Taxes Payable	1,251	

Total current liabilities:			$ 6,639
Long-term Liabilities:			
Notes Payable:			10,000
Owner's Equity:			
Jack Fraser, Capital, July 1, 1997		$13,619	
Net Income	$6,600		
Less: Jack Fraser, Drawings	1,300	5,300	
Jack Fraser, Capital, July 31, 1997			18,919
			$35,288

INCOME TAXES FOR JULY

From our preliminary income statement in Exhibit 6-22, net income for the month of July is $6,600. Knowing the amount of net income, we may compute the amount of income taxes as follows:

Income taxes = $6,600 x 30% = $1,980

This amount of income taxes for the month of July, plus income taxes owing from previous months that have not yet been paid, are all remitted to the income tax department at this time. The journal entry to record income taxes for July is illustrated in Exhibit 6-24.

Journal **Page 9**

1997					
July	31	Income Taxes	349	1,980	
		Cash	101		1,980
		Paid income taxes for July.			

Exhibit 6-24: Entry to record payment of income taxes.

The Income Taxes Payable account is examined to determine its balance as income taxes accrued from previous months must also now be paid. The entry to record payment of accrued income taxes is illustrated in Exhibit 6-25.

Journal					Page 9
1997					
July	31	Income Taxes Payable	236	1,251	
		Cash	101		1,251
		Paid accrued income taxes.			

Exhibit 6-25: Journal entry to record payment of accrued income taxes.

After posting these entries, the Income Taxes Payable account appears as shown in Exhibit 6-26 and the Income Taxes account appears as shown in Exhibit 6-27.

Income Taxes Payable 236

1997				1997				
July	31	9	1,251	May	31		5	827
				June	30	1,251	8	424

Exhibit 6-26: Income Taxes Payable account after income taxes are paid at the end of July.

Be certain that you understand the difference between the *Income Taxes Payable* account and the *Income Taxes* account. The Income Taxes Payable account is a liability account, just like any other liability account. When this debt is paid the liability is eliminated. The Income Taxes account, on the other hand, is an equity account. It serves to keep track of the amount of business growth that is handed over to the government in the form of income taxes. It is a measure of the amount by which equity is reduced due to income taxes.

Income Taxes								349
1997 April	30		4	1,205	1997 April	30	4	1,205
1997 May	31		5	827	1997 May	31	6	827
1997 June	30		8	424	1997 June	30	8	424
1997 July	31		9	1,980				

Exhibit 6-27: Income Taxes account at the end of July.

RECONCILING THE BANK STATEMENT

When the bank statement for the month of July is received, not all checks written have yet cleared the account, nor have all deposits been recorded. This means that the balance on the bank statement, which is $19,710 will not agree with the balance in the Cash account in our ledger. Thus the balance on the bank statement must be reconciled with the balance in the Cash account.

In addition to the Cash and Petty Cash accounts, we must also keep a check register. The check register, Exhibit 6-28, serves as a control device whereby all checks issued are listed in chronological order by serial number. Any spoiled checks should be marked *Void* with heavy pen and filed with the canceled checks. In the check register we also list all deposits and maintain a running balance. The final balance in the check register at the end of each month will be equal to the balance in the Cash ledger account. The balances in the Cash account and the Petty Cash account are combined and simply listed as *Cash* on the balance sheet. If any checks that were deposited are returned marked N.S.F. a notation must be made in the check register, with the amount in parenthesis. This means that the amount of the returned item must be subtracted in arriving at the balance. The amount of service charges must be obtained from the bank statement and also recorded in the check register.

The first step in reconciling the balance in the bank statement with the balance in the Cash account is to ensure that the check register is up to date with no entries missing. If this is the case, the balance in the check register will equal the balance in the Cash account. The balance in the check register at the end of July, from Exhibit 6-28, is $12,467. The balance in the Cash account at the end of July, from Exhibit 6-32 is also $12,467.

The balance on the bank statement at the end of July, from Exhibit 6-29, is $19,710.

This balance differs from the balance in the check register because all of the deposits have not been recorded on the statement for July; the missing deposits will appear on the statement for August. Similarly, all of the checks written have not yet cleared the account; they will likely clear the account in August. Taking these factors into consideration, the question remains whether the balance on the bank statement is consistent with that on the Cash account. We may determine the answer through the reconciliation illustrated in Exhibit 6-30. To the final balance on the bank statement we add any deposits made but which do not appear on the statement and obtain a subtotal. From this subtotal, we subtract the sum of all outstanding checks which have not yet cleared the account, to arrive at a final total. This final total, as can be seen in Exhibit 6-30, equals the final balance in the check register, which in turn is equal to the balance in the Cash account. The purpose of bank statement reconciliation is to ensure that the balance in the bank statement continues to be in agreement with our balance in the Cash ledger account and that no errors have been made by the bank or by ourselves.

Exhibit 6-28: Check register for the month of July.

Check Register

Date	Check Number	Description	Checks	Deposits	Balance Forward
1997					
July 1	---	Balance Forward	---	---	14,295
2	201	Fastic Freight Corporation	200	532	14,627
3	202	Ralph Black	1,500	1,281	14,408
6	---	---	---	961	15,369
7	---	---	---	1,152	16,521
8	---	---	---	1,580	18,101
9	---	---	---	1,080	19,181
10	203	Reliable Stationers Inc.	40	---	19,141
10	204	Alpha Wholesale Inc.	4,214	889	15,816
13	205	The Daily Bugle	220	323	15,919
14	---	---	---	952	16,871
15	206	Petty Cash	50	---	16,821
15	207	Delta Distributors Inc.	2,000	1,477	16,298
16	---	---	---	1,257	17,555
17	---	---	---	1,061	18,616
18	---	---	---	18	18,634
20	---	Deposit returned N.S.F.	---	(212)	18,422
20	---	Deposit returned N.S.F.	---	(106)	18,316
23	---	---	---	851	19,167
24	208	Racey Motors Inc.	60	---	19,107

July 28	---	---	---	106	19,213
29	---	---	---	1,045	20,258
30	---	---	---	858	21,116
31	209	ACME Wholesale Inc.	4,800	2,042	18,358
31	210	Superior Office Prod. Inc.	500	---	17,858
31	211	Petty Cash	22	---	17,836
31	212	June Jones	600	---	17,236
31	213	Advance Realty Corporation	400	---	16,836
31	214	Bell Intl. Telephone Corp.	54	---	16,782
31	215	Pyramid Power Corp.	80	---	16,702
31	216	Jack Fraser	1,000	---	15,702
31	217	Public Controller	3,231	---	12,471
31	---	Service Charges	4	---	12,467

Exhibit 6-29: **Bank statement for the month of July.**

New York Mutual Bank

Monthly Statement

Account Number: 2017-90
Date of Statement: July 31, 1997

Date of Previous Statement: June 30
Balance Forward: $14,295

Code	Description	Date	Debits	Credits	Balance
CK		07 02	200		14,095
CD		07 02		532	14,627
CK		07 03	1,500		13,127
CD		07 03		1,281	14,408
CD		07 06		961	15,369
CD		07 07		1,152	16,521
CD		07 08		1,580	18,101
CD		07 09		1,080	19,181
CK		07 10	40		19,141
CK		07 10	4,214		14,927
CD		07 10		889	15,816
CD		07 13		323	16,139
CD		07 14		952	17,091
CK		07 15	50		17,041
CK		07 15	2,000		15,041
CD		07 15		1,477	16,518
CD		07 16		1,257	17,775
CD		07 17		1,061	18,836

CD		07	18		18	18,854
RT	Deposit returned N.S.F.	07	20	212		18,642
RT	Deposit returned N.S.F.	07	20	106		18,536
CD		07	23		851	19,387
CK		07	24	60		19,327
CD		07	28		106	19,433
CD		07	29		1,045	20,478
CD		07	30		858	21,336
CK		07	31	22		21,314
CK		07	31	600		20,714
CK		07	31	1,000		19,714
SC	Service Charges	07	31	4		19,710

Exhibit 6-30: Reconciliation of the bank statement balance with the balance in the check register.

Reconciliation of Bank Statement Balance

Final balance from bank statement:			$19,710
Add: Deposits made which do not appear on statement:			
	July 31	$2,042	2,042
Subtotal:			$21,752
Subtract: Outstanding checks, not yet processed:			
	205	$ 220	
	209	4,800	
	210	500	
	213	400	
	214	54	
	215	80	
	217	3,231	9,285
Total:			$12,467
Final balance from check register:			$12,467
Difference:			Nil

CLOSING THE BOOKS

To close the books we go through the ledger and make journal entries to close all of the income statement accounts and beginning inventory. Ending inventory is placed on the books, and the Income Summary account, the drawings account, and the income taxes account, are all closed by means of the journal entries which are illustrated in Exhibit 6-31.

Exhibit 6-31: Closing entries at the end of July.

		Journal			**Page 10**
1997					
July	31	Income Summary	600	17,946	
		Inventory	105		3,000
		Purchases	463		11,000
		Transportation-in	464		200
		Rent Expense	567		400
		Telephone Expense	568		54
		Utilities Expense	569		80
		Automobile Maintenance Expense	570		60
		Insurance Expense	571		30
		Office Supplies Expense	572		62
		Shop Supplies Expense	573		20
		Advertising and Promotion Expense	574		220
		Interest and Service Charges Expense	575		104
		Bad Debts Expense	578		412
		Salaries Expense	584		2,100
		Cash Shortage	589		9
		Depreciation Expense: Office Equipment	592		25
		Deprn. Expense: Furniture and Fixtures	593		20
		Depreciation Expense: Automobile	594		150
		To close beginning inventory and all of the income statement accounts having debit balances.			
	31	Inventory	105	4,000	
		Commissions	455	260	
		Sales	460	20,000	
		Purchase Returns and Allowances	465	200	
		Purchase Discounts	466	86	
		Income Summary	600		24,546
		To record ending inventory and to close all of the income statement accounts having credit balances.			

July	31	Income Summary	600	6,600	
		Jack Fraser, Capital	343		6,600
		To close the Income Summary account.			
	31	Jack Fraser, Capital	343	1,300	
		Jack Fraser, Drawings	344		1,300
		To close the drawings account.			
	31	Jack Fraser, Capital	343	1,980	
		Income Taxes	349		1,980
		To close the Income Taxes account.			

LEDGER AFTER POSTING CLOSING ENTRIES

The complete ledger at the end of July, after all of the closing entries have been posted from the journal, is illustrated in Exhibit 6-32.

Exhibit 6-32: Complete ledger after closing the books at the end of July.

Cash 101

1997					1997				
March	1		1	10,000	March	5		1	7,700
	31		1	250		15		1	500
April	5		2	1,200		31		1	500
	21		2	4,500	April	1		2	100
	30	16,200	2	250		7		2	30
						30		2	600
						30		2	400
						30		2	1,500
						30	13,130	2	1,800
						30	14,335	4	1,205
						30	Balance	✓	1,865
				16,200					16,200
1997					1997				
May	1	Balance	✓	1,865	May	1		5	360
	1		5	1,200		6		5	800

1		5	10,000	7		5	35
31		5	250	10		5	70
31		5	7,100	15		5	70
				22		5	150
				25		5	60
				31		5	400
				31		5	150
				31		5	80
				31		5	500
				31		5	600
				31		5	40
				31	5,315	5	2,000
				31	Balance	✓	15,100
			20,415				20,415

1997					1997				
June	1	Balance	✓	15,100	June	2		7	8,000
	2		7	400		3		7	50
	12		7	200		4		7	100
	17		7	700		5		7	1,500
	30		7	5,880		18		7	35
	30		7	5,120		20		7	980
	30		7	450		21		7	250
						30		7	600
						30		7	400
						30		7	50
						30		7	90
						30	13,555	7	1,500
						30	Balance	✓	14,295
				27,850					27,850

1997					1997				
July	1	Balance	✓	14,295	July	2		9	200
	10		9	150		3		9	1,500
	18		9	18		10		9	40
	28		9	106		10		9	4,214
	31	31,760	9	15,149		13		9	220
	31		9	2,042		15		9	50
						15		9	2,000
						20		9	212
						20		9	106
						24		9	60
						31		9	4,800
						31		9	500
						31		9	22

					31			9	600
					31			9	400
					31			9	54
					31			9	80
					31			9	4
					31	16,062		9	1,000
					31			9	1,980
					31	19,293		9	1,251
					31	Balance		✓	12,467
				31,760					31,760
1997									
August 1	Balance		✓	12,467					

Petty Cash 102

1997								
July	15		9	50				

Accounts Receivable 103

1997					1997				
March	20		1	500	March	31		1	250
April	12		2	700	April	30	500	2	250
						30	Balance	✓	700
				1,200					1,200
1997					1997				
May	1	Balance	✓	700	May	31		5	250
	31		5	200		31	Balance	✓	650
				900					900
1997					1997				
June	1	Balance	✓	650	June	12		7	200
	3		7	700		17		7	700
	25		7	6,000		30		7	6,000
	30		7	150		30	7,350	7	450
						30	Balance	✓	150
				7,500					7,500
1997					1997				
July	1	Balance	✓	150	July	10		9	150
	20		9	212		22		9	212

	20		9	106		23		9	106
	27		9	106		28		9	106
	31		9	6,042		31	2,616	9	2,042
	31	6,776	9	160		31	Balance	✓	4,160
				6,776					6,776
1997									
August	1	Balance	✓	4,160					

Allowance for Bad Debts 104

					1997				
					July	31		9	200

Inventory 105

1997					1997				
June	30		8	3,000	July	31		10	3,000
1997									
July	31		10	4,000					

Unexpired Insurance 106

1997					1997				
May	1		5	360	May	31		5	30
						31	Balance	✓	330
				360					360
1997					1997				
June	1	Balance	✓	330	June	30		7	30
						30	Balance	✓	300
				330					330
1997					1997				
July	1	Balance	✓	300	July	31		9	30
						31	Balance	✓	270
				300					300
1997									
August	1	Balance	✓	270					

Shop Supplies — 111

1997					1997				
May	6		5	800	May	31		5	40
						31	Balance	✓	760
				800					800
1997					1997				
June	1	Balance	✓	760	June	30		7	50
						30	Balance	✓	710
				760					760
1997					1997				
July	1	Balance	✓	710	July	31		9	20
						31	Balance	✓	690
				710					710
1997									
August	1	Balance	✓	690					

Office Equipment — 112

1997									
March	11		1	1,800					

Accumulated Depreciation: Office Equipment — 113

					1997				
					April	30		3	25
					May	31	50	5	25
					June	30	75	7	25
					July	31	100	9	25

Furniture and Fixtures — 114

1997									
March	15		1	2,400					

Accumulated Depreciation: Furniture and Fixtures — 115

					1997				
					April	30		3	20
					May	31	40	5	20
					June	30	60	7	20
					July	31	80	9	20

Automobile — 116

1997					1997				
March	5		1	7,700	March	20		1	500
					April	30	Balance	✓	7,200
				7,700					7,700
1997									
May	1	Balance	✓	7,200					

Accumulated Depreciation: Automobile — 117

					1997				
					April	30		3	150
					May	31	300	5	150
					June	30	450	7	150
					July	31	600	9	150

Accounts Payable — 230

1997					1997				
March	31		1	500	March	11		1	1,800
April	30	2,300	2	1,800		15		1	1,900
	30	Balance	✓	1,655	April	14		2	150
						30		2	35
						30	3,955	2	70
				3,955					3,955
1997					1997				
May	7		5	35	May	1	Balance	✓	1,655
	10		5	70					
	31		5	150					
	31	755	5	500					
	31	Balance	✓	900					
				1,655					1,655

1997					1997				
June	4		7	100	June	1	Balance	✓	900
	20	1,100	7	1,000		3		7	900
	30	Balance	✓	1,700		11		7	1,000
				2,800					2,800
1997					1997				
July	10		9	4,300	July	1	Balance	✓	1,700
	17		9	200		2		9	4,300
	31		9	4,800		14	11,000	9	5,000
	31	9,800	9	500					
	31	Balance	✓	1,200					
				11,000					11,000
					1997				
					August	1	Balance	✓	1,200

Salaries Payable 231

1997					1997				
June	5		7	1,500	May	31		5	1,500
	30	Balance	✓	1,500	June	30		7	1,500
				3,000					3,000
1997					1997				
July	3		9	1,500	July	1	Balance	✓	1,500
	31	Balance	✓	1,500		31	3,000	9	1,500
				3,000					3,000
					1997				
					August	1	Balance	✓	1,500

Interest Payable 232

					1997				
					May	31		5	100
					June	30	200	7	100
					July	31	300	9	100

Unearned Commissions 233

1997					1997				
May	31		5	100	May	1		5	1,200
	31	Balance	✓	1,100					
				1,200					1,200
1997					1997				
June	30		7	100	June	1	Balance	✓	1,100
	30	Balance	✓	1,000					
				1,100					1,100
1997					1997				
July	31		9	100	July	1	Balance	✓	1,000
	31	Balance	✓	900					
				1,000					1,000
					1997				
					August	1	Balance	✓	900

Sales Tax Payable 235

					1997				
					July	18		9	18
						31		9	858
						31	1,218	9	342

Income Taxes Payable 236

1997					1997				
July	31		9	1,251	May	31		5	827
					June	30	1,251	8	424

Notes Payable 240

					1997				
					May	1		5	10,000

Jack Fraser, Capital — 343

1997					1997				
April	30		4	1,500	March	1		1	10,000
	30		4	1,205	April	30		4	4,820
	30	Balance	✓	12,115					
				14,820					14,820
1997					1997				
May	31		6	2,000	May	1	Balance	✓	12,115
	31		6	827		31		6	4,135
	31	Balance	✓	13,423					
				16,250					16,250
1997					1997				
June	30		8	1,500	June	5	Balance	✓	13,423
	30	1,924	8	424		30	15,543	8	2,120
	30	Balance	✓	13,619					
				15,543					15,543
1997					1997				
July	31		10	1,300	July	1	Balance	✓	13,619
	31	3,280	10	1,980		31	20,219	10	6,600
	31	Balance	✓	16,939					
				20,219					20,219
					1997				
					August	1	Balance	✓	16,939

Jack Fraser, Drawings — 344

1997					1997				
April	30		2	1,500	April	30		4	1,500
1997					1997				
May	31		5	2,000	May	31		6	2,000
1997					1997				
June	30		7	1,500	June	30		8	1,500
1997					1997				
July	18		9	300	July	31		10	1,300
	31	1,300	9	1,000					
				1,300					1,300

Income Taxes 349

1997				1997			
April	30	4	1,205	April	30	4	1,205
1997				1997			
May	31	5	827	May	31	6	827
1997				1997			
June	30	8	424	June	30	8	424
1997				1997			
July	31	9	1,980	July	31	10	1,980

Commissions 455

1997				1997			
April	30	4	6,400	April	5	2	1,200
					12	2	700
					21	2	4,500
			6,400				6,400
1997				1997			
May	31	6	7,400	May	31	5	7,100
					31	5	100
					31	5	200
			7,400				7,400
1997				1997			
June	30	8	250	June	30	7	100
					30	7	150
			250				250
1997				1997			
July	31	10	260	July	31	9	100
					31	9	160
			260				260

Sales 460

1997				1997			
June	30	8	12,220	June	2	7	400
					3	7	700
					25	7	6,000
					30	7	5,120
			12,220				12,220
1997				1997			
July	31	10	20,000	July	31	9	14,300
					31	9	5,700
			20,000				20,000

Sales Returns and Allowances 461

1997				1997			
June	4	7	100	June	30	8	100

Sales Discounts 462

1997				1997			
June	30	7	120	June	30	8	120

Purchases 463

1997					1997			
June	2		7	8,000	June	30	8	9,900
	3		7	900				
	11		7	1,000				
				9,900				9,900
1997					1997			
July	2		9	4,300	July	18	9	300
	14		9	5,000		31	10	11,000
	15	11,300	9	2,000				
				11,300				11,300

Transportation-in 464

1997				1997			
June	3	7	50	June	30	8	50
1997				1997			
July	2	9	200	July	31	10	200

Purchase Returns and Allowances 465

1997				1997			
June	30	8	100	June	4	7	100
1997				1997			
July	31	10	200	July	17	9	200

Purchase Discounts 466

1997				1997			
June	30	8	20	June	20	7	20
1997				1997			
July	31	10	86	July	10	9	86

Rent Expense 567

1997				1997			
April	30	2	400	April	30	4	400
1997				1997			
May	31	5	400	May	31	6	400
1997				1997			
June	30	7	400	June	30	8	400
1997				1997			
July	31	9	400	July	31	10	400

Telephone Expense 568

1997				1997				
April	30	2	35	April	30	4	35	
1997				1997				
May	31	5	40	May	31	6	40	
1997				1997				
June	30	7	50	June	30	8	50	
1997				1997				
July	31	9	54	July	31	10	54	

Utilities Expense 569

1997				1997			
April	30	2	70	April	30	4	70
1997				1997			
May	31	5	80	May	31	6	80
1997				1997			
June	30	7	90	June	30	8	90
1997				1997			
July	31	9	80	July	31	10	80

Automobile Maintenance Expense 570

1997				1997			
July	24	9	60	July	31	10	60

Insurance Expense 571

1997				1997			
May	31	5	30	May	31	6	30

1997				1997			
June	30	7	30	June	30	8	30
1997				1997			
July	31	9	30	July	31	10	30

Office Supplies Expense 572

1997				1997			
April	7	2	30	April	30	4	30
1997				1997			
May	15	5	70	May	31	6	70
1997				1997			
June	18	7	35	June	30	8	35
1997				1997			
July	10	9	40	July	31	10	62
	31	9	22				
			62				62

Shop Supplies Expense 573

1997				1997			
May	31	5	40	May	31	6	40
1997				1997			
June	30	7	50	June	30	8	50
1997				1997			
July	31	9	20	July	31	10	20

Advertising and Promotion Expense — 574

1997				1997			
April	1	2	100	April	30	4	250
	14	2	150				
			250				250
1997				1997			
May	22	5	150	May	31	6	210
	25	5	60				
			210				210
1997				1997			
June	21	7	250	June	30	8	250
1997				1997			
July	13	9	220	July	31	10	220

Interest and Service Charges Expense — 575

1997				1997			
May	31	5	100	May	31	6	100
1997				1997			
June	30	7	100	June	30	8	100
1997				1997			
July	31	9	4	July	31	10	104
	31	9	100				
			104				104

Bad Debts Expense — 578

1997				1997			
July	22	9	212	July	27	9	106
	23	9	106		31	10	412
	31	9	200				
			518				518

Salaries Expense 584

1997				1997			
April	30	2	600	April	30	4	600
1997				1997			
May	31	5	600	May	31	6	2,100
	31	5	1,500				
			2,100				2,100
1997				1997			
June	30	7	600	June	30	8	2,100
	30	7	1,500				
			2,100				2,100
1997				1997			
July	31	9	600	July	31	10	2,100
	31	9	1,500				
			2,100				2,100

Cash Shortage 589

1997				1997			
July	31	9	9	July	31	10	9

Depreciation Expense: Office Equipment 592

1997				1997			
April	30	3	25	April	30	4	25
1997				1997			
May	31	5	25	May	31	6	25
1997				1997			
June	30	7	25	June	30	8	25
1997				1997			
July	31	9	25	July	31	10	25

Depreciation Expense: Furniture and Fixtures 593

1997				1997			
April	30	3	20	April	30	4	20
1997				1997			
May	31	5	20	May	31	6	20
1997				1997			
June	30	7	20	June	30	8	20
1997				1997			
July	31	9	20	July	31	10	20

Depreciation Expense: Automobile 594

1997				1997			
April	30	3	150	April	30	4	150
1997				1997			
May	31	5	150	May	31	6	150
1997				1997			
June	30	7	150	June	30	8	150
1997				1997			
July	31	9	150	July	31	10	150

Income Summary 600

1997				1997			
April	30	4	1,580	April	30	4	6,400
	30	4	4,820				
			6,400				6,400
1997				1997			
May	31	6	3,265	May	31	6	7,400
	31	6	4,135				
			7,400				7,400

1997				1997			
June	30	8	13,470	June	30	8	15,590
	30	8	2,120				
			15,590				15,590

1997				1997			
July	31	10	17,946	July	31	10	24,546
	31	10	6,600				
			24,546				24,546

TRIAL BALANCE AFTER CLOSING THE BOOKS

A trial balance prepared after the books have been closed is illustrated in Exhibit 6-33. The only accounts which have balances remaining in them are balance sheet accounts. No income statement accounts appear in the trial balance at this stage because their balances have all been transferred to Income Summary and the net balance of all of these accounts is now zero. Likewise the Income Summary, income taxes, and drawings accounts have all been closed and now have zero balances.

Exhibit 6-33: Trial balance after closing the books.

Pacific Printers Mart
Trial Balance
July 31, 1997

Cash	$12,467	
Petty Cash	50	
Accounts Receivable	4,160	
Allowance for Bad Debts		$ 200
Inventory (July 31, 1997)	4,000	
Unexpired Insurance	270	
Shop Supplies	690	
Office Equipment	1,800	
Accumulated Depreciation: Office Equipment		100
Furniture and Fixtures	2,400	
Accumulated Depreciation: Furniture and Fixtures		80
Automobile	7,200	
Accumulated Depreciation: Automobile		600

Accounts Payable		1,200
Salaries Payable		1,500
Interest Payable		300
Unearned Commissions		900
Sales Tax Payable		1,218
Notes Payable		10,000
Jack Fraser, Capital		16,939
	$33,037	$33,037

FINANCIAL STATEMENTS

An income statement for the month of July, after income taxes have been taken into consideration is illustrated in Exhibit 6-34. A balance sheet at the end of July, after income taxes have been taken into consideration, is illustrated in Exhibit 6-35.

Exhibit 6-34: Income statement for the month of July after income taxes have been taken into consideration.

Pacific Printers Mart
Income Statement
For the month ending July 31, 1997

Revenue:				
Commissions				$ 260
Sales				20,000
Cost of Goods Sold:				
Inventory, July 1st			$ 3,000	
Purchases		11,000		
Add: Transportation-in		200		
Delivered Cost of Purchases		11,200		
Less: Purchase Ret. & Allowances	$200			
Purchase Discounts	86	286		
Net Purchases			10,914	
Cost of Goods Available for Sale			13,914	
Less: Inventory, July 31st			4,000	
Cost of Goods Sold:				9,914
Gross Profit:				$10,346

Expenses:		
Rent Expense	$ 400	
Telephone Expense	54	
Utilities Expense	80	
Automobile Maintenance Expense	60	
Insurance Expense	30	
Office Supplies Expense	62	
Shop Supplies Expense	20	
Advertising and Promotion Expense	220	
Interest and Service Charges Expense	104	
Bad Debts Expense	412	
Salaries Expense	2,100	
Cash Shortage	9	
Depreciation Expense: Office Equipment	25	
Depreciation Expense: Furniture and Fixtures	20	
Depreciation Expense: Automobile	150	3,746
Net Income:		$ 6,600
Less: Income Taxes		1,980
Net Income after Taxes:		$4,620

Exhibit 6-35: Balance sheet at the end of July after income taxes have been taken into consideration.

Pacific Printers Mart

Balance Sheet

July 31, 1997

Assets

Current Assets:			
Cash		$12,517	
Accounts Receivable	$4,160		
Less: Allowance for Bad Debts	200	3,960	
Inventory, July 31, 1997		4,000	
Unexpired Insurance		270	
Total current assets:			$20,747
Plant and Equipment:			
Shop Supplies		$ 690	

Office Equipment		$1,800		
Less: Accumulated Depreciation: Office Equipment		100	1,700	
Furniture and Fixtures		$2,400		
Less: Accumulated Depreciation: Furniture and Fixtures		80	2,320	
Automobile		$7,200		
Less: Accumulated Depreciation: Automobile		600	6,600	
Total plant and equipment:				11,310
				$32,057

Liabilities and Owner's Equity

Current Liabilities:				
Accounts Payable			$1,200	
Salaries Payable			1,500	
Interest Payable			300	
Unearned Commissions			900	
Sales Tax Payable			1,218	
Total current liabilities:				$ 5,118
Long-term Liabilities:				
Notes Payable:				10,000
Owner's Equity:				
Jack Fraser, Capital, July 1, 1997			$13,619	
Net Income		$6,600		
Less: Jack Fraser, Drawings	$1,300			
Income Taxes	1,980	3,280	3,320	
Jack Fraser, Capital, July 31, 1997				16,939
				$32,057

Exercises

1. Does a business keep the money collected from sales tax? Explain.

2. How may a business handle the task of recording numerous sales throughout the day, especially the sale of low-priced items? Is it necessary to make an entry in the journal for the sale of each individual item?

3. Is it acceptable practice to simply pocket any cash overages resulting at the end of the day? How should cash overages be dealt with? Explain.

4. Is it an indication of bad management if a business incurs a limited amount of bad debt losses resulting from credit sales? If not, why not? Explain.

5. Stores that only sell merchandise for cash can never incur any bad debt losses. Is that statement true, in your opinion?

6. When asked to name an establishment that has never suffered a bad debt loss, one student exclaimed, "McDonald's Restaurants"! In your opinion, is that belief correct? If not, explain how a bad debt loss could arise.

7. Name two main sources of bad debt losses. In what circumstances do such losses arise?

8. Mr. Stout is a frequent customer at a local hamburger chain restaurant. He is well-known to the manager and staff who always greet him enthusiastically whenever he arrives. On June 10th he pays for his dinner with a Canadian $20 bill, which is later discovered to be counterfeit and valueless. The manager clearly remembers receiving the worthless bank note from Mr. Stout as that was the only Canadian money received that day. A telephone call to Mr. Stout brings the reassuring news that he will settle the bill the next time he visits the restaurant, six days from today. In the meantime what accounting entries should be made to account for the loss? Because of the exchange rate the $20 Canadian money was initially recorded at its equivalent of $14 American funds.

9. What should a business do if it collects an account receivable that has already been written off as uncollectible?

10. Explain the difference between the direct write off method of dealing with bad debt losses and accounting to provide for expected bad debt losses. Under what circumstances is each method used? Explain.

11. Must a proprietor account for merchandise consumed by himself or herself? Explain.

12. What are the circumstances under which a petty cash book is necessary? Explain the operation of a petty cash book.

13. What is the purpose of reconciling the bank statement with the check register? Must the balance at the end of an accounting period in the check register agree with the balance in the Cash account? If a check register is maintained, is a Cash ledger account necessary, in your opinion?

Problems

1. Prepare journal entries from the record of daily sales given below.

Record of Daily Sales

Date	Credit Sales	Sales Tax	Cash Sales	Sales Tax	Cash Overage	Cash Shortage
May 1			$ 400	$ 24	$ 4	
2	$ 200	12	500	30		$ 11
3			600	36		8
6	400	24	300	18	2	
7			800	48	9	
8	300	18	500	30	1	
9			900	54		14
10	200	12	500	30		3
13	400	24	400	24		10
14	100	6	400	24	15	
15			800	48		2
16			700	42		1
17	500	30	400	24		9
20	200	12	600	36		
21			500	30		
22			900	54	8	
23	200	12	500	30	2	
24			700	42		7
27			600	36	3	

28			800	48	5	
29	500	30	400	24		2
30			800	48		2
31			700	42	10	—
	$3,000	180	$13,700	$822	$59	$69

2. Prepare entries to record the remittance of sales tax collected during the month of May from the data in problem 1. The sales tax is remitted on June 15th and the department of government responsible for administering the collection of sales tax allows retailers to retain 3% of the sales tax collected as commission.

3. Prepare journal entries for the following transactions:
   a. July 2 Sold $400 worth of merchandise to a customer. Payment, including 6% sales tax, was by check.
   b. July 5 Check returned by the bank, stamped N.S.F.
   c. July 6 Received word that the customer has fled the country.

4. Prepare journal entries for the following transactions:
   a. June 10 Sold merchandise priced at $500 to a customer. Payment, including 6% sales tax, was by check.
   b. June 13 Check returned by the bank, stamped N.S.F.
   c. June 13 Inquiry reveals that the customer is bankrupt and the goods have been consumed.
   d. June 17 Unexpectedly hear from the customer indicating that he will pay for the merchandise.
   e. June 30 Receive payment in cash from the customer.

5. The books of Ajax Wholesalers Inc. reveal that it has $600,000 in accounts receivable outstanding on December 31st. Past experience has proven that approximately 5% of these accounts will ultimately be uncollectible and will have to be written off. Prepare appropriate journal entries on December 31st to provide for these expected bad debt losses.

6. Western Wholesale Suppliers Inc. has $60,000 in accounts receivable outstanding at year end. Wholesale sales are not subject to sales tax.
   a. Prepare appropriate journal entries to record anticipated losses from bad debts based on an average loss of 6% annually.
   b. February 2 An account receivable for $500 is written off. Record this event.
   c. February 8 An account receivable for $200 is written off. Make appropriate entries in the journal.
   d. March 7 The account receivable written off on February 8th is

reinstated. Record this event.

e. March 30 The account receivable reinstated on March 7th is collected. Make an appropriate journal entry.

7. Prepare journal entries for the following transactions:
   - a. October 10 Sales for the first ten days in October amounted to $8,416. Sales tax at the rate of 6% was collected.
   - b. October 13 A check for $318 was returned by the bank, stamped N.S.F.
   - c. October 14 Received word that the customer had moved, address unknown.

8. Make journal entries, as required, for the events listed below:

December 31	Eastern Wholesale Inc. has $30,000 in accounts receivable outstanding. It is anticipated that 5% of these accounts will ultimately prove to be uncollectible. This is the firm's first year of business. Sales not subject to sales tax.
January 28	An account receivable for $500 is written off as uncollectible.
February 3	An account receivable for $400 is written off as uncollectible.
March 10	An account receivable for $600 is written off as uncollectible.
March 15	The account written off on February 3rd is reinstated.
March 17	An account receivable for $800 is written off as uncollectible.
March 31	Collected the account which was reinstated on March 15th.
Dec. 31	Accounts receivable outstanding at the end of the second year amount to $50,000. It is expected that 6% of these accounts will ultimately have to be written off as uncollectible.

9. Journalize the following transactions:

Dec. 2	Merchandise costing $5,000 is purchased from ACME Wholesale Inc., paying cash.
Dec. 11	Two hundred dollars worth of goods are withdrawn by the owner, Sue Ace, for her own use. Sales tax is 6%.
Dec. 11	The owner pays the sales tax with money out of her own pocket.
January 15	The sales tax is remitted to the government.

10. A petty cash fund in the amount of $200 is established on November 25th. Record this event.

11. Record the following items of expenditure out of the petty cash fund. Make an appropriate journal entry to replenish the fund.

Postage stamps.	$3.60	Receipt dated August 11th.
Taxi fare.	$11.00	Receipt dated August 8th.
Fertilizer.	$8.39	Receipt dated August 31st.
Bottle of ink.	$6.48	Receipt dated August 19th.

12. Make an appropriate entry in a check register corresponding to the journal entry to replenish the petty cash fund in problem number 11.

13. Reconcile the balance on the bank statement with the balance in the check register at the end of June. Be certain to enter any bank charges into the check register.

Check Register

Date	Check Number	Description	Checks	Deposits	Balance Forward
1997					
June 1	---	Balance Forward	---	---	5,018
5	407	Advance Wholesale Inc.	2,004	---	3,014
10	---	---	---	1,400	4,414
15	408	Pacific Telephone	35	200	4,579
18	---	---	---	900	5,479
19	409	The Star Weekly	459	142	5,162
24	410	Joan Baxter	900	---	4,262
27	---	---	---	1,528	5,790
30	411	Petty Cash	41	418	6,167
30	412	Western Realty	500	---	5,667

TACOMA MUTUAL BANK
Monthly Statement

Account number: 20-0477 **Balance Forward:** $5,018
Date of statement: June 30, 1997 **Previous statement:** May 31, 1997

Code	Description	Date	Debits	Credits	Balance
CK		06 01	2,004		3,014
CD		06 10		1,400	4,414
CD		06 15		200	4,614
CD		06 18		900	5,514
CK		06 19	459		5,055
CD		06 19		142	5,197
CK		06 24	900		4,297
CD		06 27		1,528	5,825
SC	*** Service Charges***	06 30	4		5,821

14. Prepare journal entries to record the following transactions:

December	5	A $100 petty cash fund is established.
December	31	The size of the fund is reduced to $60.

15. For the business described below, do the following:
    a. Record journal entries for all operating transactions and post to the ledger.
    b. Prepare a trial balance.
    c. Compute and record adjusting entries. Post to the ledger. Prepare an adjusted trial balance.
    d. Record ending inventory and close the books.
    e. Prepare a preliminary set of financial statements.
    f. Compute the amount of income taxes. Assume that the income tax rate is 20%. Record entries for income taxes in the journal and post to the ledger.
    g. Prepare an after closing trial balance.

November	1	Susan Schuss deposits $40,000 in a bank account under the business name, the Alpine Ski Shop.
	2	Signs a three year lease on the premises. Pays the rent for the month of November, which amounts to $600.
	3	Purchases furniture and fixtures costing $4,200. Issues check number 002 in payment. Seven-year property.
	4	Leases a neon sign at a cost of $120 per month. Pays for the first month's rental on the sign at this time.
	5	Acquires $8,000 worth of merchandise from Western Outdoor Supply Inc. Pays cash for the merchandise. Pays Speedy Delivery Services Inc. $485 for transporting the merchandise to the premises.
	5	Purchases office supplies costing $82 for use in November. Paid for by check at the time of purchase.
	8	Hires a sales clerk at a rate of $400 per week. It was agreed that payment for the three weeks of work in November would not be made until December 2nd.
	10	Sales for the first ten days of business amounted to $4,600. Six percent sales tax was collected on all sales. All sales were for cash.
	13	A customer returns a pair of skis and asks for a refund. The customer had purchased these skis two days earlier at a cost of $300.
	14	Sells $4,000 worth of skis and equipment to the Grouse Mountain Ski Club, on credit. Terms are net 30 days.
	17	Purchases merchandise costing $2,000 on credit from Great West Supply Company Inc. Payment must be made by the end of the month.
	18	Receives an allowance of $160 from Great West Supply Company Inc. for damaged goods.
	19	Gives a Grouse an allowance of $100 for damage

discovered to equipment purchased a few days earlier.

November 20	Sales amounting to $5,400 were made during the second ten days of November, in addition to the credit sales made earlier. A cash shortage of $12 is discovered.
22	Receives a check from the Grouse Mountain Ski Club.
22	A check for $318 was returned by the bank stamped N.S.F.
22	Purchases merchandise costing $4,000 from Rocky Mountain Suppliers Inc. on credit. Terms are 1/5, net 15.
23	Remits $120 to City Hall for a business license. Charge the entire cost to the month of November.
23	Removes skis and equipment costing $200 for her own personal use. Places $12 of her own money in the till in payment of sales tax.
24	The statement to the customer whose check was returned by the bank on November 22nd, was returned by the post office, with the notation *Return to Sender—Address Unknown.* The entire amount, $318 was written off as bad debt.
26	Susan Schuss withdraws $1,400 from the business for her own personal use.
27	Pays Rocky Mountain Suppliers Inc.
28	Pays Great West Supply Company Inc.
28	Pays radio station KIXI $540 for spot commercials.
30	The telephone bill for November, amounting to $36 is received. Payment is due by December 10th.
30	Received the bill for electricity consumed during November amounting to $102. Payment is due by December 15th.
30	Pays her accountant $1,400 for tax planning advice.
30	A count of inventory reveals $4,000 in unsold goods.
30	Donates $100 to the United Way Charity.
30	Cash sales for the last ten days in November amounted to $6,200. Sales tax was collected on all sales made during the month.

CHAPTER SEVEN

Corporations

INTRODUCTION

In our example, employing Pacific Printers Mart, this concern is a proprietorship and Jack Fraser is the proprietor of the business. In the contemplation of the law, Pacific Printers Mart and Jack Fraser are one and the same. Pacific Printers Mart has no existence separate from that of Jack Fraser and its assets and liabilities are really those of Jack Fraser. Should the business become bankrupt, creditors may look directly to Jack Fraser, the proprietor, for payment. By its very nature, a proprietorship is owned by only one person, the sole proprietor, who may hire employees. But a proprietorship may not take on any investors. The moment it does, it is no longer a proprietorship but becomes a partnership. Should the proprietor, Jack Fraser, die or become insane, the proprietorship comes to an end. Its existence is directly dependent upon the existence of its owner.

Proprietorship is the simplest form of business organization. If a person knew nothing whatsoever about the different possible forms of business organization, but simply followed his or her instincts, the kind of business organization that would result would likely be a proprietorship. Or, it might be a partnership. Partnership is similar to a proprietorship in most respects in that its existence is dependent on the existence of its owners, which are its partners. Upon the death or legal incapacity of any one partner the partnership comes to an end, the business is dissolved and its assets are distributed among the various partners. Like a proprietorship, the assets and liabilities of the partnership are those of the individual partners. Should the partnership become bankrupt, creditors may look to the individual partners to pay off the debts of the business. Thus, a partner whose investment in the business is minor, perhaps as little as one percent, but who has financial means, would be liable to pay off all the debts of the business, if the other partners are penniless.

Accounting for a partnership is identical to accounting for a proprietorship, such as Pacific Printers Mart. There is only one difference. In the owner's equity section of the balance sheet for a partnership there are separate capital, drawings, and income taxes accounts for each partner. These accounts must be kept separate in order to keep track of the investment of each partner, and because each partner may be taxed at a different rate of personal income tax. Earnings of proprietorship and partnership are taxed as personal income. Other than this brief description, proprietorship and partnership will not be considered further in this book. You will obtain a more complete knowledge of the different forms of business organization as you continue your studies in business administration, but this description will do for the time being. The most important form of business organization, with which to carry on risky business activity, is the *limited company,* or *corporation,* as it is also known.

CORPORATIONS

Unlike proprietorship or partnership whose very existence is dependent upon that of its owner or owners, a limited company or corporation is a separate legal entity and its existence is independent of that of its shareholders who are owners. Corporation is another term for limited company. These terms may be used interchangeably. A *legal entity* means *person* in the contemplation of the law. A corporation then, exists as a legal person in the eyes of the law. It may own assets, incur liabilities, buy goods, sell goods, earn a profit, suffer a loss, etc., and do all this in its own name, just like any other person. Should one, or even all, of its shareholders die, the life of the corporation remains unaffected. Its existence is separate and distinct from the lives of its shareholders. It enjoys perpetual succession, that is, it will live forever, provided that someone files its annual report. Thus, corporations founded several hundred years ago continue to do business to this very day.

Because the existence of the corporation is separate and distinct from that of its shareholders, who own the corporation, its assets are its own and its liabilities are its own. A shareholder may not help himself or herself to the assets of the corporation. Likewise, creditors may not look to shareholders for payment of the corporation's debts, just as a creditor may not look to a friend, neighbor, or relative for payment of an individual's debts. The creditor may only look to the person to whom he has granted credit for repayment of that debt; the creditor may not look to any other person unless that other person has offered to personally guarantee or indemnify that individual's debt. Thus, when a creditor extends credit to a corporation, without obtaining a personal guarantee from some individual for the debts of the corporation, it may only look to the corporation for repayment. It may sue the corporation but not the shareholders. This concept is known as *limited liability.* The most that shareholders can lose is the amount that they have paid for the shares of the corporation. Those are some of the main features of a corporation. This description of the corporation is sufficient for our purposes at this time.

INCORPORATION OF THE BUSINESS

On August 1st, Jack Fraser files some documents with the appropriate government department and incorporates the business. It is now known by the name, *Pacific Printers Mart Inc.* All corporations may easily be identified by one of the terms, that is, *Ltd., Inc.,* or *Corp.* as the last word in the name which serves to warn creditors of its status as a company with limited liability. The complete corporate name must be included on all corporate documents.

TRANSFER OF ASSETS AND LIABILITIES

The owner of Pacific Printers Mart, Jack Fraser, decides to transfer the assets of the business, that is, the assets of his proprietorship, to the corporation, Pacific Printers Mart Inc. In exchange he will receive shares in the corporation. Creditors are contacted and they give their permission to allow the corporation to assume the liabilities of the proprietorship.

CORPORATE CHARTER RECORDED AS AN ASSET

Jack Fraser takes $200 out of his own pocket and pays for the documentation and filing fee, which results in the incorporation of the business which is now Pacific Printers Mart Inc. The journal entry to record this transaction is illustrated in Exhibit 7-1.

Journal **Page 11**

1997					
August	1	Company Charter	129	200	
		Common Share Capital	347		200
		To record issue of shares for past services.			

Exhibit 7-1: Journal entry at the time of incorporation.

Note that the corporation itself cannot pay for the fee of incorporation. This is because it is not in existence until it is incorporated and therefore cannot engage in transactions until it is incorporated. By the same principle the corporation cannot have any cash or other assets, for that matter, until it comes into existence. Therefore, the party incorporating the company must pay the costs of incorporation out of his or her own pocket. But for these past services performed, the newly formed corporation may issue shares to pay for these past services which brought it into being. The director of the corporation, Jack Fraser, sets the price of the corporation's common shares at one dollar apiece, and authorizes the corporation to issue him 200 common shares in payment for incorporating the company.

COMMON SHARES ISSUED FOR CASH

Jack Fraser decides to invest $61 of his own money in common shares of Pacific Printers Mart Inc. The journal entry to record this transaction is illustrated in Exhibit 7-2.

Journal — **Page 11**

1997					
August	1	Cash	101	61	
		Common Share Capital	347		61
		To record issue of common shares in exchange for cash.			

Exhibit 7-2: Common shares issued in exchange for cash.

PREFERRED SHARES ISSUED

Pacific Printers Mart Inc. has the ability to issue another class of shares, in addition to common shares, called preferred shares. These preferred shares carry no voting privileges, but are preferred with respect to the fact that the holders of preferred shares must receive a dividend of 20 cents per share each year, including arrears for those years in which dividends have not been declared, before common shareholders may receive any dividends. The par value of these preferred shares is one dollar per share, but because the dividend yield is twenty cents per annum, corporate director, Jack Fraser, sets the price per preferred share at two dollars each. Preferred shares may be sold at any price which is equal to par value or more, but not for a price that is less than par value. The reason is to prevent dilution of preferred share capital, so present shareholders can rest assured that their share capital will remain intact. This measure of protection is necessary because preferred shareholders virtually always have no voting privileges.

On August 1st, Jack Fraser, the director and president of Pacific Printers Mart Inc., decides to raise additional capital by the sale of preferred shares. Mrs. Fraser agrees to buy 1,000 preferred shares from Pacific Printers Mart Inc. The journal entry to illustrate this transaction is shown in Exhibit 7-3.

Journal — **Page 11**

1997					
August	1	Cash	101	2,000	
		Preferred Share Capital	345		1,000
		Premium on Preferred Shares	346		1,000
		To record issue of preferred shares with a par value of one dollar for cash.			

Exhibit 7-3: One thousand preferred shares with a par value of one dollar each, issued for cash.

ROLL OVER OF ASSETS TO CORPORATION

All of the assets and liabilities of the proprietorship are transferred to the corporation, at their present book value. Jack Fraser, president and director of Pacific Printers Mart Inc., buys the equity of the proprietorship for the corporation and issues common shares in exchange. The journal entry for this transaction is illustrated in Exhibit 7-4.

Journal **Page 11**

1997					
August	1	Jack Fraser, Capital	343	16,939	
		Common Share Capital	347		16,939
		Issued 16,939 common shares for assets of proprietorship.			

Exhibit 7-4: Journal entry to record roll over of assets to the corporation.

In exchange for his equity in the proprietorship, Jack Fraser receives 16,939 common shares in the capital of Pacific Printers Mart Inc. and the corporation now owns all of the assets that belonged to the proprietorship and has assumed all of its liabilities. The two proprietorship accounts *Jack Fraser, Capital* and *Jack Fraser, Drawings* have been closed permanently and will not be used again after this point in time.

LEDGER ACCOUNTS AT TIME OF INCORPORATION

The entire ledger is not reproduced at this time, but only those accounts affected at the time of incorporation. These accounts are illustrated in Exhibit 7-5.

Cash 101

1997					
August	1	Balance	✓	12,467	
	1		11	61	
	1	14,528	11	2,000	

Company Charter 129

1997					
August	1		11	200	

Jack Fraser, Capital — 343

1997					1997				
April	30		4	1,500	March	1		1	10,000
	30		4	1,205	April	30		4	4,820
	30	Balance	✓	12,115					
				14,820					14,820
1997					1997				
May	31		6	2,000	May	1	Balance	✓	12,115
	31		6	827		31		6	4,135
	31	Balance	✓	13,423					
				16,250					16,250
1997					1997				
June	30		8	1,500	June	5	Balance	✓	13,423
	30	1,924	8	424		30	15,543	8	2,120
	30	Balance	✓	13,619					
				15,543					15,543
1997					1997				
July	31		10	1,300	July	1	Balance	✓	13,619
	31	3,280	10	1,980		31	20,219	10	6,600
	31	Balance	✓	16,939					
				20,219					20,219
1997					1997				
August	1		11	16,939	August	1	Balance	✓	16,939

Preferred Share Capital — 345

					1997				
					August	1		11	1,000

Premium on Preferred Shares — 346

					1997				
					August	1		11	1,000

Common Share Capital					347
	1997				
	August	1		11	200
		1		11	61
		1	17,200	11	16,939

Exhibit 7-5: Ledger accounts after posting entries at the time of incorporation.

OPENING BALANCE SHEET

An opening balance sheet for Pacific Printers Mart Inc. may easily be prepared by referring to the ledger in Exhibit 6-32 and the updated accounts in Exhibit 7-5. By doing so the balance sheet in Exhibit 7-6 may be prepared as a result. This is the balance sheet at the opening of business by the corporation, after the initial transfers of share capital have been accomplished.

Exhibit 7-6: Opening balance sheet for the corporation.

Pacific Printers Mart Inc.
Balance Sheet
August 1, 1997

Assets

Current Assets:			
Cash		$14,578	
Accounts Receivable	$4,160		
Less: Allowance for Bad Debts	200	3,960	
Inventory, July 31, 1997		4,000	
Unexpired Insurance		270	
Total current assets:			$22,808
Plant and Equipment:			
Shop Supplies		$ 690	
Office Equipment	$1,800		
Less: Accumulated Depreciation: Office Equipment	100	1,700	
Furniture and Fixtures	$2,400		
Less: Accumulated Depreciation: Furniture and Fixtures	80	2,320	
Automobile	$7,200		
Less: Accumulated Depreciation: Automobile	600	6,600	
Total plant and equipment:			11,310

Other Assets:		
Company Charter		200
		$34,318

Liabilities and Shareholders' Equity

Current Liabilities:		
Accounts Payable	$1,200	
Salaries Payable	1,500	
Interest Payable	300	
Unearned Commissions	900	
Sales Tax Payable	1,218	
Total current liabilities:		$ 5,118
Long-term Liabilities:		
Notes Payable:		10,000
Shareholders' Equity:		
Preferred share capital, 10% cumulative, $1 par value, authorized 1,000,000 shares, issued and outstanding 1,000 shares		1,000
Premium on Preferred Shares		1,000
Common Share Capital, without par value, authorized 1,000,000 shares, issued and outstanding 17,200 shares		17,200
		$34,318

PURCHASE OF GOODWILL

Atlantic Trade Services Inc., a firm involved in a similar line of business to that which Pacific Printers Mart Inc. is engaged in, decides to close down its local operations if it is able to find someone to buy its already established accounts. The buyer of the accounts would receive a customer list from Atlantic Trade Services Inc. and in addition Atlantic Trade Services Inc. would agree not to re-enter the local market to do business. Pacific Printers Mart Inc. agrees to buy the established customer base from Atlantic Trade Services Inc. The journal entry to record the purchase of this goodwill by Pacific Printers Mart Inc. is illustrated in Exhibit 7-7.

Journal **Page 11**

1997					
August	5	Goodwill	127	2,000	
		Cash	101		2,000
		To record purchase of goodwill from Atlantic Trade Services Inc.			

Exhibit 7-7: Journal entry to record purchase of goodwill.

The president of Pacific Printers Mart Inc., Jack Fraser, decides not to depreciate the goodwill purchased by his company. He feels that it is very likely that business from the purchased accounts will increase over time and that the goodwill is worth more than what it cost.

Note that in our discussion, the term*accounts*in this context simply means identity of customers.

PURCHASE OF GOVERNMENT BONDS

Because the cash position of Pacific Printers Mart Inc. is very strong it is decided to acquire some interest bearing government bonds. Further business expansion is out of the question at the moment which means that the firm cannot otherwise re-invest in its internal operations. The journal entry to record the purchase of government bonds is illustrated in Exhibit 7-8.

		Journal			**Page 11**
1997					
August	9	Government Bonds	108	3,000	
		Cash	101		3,000
		To record purchase of government bonds with a coupon rate of 10%.			

Exhibit 7-8: Journal entry to record purchase of government bonds.

SHAREHOLDER'S LOAN

The expression *shareholder's loan* is often used to describe two completely different situations and it is impossible to know what is meant by the term*shareholder's loan* unless we have additional information about the transaction.

Because a corporation is a separate legal entity, shareholders may lend money to the corporation or borrow money from the corporation. When a corporation borrows money from a shareholder this transaction results in a Note Payable. On the other hand, when a corporation lends money to a shareholder this transaction results in a Note Receivable. Thus the term shareholder's loan, by itself, without specifying whether the shareholder borrowed money from the corporation, or lent money to the corporation, is ambiguous. The expression*shareholder's loan* should not be used on the balance sheet. The proper terms are Notes Receivable and Notes Payable based on the name of the account in each instance to which the transaction has been entered. If desired, transactions with shareholders may be noted as a footnote on the balance sheet or described on a separate sheet attached to the set of financial statements.

SHAREHOLDER BORROWS MONEY FROM THE CORPORATION

On August 12th, Mrs. Fraser, a shareholder in Pacific Printers Mart Inc., borrows $1,000 from the corporation. No interest is charged on the loan, but she is asked to sign a *promissory note*, promising to pay back the money on demand. The promissory note is shown in the illustration in Exhibit 7-9 and the journal entry to record this transaction is illustrated in Exhibit 7-10.

PROMISSORY NOTE

12 August 1997

I, Mrs. J. Fraser, promise to pay to Pacific Printers Mart Inc.
the sum of ONE THOUSAND DOLLARS,
on demand, and without interest.

Joan Fraser
....

Exhibit 7-9: Note signed when borrowing money from the corporation.

	Journal			**Page 11**
1997				
August 12	Notes Receivable	109	1,000	
	Cash	101		1,000
	To record loan to Joan Fraser.			

Exhibit 7-10: Journal entry to record loan made by the corporation to a shareholder.

SHAREHOLDER LENDS MONEY TO THE CORPORATION

The corporation may, of course, borrow money from its shareholders. When it does so, the shareholder will require the president and director to sign the promissory note on behalf of the corporation. On August 16, 1997, Jack Fraser, a shareholder in the corporation, lends $2,000 to Pacific Printers Mart Inc. A promissory note is signed by the president of the corporation as shown in Exhibit 7-11. The journal entry to record the loan is shown in Exhibit 7-12.

PROMISSORY NOTE

16 August 1997
Pacific Printers Mart Inc. *promises to pay to Jack Fraser*
the sum of TWO THOUSAND DOLLARS,
on demand, and without interest.

Jack Fraser
President

Exhibit 7-11: **Note signed by officer of the corporation when borrowing money from a shareholder.**

		Journal			**Page 11**
1997					
August	16	Cash	101	2,000	
		Notes Payable	240		2,000
		To record loan received from Jack Fraser.			

Exhibit 7-12: **Journal entry to record loan made by a shareholder to the corporation.**

OUT-OF-POCKET EXPENDITURES

Care must be taken to account for every penny that belongs to the corporation. In accordance with this same principle, shareholders and employees are entitled to and must be reimbursed for every cent spent out-of-pocket on behalf of the corporation. Unless this is done, the books will not balance.

On August 17th, Jack Fraser attends an auction and buys some stock for resale. Because the auction house only accepts cash in payment, Jack Fraser pays for these purchases out-of-pocket. The entry in Exhibit 7-13 is made in the journal.

Journal				Page 11
1997				
August 17	Purchases	463	200	
	Accounts Payable	230		200
	To record purchase of merchandise; paid out-of-pocket by Jack Fraser.			

Exhibit 7-13: To record out-of-pocket expenditure.

Pacific Printers Mart Inc. makes out a check to Jack Fraser and thereby reimburses him for his out-of-pocket expenditure. The journal entry to record this transaction is illustrated in Exhibit 7-14.

Journal				Page 11
1997				
August 18	Accounts Payable	230	200	
	Cash	101		200
	Reimbursed Jack Fraser for his out-of-pocket expenditure.			

Exhibit 7-14: Journal entry to record reimbursement of out-of-pocket expenditure.

PAYROLL DEDUCTIONS

There is no drawings account in a corporation. The shareholders in a corporation are its owners. But these owners own the shares of the corporation and do not own its assets directly and accordingly cannot help themselves to the asset cash, by means of drawings, so a corporation cannot have a drawings account. Shareholders who are also employees of the corporation may be paid a salary. This is possible because a corporation is an entity separate and distinct from its shareholders.

Up to this point we have simply ignored the question of payroll deductions. However, legislation requires that when an employee is paid a salary, a fraction of that salary must be withheld by the employer and remitted to the government. These are income tax deductions, withheld from the salaries of employees. In addition, both employees and employers contribute to pension and unemployment insurance plans. Deductions from salaries are required in each case. And the employer must contribute to a workers' compensation plan, in most industries, which is a form of insurance for injury on the job. A record must be kept of all salaries paid and the amount of deductions made, together with the employer's contribution, for the employees of a firm. Salaries and deductions are first recorded in a payroll book and then appropriate entries are made in the journal.

Payroll Record

Date: August 31, 1997

Name of Employee:	June Jones	Ralph Black	Jack Fraser	Total
Gross Earnings:	$600	$1,500	$2,000	$4,100
Less: Income Taxes	110	600	730	1,440
Pension Plan	10	20	24	54
Unemployment Insurance	12	18	--	30
Net Earnings:	468	862	1,246	2,576
Employer's Contributions:				
Pension Plan	12	22	28	62
Unemployment Insurance	14	20	--	34
Workers' Compensation	3	6	8	17

Exhibit 7-15: Record of payroll for the month of August, 1997.

To determine the appropriate journal entries we must examine the payroll record. This record simply lists the amount of salary paid to each employee, the amount of deductions from salary, and the contributions made by the employer on each employee's behalf. The payroll record for Pacific Printers Mart Inc., for the month of August is illustrated in Exhibit 7-15. Either a vertical or horizontal format may be used. The appropriate journal entries are illustrated in Exhibit 7-16. Employee, Ralph Black, who used to be paid at the end of the first week in the month following the month in which he earned his wages is now being paid immediately at the end of each month in which his wages are earned. So we no longer have to make an adjusting entry, as we did in previous months, to record his salary, but we now make an operating entry at the end of each month.

Journal					Page 11
1997					
August	31	Salaries Expense	584	4,100	
		Cash	101		2,576
		Accounts Payable	230		1,524
		To record salaries expense for August and payroll deductions withheld at source.			
	31	Pension Plan Expense	585	62	
		Unemployment Insurance Plan Expense	586	34	
		Workers' Compensation Plan Expense	587	17	
		Accounts Payable	230		113
		To record employer's contributions to payroll benefit plans.			

Exhibit 7-16: Entries to record salaries expense and related payroll deductions and contributions.

The payroll deductions and employer's contributions are remitted early in the next accounting period. At that time the journal entry which is illustrated in Exhibit 7-17 must be made.

Journal					Page 13
1997					
September	10	Accounts Payable	230	1,637	
		Cash	101		1,637
		Remitted payroll deductions and employer's contributions.			

Exhibit 7-17: Journal entry to record remittance of payroll deductions and employer's contributions.

We account for other deductions from payroll in a similar manner. These other deductions might include union dues, professional organization fees, etc. For accounting purposes it is essential to distinguish between deductions from gross salary and contributions made by the employer on behalf of an employee. Otherwise the procedure is basically straightforward.

RETAINED EARNINGS ACCOUNT

When the books are closed at the end of an accounting period in a corporation, the income statement accounts are closed in the Income Summary account in the usual manner and the Income Summary account is closed into an account called *Retained Earnings*. The Income Taxes account is also closed into Retained Earnings. In general it may be stated that all increases or decreases to shareholders' equity, resulting from the operations of the business, are transferred to the equity account, Retained Earnings.

OPERATING ENTRIES FOR THE MONTH OF AUGUST

All of the operating entries for the month of August are illustrated in Exhibit 7-18. This exhibit is followed by adjusting entries for the month of August, illustrated in Exhibit 7-19. A trial balance is illustrated in Exhibit 7-20; an income statement for the month of August is illustrated in Exhibit 7-21; and, a balance sheet as of August 31, 1997 is illustrated in Exhibit 7-22. The financial statements are preliminary in that they have been prepared before income taxes have been taken into consideration.

Exhibit 7-18: Operating entries for the month of August.

Journal **Page 11**

1997					
August	1	Company Charter	129	200	
		Common Share Capital	347		200
		To record issue of shares for past services.			
	1	Cash	101	61	
		Common Share Capital	347		61
		To record issue of common shares in exchange for cash.			
	1	Cash	101	2,000	
		Preferred Share Capital	345		1,000
		Premium on Preferred Shares	346		1,000
		To record issue of preferred shares with a par value of one dollar for cash.			
	1	Jack Fraser, Capital	343	16,939	
		Common Share Capital	347		16,939
		Issued 16,939 common shares for the assets of the proprietorship.			

August	1	Purchases	463	5,000	
		Accounts Payable	230		5,000
		To record purchase from Alpha Wholesale Inc. Terms 2/10, net 30.			
	1	Transportation-in	464	300	
		Cash	101		300
		Paid Fastic Freight Corporation for delivery of merchandise.			
	5	Salaries Payable	231	1,500	
		Cash	101		1,500
		Paid employee his salary for work in July.			
	5	Cash	101	4,000	
		Accounts Receivable	103		4,000
		Collected on remainder of credit sales made in July.			
	5	Goodwill	127	2,000	
		Cash	101		2,000
		To record purchase of goodwill from Atlantic Trade Services Inc.			
	8	Office Supplies Expense	572	131	
		Cash	101		131
		Purchased office supplies.			
	9	Government Bonds	108	3,000	
		Cash	101		3,000
		To record purchase of government bonds with a coupon rate of 10%.			
	9	Accounts Payable	230	5,000	
		Cash	101		4,900
		Purchase Discounts	466		100
		Paid Alpha Wholesale Inc. for merchandise purchased on August 1st.			
	12	Notes Receivable	109	1,000	
		Cash	101		1,000
		To record loan to Joan Fraser.			
	12	Advertising and Promotion Expense	574	300	
		Cash	101		300
		Placed ads in the newspaper.			

August	13	Purchases	463	4,000	
		Accounts Payable	230		4,000
		Purchased merchandise from ACME Wholesale Inc. No terms. Payment due August 31st.			
	14	Cash	101	160	
		Accounts Receivable	103		160
		Check for commissions earned on photocopying in July received from Rapid Photocopiers Inc.			
	15	Accounts Payable	230	300	
		Purchase Returns and Allowances	465		300
		To record allowance from ACME Wholesale Inc. for damaged merchandise.			
	15	Sales Tax Payable	235	1,200	
		Cash	101		1,164
		Commissions	455		36
		Remitted sales tax collectible for the month of July.			
	15	Sales Tax Payable	235	18	
		Cash	101		18
		Remitted sales tax on goods removed for personal consumption in July.			
	15	Accounts Receivable	103	5,300	
		Sales	460		5,300
		Sales Tax Payable	235		300
		To record taxable sales made on credit. Terms: 2/10, net 30.			
	15	Cash	101	5,300	
		Sales	460		5,000
		Sales Tax Payable	235		300
		To record taxable cash sales during the first half of August.			
	16	Sales Returns and Allowances	461	300	
		Sales Tax Payable	235	18	
		Cash	101		318
		Gave customer a refund.			

August	16	Cash	101	2,000	
		Notes Payable	240		2,000
		To record loan received from Jack Fraser.			
	17	Purchases	463	200	
		Accounts Payable	230		200
		To record purchase of merchandise; paid out-of-pocket by Jack Fraser.			
	18	Accounts Payable	230	200	
		Cash	101		200
		Reimbursed Jack Fraser for his out-of-pocket expenditure.			
	19	Accounts Receivable	103	318	
		Cash	101		318
		N.S.F. check returned by the bank.			
	20	Bad Debts Expense	578	318	
		Accounts Receivable	103		318
		To write off an uncollectible account.			
	21	Automobile Maintenance Expense	570	50	
		Cash	101		50
		Purchased gasoline for the truck.			
	25	Cash	101	5,194	
		Sales Discounts	462	106	
		Accounts Receivable	103		5,300
		Collected on sales made on Aug. 15th.			
	25	Allowance for Bad Debts	104	180	
		Accounts Receivable	103		180
		To write off an account receivable as uncollectible.			
	31	Accounts Payable	230	3,700	
		Cash	101		3,700
		Paid ACME Wholesale Inc. for merchandise purchased on August 13th.			
	31	Cash	101	5,310	
		Sales	460		5,000
		Sales Tax Payable	235		300
		Cash Overage	457		10
		To record taxable cash sales.			

August	31	Accounts Receivable	103	6,360	
		Sales	460		6,000
		Sales Tax Payable	235		360
		To record taxable sales made on credit.			
	31	Office Supplies Expense	572	15	
		Cash	101		15
		To record office supplies expense paid for from the petty cash fund; petty cash fund replenished.			
	31	Rent Expense	567	400	
		Cash	101		400
		Paid rent for the month of August; check issued in payment.			
	31	Telephone Expense	568	52	
		Cash	101		52
		Paid telephone bill.			
	31	Utilities Expense	569	70	
		Cash	101		70
		Paid bill for electricity and gas consumed during August.			
	31	Interest and Service Charges Expense	575	6	
		Cash	101		6
		To record bank service charges for the month of August.			
	31	Accounts Payable	230	800	
		Cash	101		800
		Paid for purchases made in June from XYZ Wholesale Inc.			
	31	Cash	101	1,360	
		Accounts Receivable	103		1,360
		Collected some of the receivables for sales made in August.			
	31	Salaries Expense	584	4,100	
		Cash	101		2,576
		Accounts Payable	230		1,524
		To record salaries expense for August and payroll deductions withheld at source.			

August 31	Pension Plan Expense	585	62	
	Unemployment Insurance Plan Expense	586	34	
	Workers' Compensation Plan Expense	587	17	
	Accounts Payable	230		113
	To record employer's contributions to payroll benefit plans.			

Exhibit 7-19: Adjusting entries for the month of August.

Journal — **Page 11**

1997				
August 31	Unearned Commissions	233	100	
	Commissions	455		100
	To record commissions earned in August from arrangement with Compatible Darkroom Company.			
31	Accounts Receivable	103	120	
	Commissions	455		120
	Commissions earned on photocopying in August; to be collected in September.			
31	Insurance Expense	571	30	
	Unexpired Insurance	106		30
	To record insurance expense for August.			
31	Shop Supplies Expense	573	50	
	Shop Supplies	111		50
	To record shop supplies used up during August.			
31	Interest and Service Charges Expense	575	100	
	Interest Payable	232		100
	To record interest charges accrued during the month of August.			
31	Bad Debts Expense	578	230	
	Allowance for Bad Debts	104		230
	To record bad debts expense estimated at 5% of outstanding accounts receivable resulting from sales made in August.			

August	31	Depreciation Expense: Office Equipment	592	25	
		Accum. Deprn.: Office Equipment	113		25
		To record depreciation for August.			
	31	Deprn. Expense: Furniture and Fixtures	593	20	
		Accum. Deprn.: Furniture and Fixtures	115		20
		To record depreciation for August.			
	31	Depreciation Expense: Automobile	594	150	
		Accumulated Depreciation: Automobile	117		150
		To record depreciation for August.			

Exhibit 7-20: Trial balance after adjusting entries have been posted at the end of August.

Pacific Printers Mart Inc.
Trial Balance
August 31, 1997

Cash	$15,034	
Petty Cash	50	
Accounts Receivable	4,940	
Allowance for Bad Debts		$ 250
Inventory (July 31, 1997)	4,000	
Unexpired Insurance	240	
Government Bonds	3,000	
Notes Receivable	1,000	
Shop Supplies	640	
Office Equipment	1,800	
Accumulated Depreciation: Office Equipment		125
Furniture and Fixtures	2,400	
Accumulated Depreciation: Furniture and Fixtures		100
Automobile	7,200	
Accumulated Depreciation: Automobile		750
Goodwill	2,000	
Company Charter	200	
Accounts Payable		2,037
Interest Payable		400
Unearned Commissions		800
Sales Tax Payable		1,242
Notes Payable		12,000

Preferred Share Capital		1,000
Premium on Preferred Shares		1,000
Common Share Capital		17,200
Commissions		256
Cash Overage		10
Sales		21,000
Sales Returns and Allowances	300	
Sales Discounts	106	
Purchases	9,200	
Transportation-in	300	
Purchase Returns and Allowances		300
Purchase Discounts		100
Rent Expense	400	
Telephone Expense	52	
Utilities Expense	70	
Automobile Maintenance Expense	50	
Insurance Expense	30	
Office Supplies Expense	146	
Shop Supplies Expense	50	
Advertising and Promotion Expense	300	
Interest and Service Charges Expense	106	
Bad Debts Expense	548	
Salaries Expense	4,100	
Pension Plan Expense	62	
Unemployment Insurance Plan Expense	34	
Workers' Compensation Plan Expense	17	
Depreciation Expense: Office Equipment	25	
Depreciation Expense: Furniture and Fixtures	20	
Depreciation Expense: Automobile	150	
	$58,570	$58,570

Exhibit 7-21: Income statement before income taxes for the month of August have been computed.

Pacific Printers Mart Inc.
Income Statement
For the month ending August 31, 1997

Revenue:

Commissions	$ 256
Cash Overage	10

Sales			$21,000	
Less: Sales Returns and Allowances		$300		
Sales Discounts		106	406	
Net Sales:				20,594
Cost of Goods Sold:				
Inventory, August 1st			4,000	
Purchases		9,200		
Add: Transportation-in		300		
Delivered Cost of Purchases		9,500		
Less: Purchase Ret. & Allowances	$300			
Purchase Discounts	100	400		
Net Purchases			9,100	
Cost of Goods Available for Sale			13,100	
Less: Inventory, August 31st			5,000	
Cost of Goods Sold:				8,100
Gross Profit:				$12,760
Expenses:				
Rent Expense			$ 400	
Telephone Expense			52	
Utilities Expense			70	
Automobile Maintenance Expense			50	
Insurance Expense			30	
Office Supplies Expense			146	
Shop Supplies Expense			50	
Advertising and Promotion Expense			300	
Interest and Service Charges Expense			106	
Bad Debts Expense			548	
Salaries Expense			4,100	
Pension Plan Expense			62	
Unemployment Insurance Plan Expense			34	
Workers' Compensation Plan Expense			17	
Depreciation Expense: Office Equipment			25	
Depreciation Expense: Furniture and Fixtures			20	
Depreciation Expense: Automobile			150	6,160
Net Income:				$ 6,600

Exhibit 7-22: Balance sheet before computation of income taxes.

Pacific Printers Mart Inc.
Balance Sheet
August 31, 1997

Assets

Current Assets:			
Cash		$15,084	
Accounts Receivable	$4,940		
Less: Allowance for Bad Debts	250	4,690	
Inventory, August 31, 1997		5,000	
Unexpired Insurance		240	
Government Bonds		3,000	
Notes Receivable		1,000	
Total current assets:			$29,014
Plant and Equipment:			
Shop Supplies		$ 640	
Office Equipment	$1,800		
Less: Accumulated Depreciation: Office Equipment	125	1,675	
Furniture and Fixtures	$2,400		
Less: Accumulated Depreciation: Furniture and Fixtures	100	2,300	
Automobile	$7,200		
Less: Accumulated Depreciation: Automobile	750	6,450	
Total plant and equipment:			11,065
Other Assets:			
Goodwill		2,000	
Company Charter		200	
Total other assets:			2,200
			$42,279

Liabilities and Shareholders' Equity

Current Liabilities:		
Accounts Payable	$2,037	
Interest Payable	400	
Unearned Commissions	800	
Sales Tax Payable	1,242	
Total current liabilities:		$ 4,479
Long-term Liabilities:		
Notes Payable:		12,000

Shareholders' Equity:	
Preferred share capital, 10% cumulative, $1 par value, authorized 1,000,000 shares, issued and outstanding 1,000 shares	1,000
Premium on Preferred Shares	1,000
Common Share Capital, without par value, authorized 1,000,000 shares, issued and outstanding 17,200 shares	17,200
Retained Earnings	6,600
	$42,279

INCOME TAXES FOR AUGUST

From the preliminary income statement in Exhibit 7-21, net income for Pacific Printers Mart Inc., for the month of August is $6,600. For income that was earned in July, recall that the income tax rate was 30%. Now that the business is incorporated, the corporate rate of income tax applies, which is simply a flat rate of 23%, which is the rate applied to the earnings of small businesses, which are incorporated. Thus, incorporation provides a significant income tax advantage, particularly at higher income levels. The amount of income taxes for Pacific Printers Mart Inc., may be computed as follows:

Income taxes = $6,000 x 23% = $1,518

These income taxes need not be remitted to the income tax department until the following month, that is, the month of September. Hence, our journal entry to record income taxes appears as shown in Exhibit 7-23.

Journal **Page 11**

1997				
August 31	Income Taxes	349	1,518	
	Income Taxes Payable	236		1,518
	To record income taxes for August.			

Exhibit 7-23: Entry to record income taxes for the month of August.

The debit and credit items of the journal entry in Exhibit 7-23 are posted to the appropriate ledger accounts, and the books may now be closed. Before this is done, however, the directors of Pacific Printers Mart Inc. decide to declare dividends.

DECLARATION OF DIVIDENDS

Operations have been profitable and the directors of Pacific Printers Mart Inc. decide to declare dividends. A dividend of 10 cents per share is declared on the preferred shares and a dividend of 5 cents per share is declared on common shares. Dividends are a distribution of after-tax income to the shareholders in a corporation. The journal entries for the declaration of dividends are illustrated in Exhibit 7-24.

Journal — **Page 11**

Date		Account	Ref.	Debit	Credit
1997					
August	31	Dividends on Preferred Shares	350	100	
		Dividends Payable on Preferred Shares	237		100
		To record declaration of a dividend of 10 cents per share on preferred shares outstanding.			
	31	Dividends on Common Shares	351	860	
		Dividends Payable on Common Shares	238		860
		To record declaration of a dividend of 5 cents per share on common shares outstanding.			

Exhibit 7-24: Journal entries to record declaration of dividends.

DIVIDENDS PAID TO SHAREHOLDERS

Once dividends have been declared by the directors of a corporation, they become a debt of that corporation and shareholders may sue the corporation if these dividends are not paid. Such action is not necessary, in this case, as Pacific Printers Mart Inc. pays the dividends that were declared on August 31st. This transaction is illustrated by the journal entry in Exhibit 7-25.

Journal — **Page 11**

Date		Account	Ref.	Debit	Credit
1997					
September	8	Dividends Payable on Preferred Shares	237	100	
		Dividends Payable on Common Shares	238	860	
		Cash	101		960
		Paid the dividends declared on August 31st.			

Exhibit 7-25: Journal entry to record payment of dividends.

CLOSING THE DIVIDEND ACCOUNTS

The dividend accounts are closed directly into the Retained Earnings account as they are a distribution of after-tax income to shareholders. The dividend accounts are closed by the journal entry illustrated in Exhibit 7-26.

Journal **Page 12**

1997				
August 31	Retained Earnings	348	960	
	Dividends on Preferred Shares	350		100
	Dividends on Common Shares	351		860
	To close the dividend accounts.			

Exhibit 7-26: Journal entry to close dividend accounts.

The dividend accounts are actually closed at the time the books are closed (see Exhibit 7-27) but are illustrated separately in Exhibit 7-26 so that you may become familiar with the procedure.

CLOSING THE BOOKS

After all operating, adjusting, income tax, and dividend entries have been recorded and posted, the books may be closed. Beginning inventory is taken off the books and ending inventory is placed on the books. All of the income statement accounts are closed into the Income Summary account. The balance in the Income Summary account is closed into the Retained Earnings account. There is no drawings account in a corporation. The Income Taxes account and the dividend accounts are closed into Retained Earnings, and this completes the closing procedure. The entries to close the books at the end of August are illustrated in Exhibit 7-27.

The complete ledger after the closing entries have been posted is illustrated in Exhibit 7-28 and the trial balance after the books are closed is illustrated in Exhibit 7-29.

Exhibit 7-27: Journal entries to close the books.

Journal **Page 12**

1997					
August	31	Income Summary	600	20,066	
		Inventory	105		4,000
		Sales Returns and Allowances	461		300
		Sales Discounts	462		106
		Purchases	463		9,200
		Transportation-in	464		300
		Rent Expense	567		400
		Telephone Expense	568		52
		Utilities Expense	569		70
		Automobile Maintenance Expense	570		50
		Insurance Expense	571		30
		Office Supplies Expense	572		146
		Shop Supplies Expense	573		50
		Advertising and Promotion Expense	574		300
		Interest and Service Charges Expense	575		106
		Bad Debts Expense	578		548
		Salaries Expense	584		4,100
		Pension Plan Expense	585		62
		Unemployment Insurance Plan Exp.	586		34
		Workers' Compensation Plan Expense	587		17
		Depreciation Expense: Office Equip.	592		25
		Deprn. Expense: Furniture and Fixtures	593		20
		Depreciation Expense: Automobile	594		150
		To close beginning inventory and all of the income statement accounts having debit balances.			
	31	Inventory	105	5,000	
		Commissions	455	256	
		Cash Overage	457	10	
		Sales	460	21,000	
		Purchase Returns and Allowances	465	300	
		Purchase Discounts	466	100	
		Income Summary	600		26,666
		To record ending inventory and to close all of the income statement accounts having credit balances.			

August	31	Income Summary	600	6,600	
		Retained Earnings	348		6,600
		To close the Income Summary account.			
	31	Retained Earnings	348	1,518	
		Income Taxes	349		1,518
		To close the Income Taxes account.			
	31	Retained Earnings	348	960	
		Dividends on Preferred Shares	350		100
		Dividends on Common Shares	351		860
		To close the dividend accounts.			

Exhibit 7-28: Complete ledger after closing the books at the end of August.

Cash 101

1997					1997				
March	1		1	10,000	March	5		1	7,700
	31		1	250		15		1	500
April	5		2	1,200		31		1	500
	21		2	4,500	April	1		2	100
	30	16,200	2	250		7		2	30
						30		2	600
						30		2	400
						30		2	1,500
						30	13,130	2	1,800
						30	14,335	4	1,205
						30	Balance	✓	1,865
				16,200					16,200
1997					1997				
May	1	Balance	✓	1,865	May	1		5	360
	1		5	1,200		6		5	800
	1		5	10,000		7		5	35
	31		5	250		10		5	70
	31		5	7,100		15		5	70
						22		5	150
						25		5	60
						31		5	400
						31		5	150
						31		5	80

						31		5	500
						31		5	600
						31		5	40
						31	5,315	5	2,000
						31	Balance	✓	15,100
				20,415					20,415

1997					1997				
June	1	Balance	✓	15,100	June	2		7	8,000
	2		7	400		3		7	50
	12		7	200		4		7	100
	17		7	700		5		7	1,500
	30		7	5,880		18		7	35
	30		7	5,120		20		7	980
	30		7	450		21		7	250
						30		7	600
						30		7	400
						30		7	50
						30		7	90
						30	13,555	7	1,500
						30	Balance	✓	14,295
				27,850					27,850

1997					1997				
July	1	Balance	✓	14,295	July	2		9	200
	10		9	150		3		9	1,500
	18		9	18		10		9	40
	28		9	106		10		9	4,214
	31	31,760	9	15,149		13		9	220
	31		9	2,042		15		9	50
						15		9	2,000
						20		9	212
						20		9	106
						24		9	60
						31		9	4,800
						31		9	500
						31		9	22
						31		9	600
						31		9	400
						31		9	54
						31		9	80
						31		9	4
						31	16,062	9	1,000
						31		9	1,980
						31	19,293	9	1,251

						31	Balance	✓	12,467
				31,760					31,760
1997					1997				
August	1	Balance	✓	12,467	August	1		11	300
	1		11	61		5		11	1,500
	1		11	2,000		5		11	2,000
	5		11	4,000		8		11	131
	14		11	160		9		11	3,000
	15		11	5,300		9		11	4,900
	16		11	2,000		12		11	1,000
	25		11	5,194		12		11	300
	31		11	5,310		15		11	1,164
	31	37,852	11	1,360		15		11	18
						16		11	318
						18		11	200
						19		11	318
						21		11	50
						31		11	3,700
						31		11	15
						31		11	400
						31		11	52
						31		11	70
						31		11	6
						31		11	800
						31	22,818	11	2,576
						31	Balance	✓	15,034
				37,852					37,852
1997									
Sept.	1	Balance	✓	15,034					

Petty Cash 102

1997									
July	15		9	50					

Accounts Receivable 103

1997					1997				
March	20		1	500	March	31		1	250
April	12		2	700	April	30	500	2	250
						30	Balance	✓	700
				1,200					1,200

1997					1997				
May	1	Balance	✓	700	May	31		5	250
	31		5	200		31	Balance	✓	650
				900					900
1997					1997				
June	1	Balance	✓	650	June	12		7	200
	3		7	700		17		7	700
	25		7	6,000		30		7	6,000
	30		7	150		30	7,350	7	450
						30	Balance	✓	150
				7,500					7,500
1997					1997				
July	1	Balance	✓	150	July	10		9	150
	20		9	212		22		9	212
	20		9	106		23		9	106
	27		9	106		28		9	106
	31		9	6,042		31	2,616	9	2,042
	31	6,776	9	160		31	Balance	✓	4,160
				6,776					6,776
1997					1997				
August	1	Balance	✓	4,160	August	5		11	4,000
	15		11	5,300		14		11	160
	19		11	318		19		11	318
	31		11	6,360		25		11	5,300
	31	16,258	11	120		25		11	180
						31	11,318	11	1,360
						31	Balance	✓	4,940
				16,258					16,258
1997									
Sept.	1	Balance	✓	4,940					

Allowance for Bad Debts 104

1997					1997				
August	25		11	180	July	31		9	200
	31	Balance	✓	250	August	31	430	11	230
				430					430
					1997				
					Sept.	1	Balance	✓	250

Inventory 105

Date		Explanation	Ref.	Amount	Date		Explanation	Ref.	Amount
1997					1997				
June	30		8	3,000	July	31		10	3,000
1997					1997				
July	31		10	4,000	August	31		12	4,000
1997									
August	31		12	5,000					

Unexpired Insurance 106

Date		Explanation	Ref.	Amount	Date		Explanation	Ref.	Amount
1997					1997				
May	1		5	360	May	31		5	30
						31	Balance	✓	330
				360					360
1997					1997				
June	1	Balance	✓	330	June	30		7	30
						30	Balance	✓	300
				330					330
1997					1997				
July	1	Balance	✓	300	July	31		9	30
						31	Balance	✓	270
				300					300
1997					1997				
August	1	Balance	✓	270	August	31		11	30
						31	Balance	✓	240
				270					270
1997									
Sept.	1	Balance	✓	240					

Government Bonds 108

Date		Explanation	Ref.	Amount	Date		Explanation	Ref.	Amount
1997									
August	9		11	3,000					

Notes Receivable — 109

Date		Item	Ref.	Debit	Date		Item	Ref.	Credit
1997									
August	12		11	1,000					

Shop Supplies — 111

Date		Item	Ref.	Debit	Date		Item	Ref.	Credit
1997					1997				
May	6		5	800	May	31		5	40
						31	Balance	✓	760
				800					800
1997					1997				
June	1	Balance	✓	760	June	30		7	50
						30	Balance	✓	710
				760					760
1997					1997				
July	1	Balance	✓	710	July	31		9	20
						31	Balance	✓	690
				710					710
1997					1997				
August	1	Balance	✓	690	August	31		11	50
						31	Balance	✓	640
				690					690
1997									
Sept.	1	Balance	✓	640					

Office Equipment — 112

Date		Item	Ref.	Debit	Date		Item	Ref.	Credit
1997									
March	11		1	1,800					

Accumulated Depreciation: Office Equipment — 113

Date		Item	Ref.	Debit	Date		Item	Ref.	Credit
					1997				
					April	30		3	25
					May	31	50	5	25
					June	30	75	7	25
					July	31	100	9	25
					August	31	125	11	25

Furniture and Fixtures 114

1997								
March 15		1	2,400					

Accumulated Depreciation: Furniture and Fixtures 115

				1997				
				April 30			3	20
				May 31		40	5	20
				June 30		60	7	20
				July 31		80	9	20
				August 31		100	11	20

Automobile 116

1997				1997			
March 5		1	7,700	March 20		1	500
				April 30	Balance	✓	7,200
			7,700				7,700
1997							
May 1	Balance	✓	7,200				

Accumulated Depreciation: Automobile 117

				1997				
				April 30			3	150
				May 31		300	5	150
				June 30		450	7	150
				July 31		600	9	150
				August 31		750	11	150

Goodwill 127

1997							
August 5		11	2,000				

Company Charter 129

1997							
August 1		11	200				

Accounts Payable 230

1997					1997				
March	31		1	500	March	11		1	1,800
April	30	2,300	2	1,800		15		1	1,900
	30	Balance	✓	1,655	April	14		2	150
						30		2	35
						30	3,955	2	70
				3,955					3,955
1997					1997				
May	7		5	35	May	1	Balance	✓	1,655
	10		5	70					
	31		5	150					
	31	755	5	500					
	31	Balance	✓	900					
				1,655					1,655
1997					1997				
June	4		7	100	June	1	Balance	✓	900
	20	1,100	7	1,000		3		7	900
	30	Balance	✓	1,700		11		7	1,000
				2,800					2,800
1997					1997				
July	10		9	4,300	July	1	Balance	✓	1,700
	17		9	200		2		9	4,300
	31		9	4,800		14	11,000	9	5,000
	31	9,800	9	500					
	31	Balance	✓	1,200					
				11,000					11,000
1997					1997				
August	9		11	5,000	August	1	Balance	✓	1,200
	15		11	300		1		11	5,000
	18		11	200		13		11	4,000
	31		11	3,700		17		11	200
	31	10,000	11	800		31		11	1,524
	31	Balance	✓	2,037		31	12,037	11	113
				12,037					12,037
					1997				
					Sept.	1	Balance	3	2,037

Salaries Payable 231

1997					1997				
June	5		7	1,500	May	31		5	1,500
	30	Balance	✓	1,500	June	30		7	1,500
				3,000					3,000
1997					1997				
July	3		9	1,500	July	1	Balance	✓	1,500
	31	Balance	✓	1,500		31	3,000	9	1,500
				3,000					3,000
1997					1997				
August	5		11	1,500	August	1	Balance	✓	1,500

Interest Payable 232

					1997				
					May	31		5	100
					June	30	200	7	100
					July	31	300	9	100
					August	31	400	11	100

Unearned Commissions 233

1997					1997				
May	31		5	100	May	1		5	1,200
	31	Balance	✓	1,100					
				1,200					1,200
1997					1997				
June	30		7	100	June	1	Balance	✓	1,100
	30	Balance	✓	1,000					
				1,100					1,100
1997					1997				
July	31		9	100	July	1	Balance	✓	1,000
	31	Balance	✓	900					
				1,000					1,000
1997					1997				
August	31		11	100	August	1	Balance	✓	900
	31	Balance	✓	800					

				900					900
					1997				
					Sept.	1	Balance	✓	800

Sales Tax Payable 235

1997					1997				
August	15		11	1,200	July	18		9	18
	15		11	18		31		9	858
	16	1,236	11	18		31	1,218	9	342
	31	Balance	✓	1,242	August	15		11	300
						15		11	300
						31		11	300
						31	2,478	11	360
				2,478					2,478
					1997				
					Sept.	1	Balance	✓	1,242

Income Taxes Payable 236

1997					1997				
July	31		9	1,251	May	31		5	827
					June	30	1,251	8	424
					1997				
					August	31		11	1,518

Dividends Payable on Preferred Shares 237

					1997				
					August	31		11	100

Dividends Payable on Common Shares 238

					1997				
					August	31		11	860

Notes Payable 240

					1997				
					May	1		5	10,000
					August	16	12,000	11	2,000

Jack Fraser, Capital 343

1997						1997				
April	30		4	1,500		March	1		1	10,000
	30		4	1,205		April	30		4	4,820
	30	Balance	✓	12,115						
				14,820						14,820
1997						1997				
May	31		6	2,000		May	1	Balance	✓	12,115
	31		6	827			31		6	4,135
	31	Balance	✓	13,423						
				16,250						16,250
1997						1997				
June	30		8	1,500		June	5	Balance	✓	13,423
	30	1,924	8	424			30	15,543	8	2,120
	30	Balance	✓	13,619						
				15,543						15,543
1997						1997				
July	31		10	1,300		July	1	Balance	✓	13,619
	31	3,280	10	1,980			31	20,219	10	6,600
	31	Balance	✓	16,939						
				20,219						20,219
1997						1997				
August	1		11	16,939		August	1	Balance	✓	16,939
						***** *DISCONTINUED* *****				

Jack Fraser, Drawings 344

1997					1997			
April	30	2	1,500		April	30	4	1,500
1997					1997			
May	31	5	2,000		May	31	6	2,000
1997					1997			
June	30	7	1,500		June	30	8	1,500
1997					1997			
July	18	9	300		July	31	10	1,300

	31	1,300	9	1,000					
				1,300					1,300

***** *DISCONTINUED* *****

Preferred Share Capital 345

					1997				
					August	1		11	1,000

Premium on Preferred Shares 346

					1997				
					August	1		11	1,000

Common Share Capital 347

					1997				
					August	1		11	200
						1		11	61
						1	17,200	11	16,939

Retained Earnings 348

1997					1997				
August	31		12	1,518	August	31		12	6,600
	31	2,478	12	960					
	31	Balance	✓	4,122					
				6,600					6,600
					1997				
					Sept.	1	Balance	✓	4,122

Income Taxes 349

1997					1997				
April	30		4	1,205	April	30		4	1,205

1997				1997			
May	31	5	827	May	31	6	827
1997				1997			
June	30	8	424	June	30	8	424
1997				1997			
July	31	9	1,980	July	31	10	1,980
1997				1997			
August	31	11	1,518	August	31	12	1,518

Dividends on Preferred Shares 350

1997				1997			
August	31	11	100	August	31	12	100

Dividends on Common Shares 351

1997				1997			
August	31	11	860	August	31	12	860

Commissions 455

1997				1997			
April	30	4	6,400	April	5	2	1,200
					12	2	700
					21	2	4,500
			6,400				6,400
1997				1997			
May	31	6	7,400	May	31	5	7,100
					31	5	100
					31	5	200
			7,400				7,400
1997				1997			
June	30	8	250	June	30	7	100

					30		7	150
			250					250
1997				1997				
July	31	10	260	July	31		9	100
					31		9	160
			260					260
1997				1997				
August	31	12	256	August	15		11	36
					31		11	100
					31	256	11	120
			256					256

Cash Overage 457

1997				1997			
August	31	12	10	August	31	11	10

Sales 460

1997				1997				
June	30	8	12,220	June	2		7	400
					3		7	700
					25		7	6,000
					30		7	5,120
			12,220					12,220
1997				1997				
July	31	10	20,000	July	31		9	14,300
					31		9	5,700
			20,000					20,000
1997				1997				
August	31	12	21,000	August	15		11	5,000
					15		11	5,000
					31		11	5,000
					31	21,000	11	6,000
			21,000					21,000

Sales Returns and Allowances 461

1997					1997			
June	4		7	100	June	30	8	100
1997					1997			
August	16		11	300	August	31	12	300

Sales Discounts 462

1997					1997			
June	30		7	120	June	30	8	120
1997					1997			
August	25		11	106	August	31	12	106

Purchases 463

1997					1997			
June	2		7	8,000	June	30	8	9,900
	3		7	900				
	11		7	<u>1,000</u>				
				9,900				9,900
1997					1997			
July	2		9	4,300	July	18	9	300
	14		9	5,000		31	10	11,000
	15	11,300	9	<u>2,000</u>				
				11,300				11,300
1997					1997			
August	1		11	5,000	August	31	12	9,200
	13		11	4,000				
	17	9,200	11	<u>200</u>				
				9,200				9,200

Transportation-in 464

1997					1997				
June	3		7	50	June	30		8	50
1997					1997				
July	2		9	200	July	31		10	200
1997					1997				
August	1		11	300	August	31		12	300

Purchase Returns and Allowances 465

1997					1997				
June	30		8	100	June	4		7	100
1997					1997				
July	31		10	200	July	17		9	200
1997					1997				
August	31		12	300	August	31		11	300

Purchase Discounts 466

1997					1997				
June	30		8	20	June	20		7	20
1997					1997				
July	31		10	86	July	10		9	86
1997					1997				
August	31		12	100	August	9		11	100

Rent Expense 567

1997					1997				
April	30		2	400	April	30		4	400
1997					1997				
May	31		5	400	May	31		6	400

1997 June	30	7	400	1997 June	30	8	400
1997 July	31	9	400	1997 July	31	10	400
1997 August	31	11	400	1997 August	31	12	400

Telephone Expense 568

1997 April	30	2	35	1997 April	30	4	35
1997 May	31	5	40	1997 May	31	6	40
1997 June	30	7	50	1997 June	30	8	50
1997 July	31	9	54	1997 July	31	10	54
1997 August	31	11	52	1997 August	31	12	52

Utilities Expense 569

1997 April	30	2	70	1997 April	30	4	70
1997 May	31	5	80	1997 May	31	6	80
1997 June	30	7	90	1997 June	30	8	90
1997 July	31	9	80	1997 July	31	10	80

1997 August 31	11	70	1997 August 31	12	70

Automobile Maintenance Expense 570

1997 July 24	9	60	1997 July 31	10	60
1997 August 21	11	50	1997 August 31	12	50

Insurance Expense 571

1997 May 31	5	30	1997 May 31	6	30
1997 June 30	7	30	1997 June 30	8	30
1997 July 31	9	30	1997 July 31	10	30
1997 August 31	11	30	1997 August 31	12	30

Office Supplies Expense 572

1997 April 7	2	30	1997 April 30	4	30
1997 May 15	5	70	1997 May 31	6	70
1997 June 18	7	35	1997 June 30	8	35
1997 July 10	9	40	1997 July 31	10	62

	31		9	22			
				62			62
1997					1997		
August	8		11	131	August 31	12	146
	31	146	11	15			
				146			146

Shop Supplies Expense 573

1997				1997		
May	31	5	40	May 31	6	40
1997				1997		
June	30	7	50	June 30	8	50
1997				1997		
July	31	9	20	July 31	10	20
1997				1997		
August	31	11	50	August 31	12	50

Advertising and Promotion Expense 574

1997				1997		
April	1	2	100	April 30	4	250
	14	2	150			
			250			250
1997				1997		
May	22	5	150	May 31	6	210
	25	5	60			
			210			210
1997				1997		
June	21	7	250	June 30	8	250
1997				1997		
July	13	9	220	July 31	10	220
1997				1997		
August	12	11	300	August 31	12	300

Interest and Service Charges Expense — 575

1997					1997			
May	31		5	100	May	31	6	100
1997					1997			
June	30		7	100	June	30	8	100
1997					1997			
July	31		9	4	July	31	10	104
	31		9	100				
				104				104
1997					1997			
August	31		11	6	August	31	12	106
	31	106	11	100				
				106				106

Bad Debts Expense — 578

1997					1997			
July	22		9	212	July	27	9	106
	23		9	106		31	10	412
	31		9	200				
				518				518
1997					1997			
August	20		11	318	August	31	12	548
	31	548	11	230				
				548				548

Salaries Expense — 584

1997					1997			
April	30		2	600	April	30	4	600
1997					1997			
May	31		5	600	May	31	6	2,100
	31		5	1,500				
				2,100				2,100
1997					1997			
June	30		7	600	June	30	8	2,100

30		7	1,500				
			2,100				2,100
1997				1997			
July	31	9	600	July	31	10	2,100
	31	9	1,500				
			2,100				2,100
1997				1997			
August	31	11	4,100	August	31	12	4,100

Pension Plan Expense 585

1997				1997			
August	31	11	62	August	31	12	62

Unemployment Insurance Plan Expense 586

1997				1997			
August	31	11	34	August	31	12	34

Workers' Compensation Plan Expense 587

1997				1997			
August	31	11	17	August	31	12	17

Cash Shortage 589

1997				1997			
July	31	9	9	July	31	10	9

Depreciation Expense: Office Equipment 592

1997 April	30	3	25	1997 April	30	4	25
1997 May	31	5	25	1997 May	31	6	25
1997 June	30	7	25	1997 June	30	8	25
1997 July	31	9	25	1997 July	31	10	25
1997 August	31	11	25	1997 August	31	12	25

Depreciation Expense: Furniture and Fixtures 593

1997 April	30	3	20	1997 April	30	4	20
1997 May	31	5	20	1997 May	31	6	20
1997 June	30	7	20	1997 June	30	8	20
1997 July	31	9	20	1997 July	31	10	20
1997 August	31	11	20	1997 August	31	12	20

Depreciation Expense: Automobile 594

1997 April	30	3	150	1997 April	30	4	150
1997 May	31	5	150	1997 May	31	6	150

1997				1997			
June	30	7	150	June	30	8	150
1997				1997			
July	31	9	150	July	31	10	150
1997				1997			
August	31	11	150	August	31	12	150

Income Summary 600

1997				1997			
April	30	4	1,580	April	30	4	6,400
	30	4	4,820				
			6,400				6,400
1997				1997			
May	31	6	3,265	May	31	6	7,400
	31	6	4,135				
			7,400				7,400
1997				1997			
June	30	8	13,470	June	30	8	15,590
	30	8	2,120				
			15,590				15,590
1997				1997			
July	31	10	17,946	July	31	10	24,546
	31	10	6,600				
			24,546				24,546
1997				1997			
August	31	12	20,066	August	31	12	26,666
	31	12	6,600				
			26,666				26,666

TRIAL BALANCE

A trial balance after closing the books at the end of August is illustrated in Exhibit 7-29. Only balance sheet accounts appear in the trial balance as all the other accounts have been closed and have zero balances. Because the business is a corporation the owner's equity accounts *Jack Fraser, Capital* and *Jack Fraser, Drawings* have been closed permanently and use of these accounts has been discontinued.

Exhibit 7-29: Trial balance after closing the books.

Pacific Printers Mart Inc.
Trial Balance
August 31, 1997

Cash	$15,034	
Petty Cash	50	
Accounts Receivable	4,940	
Allowance for Bad Debts		$ 250
Inventory (August 31, 1997)	5,000	
Unexpired Insurance	240	
Government Bonds	3,000	
Notes Receivable	1,000	
Shop Supplies	640	
Office Equipment	1,800	
Accumulated Depreciation: Office Equipment		125
Furniture and Fixtures	2,400	
Accumulated Depreciation: Furniture and Fixtures		100
Automobile	7,200	
Accumulated Depreciation: Automobile		750
Goodwill	2,000	
Company Charter	200	
Accounts Payable		2,037
Interest Payable		400
Unearned Commissions		800
Sales Tax Payable		1,242
Income Taxes Payable		1,518
Dividends Payable on Preferred Shares		100
Dividends Payable on Common Shares		860
Notes Payable		12,000
Preferred Share Capital		1,000
Premium on Preferred Shares		1,000
Common Share Capital		17,200
Retained Earnings		4,122
	$43,504	$43,504

FINANCIAL STATEMENTS

The final set of financial statements for the month of August may now be prepared. The income statement is presented in Exhibit 7-30 and the balance sheet is presented in Exhibit 7-31.

Exhibit 7-30: Income statement for the month of August after income taxes and dividends have been taken into consideration.

Pacific Printers Mart Inc.
Income Statement
For the month ending August 31, 1997

Revenue:				
Commissions				$ 256
Cash Overage				10
Sales			$21,000	
Less: Sales Returns and Allowances		$300		
Sales Discounts		106	406	
Net Sales:				20,594
Cost of Goods Sold:				
Inventory, August 1st			4,000	
Purchases		9,200		
Add: Transportation-in		300		
Delivered Cost of Purchases		9,500		
Less: Purchase Ret. & Allowances	$300			
Purchase Discounts	100	400		
Net Purchases			9,100	
Cost of Goods Available for Sale			13,100	
Less: Inventory, August 31st			5,000	
Cost of Goods Sold:				8,100
Gross Profit:				$12,760
Expenses:				
Rent Expense			$ 400	
Telephone Expense			52	
Utilities Expense			70	
Automobile Maintenance Expense			50	
Insurance Expense			30	
Office Supplies Expense			146	
Shop Supplies Expense			50	
Advertising and Promotion Expense			300	
Interest and Service Charges Expense			106	

Bad Debts Expense	548	
Salaries Expense	4,100	
Pension Plan Expense	62	
Unemployment Insurance Plan Expense	34	
Workers' Compensation Plan Expense	17	
Depreciation Expense: Office Equipment	25	
Depreciation Expense: Furniture and Fixtures	20	
Depreciation Expense: Automobile	150	6,160
Net Income:		$ 6,600
Less: Income Taxes	$1,518	
Dividends on Preferred Shares	100	
Dividends on Common Shares	860	2,478
Net Income after Taxes and Dividends:		$4,122

Exhibit 7-31: Balance sheet at the end of August.

Pacific Printers Mart Inc.
Balance Sheet
August 31, 1997

Assets

Current Assets:			
Cash		$15,084	
Accounts Receivable	$4,940		
Less: Allowance for Bad Debts	250	4,690	
Inventory, August 31, 1997		5,000	
Unexpired Insurance		240	
Government Bonds		3,000	
Notes Receivable		1,000	
Total current assets:			$29,014
Plant and Equipment:			
Shop Supplies		$ 640	
Office Equipment	$1,800		
Less: Accumulated Depreciation: Office Equipment	125	1,675	
Furniture and Fixtures	$2,400		
Less: Accumulated Depreciation: Furniture and Fixtures	100	2,300	
Automobile	$7,200		
Less: Accumulated Depreciation: Automobile	750	6,450	
Total plant and equipment:			11,065

Other Assets:		
Goodwill	2,000	
Company Charter	200	
Total other assets:		2,200
		$42,279

Liabilities and Shareholders' Equity

Current Liabilities:		
Accounts Payable	$2,037	
Interest Payable	400	
Unearned Commissions	800	
Sales Tax Payable	1,242	
Income Taxes Payable	1,518	
Dividends Payable on Preferred Shares	100	
Dividends Payable on Common Shares	860	
Total current liabilities:		$ 6,947
Long-term Liabilities:		
Notes Payable:		12,000
Shareholders' Equity:		
Preferred share capital, 10% cumulative, $1 par value, authorized 1,000,000 shares, issued and outstanding 1,000 shares		1,000
Premium on Preferred Shares		1,000
Common Share Capital, without par value, authorized 1,000,000 shares, issued and outstanding 17,200 shares		17,200
Retained Earnings		4,122
		$42,279

ACCOUNTING CYCLE FOR A CORPORATION

The complete accounting cycle for a corporation, engaged in merchandising, may be summarized as follows:

1. Record all operating transactions in the journal and post these entries to the ledger.

2. Record all adjusting transactions in the journal and post these entries to the ledger.

3. Prepare a trial balance.

4. Close the books in the following sequence, by making entries in the journal and by posting these entries to the ledger:
   a. Close all of the income statement accounts that have debit

balances, and beginning inventory, into the Income Summary account.

b. Record ending inventory, and close all of the income statement accounts that have credit balances into the Income Summary account.

c. Compute the net balance of the Income Summary account and close Income Summary into Retained Earnings.

5. Prepare a preliminary set of financial statements. Compute the amount of income taxes. Make entries for income taxes in the journal and post to the ledger.

6. Record declaration of dividends, if any, in the journal and post these entries to the ledger.

7. a. Close the Income Taxes account into Retained Earnings.

   b. Close the dividends accounts, if dividends have been declared, into Retained Earnings.

8. Prepare a final set of financial statements, that is, an income statement and a balance sheet.

Exercises

1. What are the characteristics of a proprietorship? In what way is a partnership different from a proprietorship?

2. Describe the main attributes of a corporation. What are the main advantages of incorporating a business?

3. List some ways in which a corporation may raise money with which to carry on business activity.

4. A shareholder borrows money from a corporation. Name the accounts that are affected.

5. A shareholder lends money to a corporation. Name the accounts involved in the transaction.

6. Why is it essential to account for all out-of-pocket expenditures when making purchases on behalf of the corporation?

7. What is gross salary? What is meant by net salary? Which of the two must be recorded in the journal?

8. Are amounts withheld from an employee's salary for income taxes, pension plan, union dues, and medical plan recorded in the journal? If so, how are they recorded? If not, why not?

9. Why must contributions made by an employer on behalf of its employees, for workers' compensation, pension plan, and an unemployment insurance plan be recorded in the journal while similar deductions from the employee's salary are not recorded in the journal? Explain.

10. Describe the nature of the Retained Earnings account. In what situation is a Retained Earnings account employed?

11. What are dividends? May a corporation have a drawings account?

12. Name two kinds of share capital.

Problems

1. Jim Smith spends $200 of his own money to incorporate a limited company. The limited company was formed on February 22nd and has the ability to

issue 1,000,000 common shares, if it desires. Make an appropriate journal entry to record this event.

2. Robert Riley incorporates his business on June 10th. The corporation has a 100,000 common share capital and a 100,000 preferred share capital. Preferred shares have a par value of one dollar each. The cost of incorporation was $210 which came from the personal funds of Robert Riley. Make appropriate journal entries to record this event.

3. August 9th: A corporation issues 1,000 common shares for cash at a price of ten dollars per share. Journalize this transaction.

4. October 11th: A corporation issues 800 common shares in exchange for shop equipment valued at $4,000. Make appropriate journal entries to record this transaction.

5. December 10th: Two thousand preferred shares with a par value of one dollar per share are issued for $2,000. Record journal entries for this transaction.

6. February 28th: Seven hundred preferred shares with a par value of $5.00 per share are issued at a price of $7.50 per share. Make appropriate journal entries to record this transaction.

7. On November 14th Arctic Airlines Inc. purchases the remaining goodwill from North West Airfreight Services Inc. for $20,000. Record this transaction.

8. A business with surplus cash purchases $6,000 worth of government bonds on November 15th. Make appropriate journal entries to record this transaction.

9. On March 9th, John Smith borrows $2,000 from a corporation in which he is the sole shareholder. He signs a note promising to pay back the money on demand. Make appropriate journal entries to record this transaction.

10. Advance Enterprises Inc. lends $4,000 to its president on May 10th. A promissory note is signed. Record this transaction.

11. Jack Jockey, president, lends $25,000 to his own limited company on July 11th. Make appropriate journal entries to record this transaction.

12. XYZ Enterprises Corporation borrows $500,000 from the president of the company Wayne Hockey on May 10th. On July 5th the president lends the corporation $200,000. Prepare appropriate journal entries to record these transactions.

13. Dobson Industries Inc. calls a demand loan for $5,000 which was made to its

president earlier in the year. Tom Dobson pays back the loan on January 15th.

14. Delbert Ho purchases office supplies on May 9th at an auction, paying the bid price of $80 out-of-pocket. Record this transaction employing appropriate journal entries.

15. Make appropriate journal entries, from the data in the payroll book below, for the month of June.

Payroll Record

Name of Employee:	Jack Smith	Robert Jones
Gross Earnings:	$2,400	$3,000
Less: Income Taxes	480	700
Pension Plan	20	24
Unemployment Insurance	10	12
Net Earnings:	1,890	2,264
Employer's Contributions:		
Pension Plan	20	24
Unemployment Insurance	15	18
Workers' Compensation	12	15

16. On December 31st dividends of 5 cents per share are declared on 7,400 common shares issued and outstanding. Journalize this transaction.

17. A dividend of 10 cents per share is declared on all outstanding preferred shares payable to shareholders of record on December 31st. Two thousand preferred shares with a par value of $2.00 each are outstanding at this time. Make appropriate journal entries for this transaction.

18. On February 2nd of the following year, the dividends declared in problems 16 and 17 are paid. Record these transactions.

19. Make appropriate journal entries at year end to close the dividend accounts in problems 16 and 17.

20. On June 2nd a dividend of ten cents per share is declared on 900 outstanding preferred shares. This dividend is paid, to all shareholders of record on the date the dividends were declared, on June 15th. Make appropriate journal entries to record these transactions.

21. For the corporation described below, do the following:
    a. Record and post all operating transactions.
    b. Record and post all adjusting entries.
    c. Prepare a trial balance.
    d. Prepare a preliminary set of financial statements. Compute the

amount of income taxes based on a rate of 20%. Make entries for income taxes in the journal and post to the ledger.

e. Record declaration of dividends in the journal and post to the ledger.

f. Close the books.

g. Prepare a final set of financial statements, after income taxes and dividends have been taken into consideration.

December 1: Jack Sterling incorporates a limited company, Kansas Money Changers Inc. He pays the cost of incorporation, which amounts to $200 out of his own pocket. Kansas Money Changers Inc. is authorized to issue 100,000 common shares without par value. Jack Sterling receives 200 shares from the corporation for his service performed in incorporating the company.

December 2: Purchases 40,000 common shares from the corporation at a price of one dollar each. Pays for these shares in cash.

December 3: Lends $20,000 to the corporation. Jack Sterling, as company president, signs a promissory note promising to pay back the money on demand and without interest.

December 3: The company purchases land costing $30,000. A down payment of $20,000 is made with the balance to be paid in equal monthly installments of $1,000 each beginning with the month of January. A promissory note is signed.

December 4: A building is erected on the site, costing $18,720 and paid for in cash. Depreciate over 39 years.

December 5: Furnishings and fixtures are purchased at a cost of $2,520 on credit. To be paid for in 90 days time. Seven-year property.

December 5: Office supplies costing $72 are purchased from the local stationery store. Check number 104 is issued in payment.

December 5: A sturdy vault is purchased from the Great West Steel Company Inc. at a cost of $3,948. It was set in the building as a fixture. A down payment of $1,000 is made with the balance to be paid in equal monthly installments of $500 each commencing with the end of this month. Seven-year property.

December 5: A $10,000 loan is negotiated with the First Kansas Bank. Both principal and interest at the rate of 6% per annum are to be repaid at the end of a five year period.

December 8: Mrs. Sterling purchases 20,000 common shares at a price of one dollar per share, paying cash.

December 10: Fees for the first ten days of operations amount to $3,419.

December 11: A 12-month insurance policy, retroactive to the beginning of the month, is purchased for $360, paying cash.

December 12: Advertisements are placed in the Kansas Times at a cost of $484. Payment is due at the end of the month.

December 13: Spends $640 on a trip to the Money Makers Convention in Vancouver.

December 17: Purchases government bonds costing $3,000, paying cash.

December 18: Pays an attorney $4,800 for legal advice.

December 20: Fees for the second ten days in December amount to $4,918.

December 24: Kansas Money Changers Inc. lends Mrs. Sterling $2,000. Mrs. Sterling signs a promissory note promising to pay back the money on demand and without interest.

December 27: Pays an accountant $900 for advice on setting up the payroll records.

December 31: Fees for the final eleven days in the month amount to $9,817.

December 31: Jack Sterling forgoes his salary for the month of December.

December 31: Receives the telephone bill amounting to $35. Payment is due by January 10th.

December 31: Receives the bill for gas and electricity amounting to $206. Payment is due by January 15th.

December 31: Makes installment payments to the company's creditors.

December 31: Declares a dividend of two cents per share to the holders of common shares on this date.

CHAPTER EIGHT

Organizing the Books and Records; and the Worksheet

INTRODUCTION

By its very nature paperwork accompanies the operation of a business. Correspondence and business paper such as invoices are sent out and correspondence, bills and statements are received. The activity that a particular business engages in will dictate what forms, etc., it requires. A filing system must be set up. Some of the files and records are accounting related while others are not related to accounting at all.

GENERAL CORRESPONDENCE

A file should be set up for all correspondence received and should contain copies of all correspondence sent out. Anything, except confidential information, which does not seem to belong to a particular file may be included in this file.

A good way of organizing any file is to place a file pin through the upper left-hand corner of a letter size sheet of *file back* paper, available at any stationery store. As correspondence is received or as letters are sent out, the letter or carbon copy is secured in the file, layer upon layer, from the file back upwards. Thus you end up with a stack of letters in reverse chronological order, with the latest correspondence at the top of the file. The file pin secures the letters and carbon copies in one file unit so that nothing can get misplaced or lost. The front cover of the file is made from a sheet of file back paper upon which is written the name of the file and a file number. With a thick felt-tipped pen we neatly print*General Correspondence* on the file cover and may include a file number such as *G.C.-1* if we wish.

Virtually every business needs letterhead paper containing the name, address, and telephone number of the business, along with envelopes and business cards. This material, of course, is not accounting related but is nevertheless a vital part of the information system in the business.

RECORD OF ASSETS

Every business must keep a separate record of all depreciable assets. The record should show from whom each depreciable asset was acquired as well as the cost and date of acquisition. When an asset is sold or traded-in, the date of disposal must be indicated together with the amount received or allowed on trade-in. No special record book or paper is necessary—a simple ruled exercise book, available at any stationery store or wherever school supplies are sold, is eminently suitable for this purpose. The record of assets for Pacific Printers Mart Inc. is illustrated in Exhibit 8-1.

Exhibit 8-1: Record of depreciable assets for Pacific Printers Mart Inc.

RECORD OF DEPRECIABLE ASSETS

Description, including name of supplier.	Cost	Date Acquired	Proceeds from Disposal	Date of Disposal
1984 Ford truck, including canopy; purchased from Surrey Motors Inc.	$7,700	March 5 1997		
Canopy sold to Don Robson			$500	March 20 1997
Canon photocopier and Facit typewriter; purchased from Dandy Discounts Inc.	$1,800	March 11 1997		

Office desks and chairs; acquired from Superior Office Products Inc.	$2,400	March 15 1997
Goodwill; acquired from Atlantic Trade Services Inc.	$2,000	August 5 1997

EXPENDITURES FILE AND ACCOUNTS PAYABLE FILE

This file is very important. Make sure that you obtain a receipt for every expenditure and file these receipts in an orderly manner. The best way is to set up a file as before with file covers and a file pin in the upper left-hand corner, but this time use thin *onion skin* paper to make up the leaves of the file. Tape every receipt into this file, as receipts are received, to maintain proper sequence working from the back cover upwards. If it is not clear from the bill as to what a particular expenditure was for, then make a notation on the receipt, such as *Shop Supplies*, to indicate what the particular expenditure was for. Pages are added to the top of the file as required so you end up with an expenditures file in reverse chronological sequence. The front cover should be labeled *Expenditures 1997*, for example.

Some people mistakenly think that it is better to have a separate file for each kind of expenditure. But this is not so for a small business, and organizing the expenditures file in that manner may lead to regrets later on. Some bills, such as the telephone bill, for example, contain more than one kind of expense. The telephone bill, of course, lists both telephone expense and advertising expense for the Yellow Pages advertisement. So in which file do you place the telephone bill—the file for telephone expense or the file for advertising expense? This same principle applies to other bills as well. When equipment is purchased supplies are often purchased at the same time and both are listed on the same invoice. And if you have to make a decision as to which file to place the bill in you will probably end up avoiding the need to make a decision and simply place the bill in a shoe box. Do not use a shoe box to store your bills. Set up an expenditures file in the manner indicated using onion skin paper held together securely between file covers with a stout file pin. If you wish you may write the account number on each receipt and that way there will be no doubt as to which account the amount has been applied to. Again, it is preferable to have one general file for expenditures than to have several separate files. This manner of filing the receipts is more efficient, takes up less space, and has proven itself workable, while the opposite may be said of the several-file situation.

Never include more than one copy of each bill of sale for each item of expenditure in the expenditures file, even though you may have several copies of a particular bill. Only one piece of paper is to be included in the expenditures file for each transaction regardless of the number of copies of invoices, etc., that you may have received. The surplus copies are redundant. Receiving several pieces of paper to represent one and the same transaction is commonplace. For example, suppose that you have ordered advertising time from a local radio station. You will undoubtedly sign a contract to begin with and receive at least one copy of this contract listing the amount of the intended expenditure. In addition to this contract you will also receive a statement listing the amount of cost to a certain date, such as the cost of advertising to the end of the month. In addition to these two items, you will also receive an invoice or *bill.* One copy, and only one copy, of this bill is to be included in the expenditures file. The remaining copies of contracts, statements, and invoices—in various colors—should be filed elsewhere. Contracts, statements, and extra copies of the invoice may be filed in the *General Correspondence* file or some other file devised for this purpose. Perhaps the spare copies should be placed in a redundant copies file. The objective of the expenditures file is to prove the source and cost of each item of expenditure—one time only so as not to cause confusion—with an appropriate piece of paper, that is, with a receipt. If no receipt is available, then make a notation in the file where the receipt should have been placed, to the effect, for example, *Office Supplies Expense $214—see canceled check number 304.*

One copy of every bill must be included in the expenditures file. Some items will have been paid for in cash at the time the item or service was acquired; other items will have been acquired on credit resulting in accounts payable. Unless accounts payable are few in number, it is advisable to set up an accounts payable file. This may consist of blank or ruled file cards of a convenient size that can be assembled in alphabetical order in a file box. One card is made up for each supplier from whom goods or services have been acquired on credit. At the very top of the card the name and address of the supplier is inserted, along with other particulars such as name of person to contact, telephone number, and account number, if applicable. In the body of each card the particulars of the transaction are entered, such as the date and description of the item, amount of the transaction, terms, when each payment is due, and the date and amount of each payment made.

Only those cards on which accounts payable are outstanding are kept in the file box comprising the accounts payable file. When no further payments are due to a supplier listed on a particular card, that card is removed from the file and placed in a separate section of this same file box or removed from the file box altogether. The latter procedure is the best remedy. The objective of the accounts payable file is to enable the business owner to determine to whom money is owed, etc., and to determine the total amount of accounts payable outstanding at the end of the year. This is especially the case if a journal and ledger are not kept, and if the number of accounts payable are numerous.

CHECK REGISTER

Maintain a check register and reconcile the balance on the bank statement with the balance in the check register and the Cash account. Check registers are available from most banks and may also be purchased at stationery stores. The check register is not meant to replace the Cash account, but provides a detailed record of each check drawn and deposit made, together with the date of each transaction. As monthly bank statements contain items of service charges expense they should be filed in the expenditures file unless there is some reason to file them separately. Checks should be serialized and canceled checks should be filed in proper sequence and should be stored for future reference.

SALES BOOK, SALES FILE, AND ACCOUNTS RECEIVABLE FILE

A record of all sales must be kept. This record includes the cash register tape, with date and totals clearly shown, stored and filed in sequence, usually reverse chronological order with the latest material on top. For a merchandising business in particular, a sales book is necessary. One may be devised from an ordinary notebook or a commercial sales book may be purchased.

A supply of invoice forms, with serialized numbers, is also required. These are the *bills of sale* that your business issues, when necessary, for large sales and for credit sales. Serialization is a control device which prevents someone from making a large cash sale and pocketing the money.

Carbon copies of all invoices that your business issues must be kept in sequence in a file, and spoiled invoices should be placed in the file marked *void* and with a diagonal line drawn across the sheet from corner to corner. In this manner, every invoice number is accounted for and a dishonest employee cannot crumple up an invoice and pocket the money on a cash sale. Supplies of invoices are usually custom printed for a particular business.

The objective of the sales book and file is to have a complete record of every item of revenue earned by the firm. A copy of each sales tax report form is kept in this file, so that the amount of commissions earned for remitting sales tax may be readily determined. Details of sales returns and allowances are entered on blank sheets of paper and are included as memos to the sales book. The sales book may also serve as an accounts receivable file.

Virtually all accounts receivable result from transactions in which revenue has been earned. Thus an accounts receivable file should be set up and kept in conjunction with the sales book, especially if credit sales are numerous. This file is set up in the same manner as the accounts payable file. A separate card is completed for each customer to whom a sale has been made on credit. The customer's name, address, and telephone number are included in the heading at the top of the card along with other pertinent data such as account number, credit rating, etc. Cards are filed in alphabetical order. In the body of the card are included particulars of the transaction such as description of the item purchased, date, amount of the sale and the date and amount of each payment received.

When no further moneys are receivable from a particular customer, that customer's card is removed from the accounts receivable file. The sum of all accounts receivable as calculated by adding up all the amounts from the cards in the file must be equal to the balance in the accounts receivable ledger account. A separate accounts receivable file is especially important where credit sales are numerous or where no journal and ledger are kept.

PERSONNEL FILES

These are confidential files and must be kept locked away. In the personnel file are kept contracts and other details of hiring, firing, resumes, and other confidential personal data. Details of personal data such as marital status and number of dependents along with amount of salary are kept in this file, but this file is not to be confused with the payroll book as payroll accounting data is not the purpose of this file.

PAYROLL BOOK

The objective of a payroll book is to keep orderly track of all salaries paid out, amounts withheld from salaries as payroll deductions, and amounts remitted on behalf of employees, including employers' contributions.

Entries for the sum of each item should be entered in the journal. A book with ruled columns is suitable for use as a payroll book. Otherwise, payroll books are available at most stationery stores.

PETTY CASH BOOK

This book was described earlier. An ordinary notebook will suffice or a petty cash book may be purchased from a stationery store.

LOANS FILE

A *loans file* is usually kept as a separate file, but it is sometimes included in the general correspondence file. The loans file includes applications for loans along with details of any loans obtained together with the relevant correspondence.

JOURNAL AND LEDGER

These are the main books of account and contain all essential data on transactions to prepare complete and accurate financial statements.

Both journals and ledgers are available commercially and may be purchased at any stationery store. As is the case with much accounting paper, column headings are not normally printed in a journal. You must inspect column size and layout to determine if the book is suitable for your purposes. This very same principle applies to other books and records, such as the payroll book. With respect to ledger paper, it is not usually laid out in two symmetrical halves, that is with a distinct left-hand and right-hand side. Instead, it normally contains only one date, explanation and reference column.

The reference column is often titled *folio*. These columns are followed by the debit and credit money columns, and sometimes a third money column, a balance column, is included. So entries are recorded in chronological order (posted from the journal) and a running balance is maintained if desired.

The accounting procedure remains the same, only the format of the ledger has changed slightly. Use of a worksheet, to be explained later in this chapter, eliminates the need for a journal and a ledger.

INCOME TAXES FILE

This file includes copies of all financial statements prepared for the business, copies of completed tax forms, and any correspondence with the income tax department.

CORPORATION RECORDS

These consist of a minute book, registers of shareholders, and other forms used in connection with maintaining the status of a corporation. In many cases the attorney for the corporation keeps these records up to date. Financial statements must be presented and considered at the annual general meeting of shareholders and these are the product of small business accounting.

WORKSHEET METHOD OF ACCOUNTING

A workbook, consisting of pages completely ruled into columns, or individual sheets ruled into columns, called worksheets, may be used for small business accounting. The objective of the worksheet is to eliminate the large number of journal entries necessary when each item is entered in the journal separately. We have already encountered a form of worksheet used for a specialized purpose, which is the sales book.

In a merchandising business with hundreds or thousands of sales made in the course of a day, it would present a formidable task to record each individual sale. Instead, sales are recorded on the cash register tape, totals are entered in a sales book at the end of each day, and the sum of these totals from the sales book is transferred to the journal once or twice a month.

Why not extend this same principle to other kinds of transactions? Instead of recording telephone expense, for example, each time we receive a bill for telephone services, we may dispense with entries to the journal altogether by simply listing the amount of each bill in one of the columns headed *Telephone Expense* in our columnar worksheet. This is in fact the way most accountants do small business accounting. For one thing, this method eliminates a lot of paperwork. However, to employ this method, you need to have a thorough knowledge of the accounting cycle and care must be taken throughout the year to ensure that absolutely every transaction is properly accounted for.

At the end of each year we compute the sum of the entries in each column and prepare an income statement and balance sheet directly from these column totals. Or, if you wish, the sum of each column may be journalized, posted to the ledger, and the books may be closed, and financial statements prepared in the usual manner.

A workbook eliminates the journal and ledger, unless you wish to journalize, etc., the sum for each account. However, all of the other files and books must, nevertheless, be kept.

We must still keep a record of assets; an expenditures file must be kept with a receipt for each expenditure as well as an accounts payable file. A check register must be maintained; a sales book, invoice and accounts receivable file must be maintained; a payroll book must be kept; where necessary, a petty cash book and a loans file is kept; and an income taxes file must be kept.

All of these files and records sound like a lot of paperwork but they are absolutely essential to support the data contained in the financial statements. The only thing that a worksheet does is eliminate the use of a journal and ledger, unless partial use of these books is desired for recording sums of transactions in each account, but even so the savings in terms of work is considerable.

EMPLOYING A WORKSHEET

To construct a worksheet use accounting paper that is completely ruled into columns, otherwise known as a columnar pad. A heading is placed at the top of each column, and the columns are arranged in the same sequence as the accounts would be if a ledger was employed. The first column is headed Cash and the balance from the check register at the end of the accounting period is copied into this column. The amount of the petty cash fund, from the petty cash book, is also entered into this column to obtain the final balance in the cash account, which will appear on the balance sheet.

The second column is headed Accounts Receivable. We go through the invoice or accounts receivable file, which is normally the sales book, and list each account receivable that remains outstanding at the end of the accounting period. We are not interested in the accounts receivable that have already been collected.

In the third column headed Allowance for Bad Debts we insert the amount of this allowance. Then we check the accounts receivable file (the sales book, or a separate supplement listing credit sales) to determine which of the accounts receivable outstanding at the end of the previous accounting period were written off during the current period. Writing off uncollectible accounts receivable, using the worksheet method of accounting, involves writing *Uncollectible* on a copy of the invoice, and that is done during the period when the account proves uncollectible. In our worksheet, under Allowance for Bad Debts, we insert the amount of accounts receivable outstanding at the end of the previous period which were written off during the current period, in parenthesis. This tells us how much we must add to the Allowance for Bad Debts account so that its balance is consistent with anticipated losses arising from accounts receivable outstanding at the end of the current accounting period. Any amounts added to the Allowance for Bad Debts column must also be added to the Bad Debts Expense column.

Merchandise purchased for resale that remains unsold at the end of the current accounting period is counted and priced at its cost to the merchant. This amount is entered into the column headed Inventory.

The cost of insurance is obtained from the receipt in the expenditures file and is listed in the column headed Unexpired Insurance. The amount of insurance used up during the current period is computed and entered in parenthesis in this same column. Amounts in parenthesis are subtracted from the regular entry in the column to arrive at the net balance. An entry must also be made in the column for Insurance Expense. A similar procedure is followed for the remaining asset accounts.

We consult our records (expenditures file, or a supplement listing accounts payable) to determine which accounts have not been paid at the end of the accounting period, to arrive at the amount of accounts payable. These amounts are listed in the column headed Accounts Payable and the sum of the individual entries is determined. Of course, only Accounts Payable outstanding at the end of the accounting period are listed in this column. We have no interest in accounts that have already been paid. We employ a similar procedure on the remaining liability accounts.

Equity accounts are handled in a similar manner. We consult the previous balance sheet to determine balances at the end of the preceding accounting period. If additional shares have been issued we make entries in the appropriate column. In the column for Retained Earnings, we include the balance at the end of the previous accounting period. In this column we enter the amount of net income. Then, in parenthesis, we enter the amount of income taxes and dividends. Net income is added to the previous balance in the Retained Earnings account while the amount of income taxes and dividends is subtracted to arrive at the current balance in this account.

The sales book and invoice file are consulted to determine the amount of sales. The expenditures file is consulted in order to determine what amounts to include in the cost of goods accounts and expense accounts. When all of this is done we end up with a worksheet as shown in Exhibit 8-2. Worksheets for most businesses will not end up as complicated, and with as many accounts, as the one shown in our example. Remember, our worksheet includes a complete business transfer of equity from proprietorship to corporation.

Exhibit 8-2: Worksheet including all entries from the time of commencement of the business.

Cash	Accounts Receivable	Allow. for Bad Debts	Inventory	Unexpired Insurance
15,034	5,000	200	5,000	360
50	120	(180)		(30)
	(180)	230		(30)
				(30)
				(30)
15,084	4,940	250	5,000	240

Government Bonds	Notes Receivable	Shop Supplies	Office Equipment	Ac. Deprn.: Of. Equip.
3,000	1,000	800	1,800	25
		(40)		25
		(50)		25
		(20)		25
		(50)		25
3,000	1,000	640	1,800	125

Furniture & Fixtures	Ac. Deprn.: Furn. & Fix.	Automobile	Ac. Deprn.: Automobile	Goodwill
2,400	20	7,700	150	2,000
	20	(500)	150	
	20		150	
	20		150	
	20		150	
2,400	100	7,200	750	2,000

Company Charter	Accounts Payable	Interest Payable	Unearned Commissions	Sales Tax Payable
200	400	100	1,200	300
	800	100	(100)	300
	113	100	(100)	(18)
	724	100	(100)	300
			(100)	360
200	2,037	400	800	1,242

Income Taxes Payable	Dividends Payable on Preferred Shares	Dividends Payable on Common Shares	Notes Payable	Jack Fraser, Capital
1,518	100	860	10,000	10,000
			2,000	17,675
				(6,300)
				(4,436)
1,518	100	860	12,000	16,939

Jack Fraser, Drawings	Preferred Share Capital	Premium on Preferred Shares	Common Share Capital	Retained Earnings
1,500	1,000	1,000	200	6,600
2,000			61	(1,518)
1,500			16,939	(100)
300				(860)
1,000				
6,300	1,000	1,000	17,200	4,122

Income Taxes	Dividends on Preferred Shares	Dividends on Common Shares	Commissions	Cash Overage
	100	860	1,200	10
Proprietorship			700	
1,205			4,500	
827			7,100	
424			100	
1,980			200	
4,436			100	
			150	
Corporation			100	
1,518			160	
			36	
			100	
			120	
1,518	100	860	14,566	10

Sales	Sales Returns and Allowances	Sales Discounts	Purchases	Transpor-tation-in
400	100	120	8,000	50
700	300	106	900	200
6,000			1,000	300
5,120			4,300	
14,300			5,000	
5,700			2,000	
5,000			(300)	
5,000			5,000	
5,000			4,000	
6,000			200	
53,220	400	226	30,100	550

Purchase Returns and Allowances	Purchase Discounts	Rent Expense	Telephone Expense	Utilities Expense
100	20	400	35	70
200	86	400	40	80
300	100	400	50	90
		400	54	80
		400	52	70
600	206	2,000	231	390

Automobile Maintenance Expense	Insurance Expense	Office Supplies Expense	Shop Supplies Expense	Advertising and Promotion Expense
60	30	30	40	100
50	30	70	50	150
	30	35	20	150
	30	40	50	60
		22		250
		131		220
		15		300
110	120	343	160	1,230

Interest and Service Charges Expense	Bad Debts Expense	Salaries Expense	Pension Plan Expense	Unemployment Insurance Plan Expense
100	212	600	62	34
100	106	600		
4	(106)	1,500		
100	200	600		
6	318	1,500		
100	230	600		
		1,500		
		4,100		
410	960	11,000	62	34

Workers' Compensation Plan Expense	Cash Shortage	Depreciation Expense: Office Equipment	Depreciation Expense: Furniture and Fixtures	Depreciation Expense: Automobile
17	9	25	20	150
		25	20	150
		25	20	150
		25	20	150
		25	20	150
17	9	125	100	750

FINANCIAL STATEMENTS

A set of financial statements may be produced directly from the data in the worksheet. The worksheet includes financial data from the time of commencement of business, March 1, 1997, to August 31, 1997, inclusive. No entries at all are made to the journal, and, accordingly, a ledger is not necessary. Thus, these two books of account may be dispensed with. The income statement and balance sheet are simply formulated from the worksheet data.

To do it this way great care must be taken throughout the year to ensure that all transactions are represented in some manner or other, such as by entries in the check register, receipts in the expenditures file, and entries in the sales book. Most accountants do small business accounting in this manner. You may do it this way too, if you wish. The main advantage of using a worksheet is that it saves an enormous amount of paper work, as compared to a journal and ledger. However, to use a worksheet, a thorough knowledge of the accounting cycle is essential.

A combined income statement, prepared from the data in the worksheet in Exhibit 8-2, is shown in Exhibit 8-3. This income statement includes all of the operating results, right from the time of commencement of business on March 1st up to August 31st.

The operating results from both the operation of the proprietorship and the corporation have been combined in our illustration. However, for taxation purposes a separate set of financial statements would have to be filed for the proprietorship and the corporation, because the corporation is a separate legal entity and must file its own income tax return. The balance sheet is illustrated in Exhibit 8-4. It is identical to the balance sheet previously illustrated in Exhibit 7-31, as it must be, as that is the financial position of Pacific Printers Mart Inc. on August 31, 1997.

Our income statement in Exhibit 8-3 is not identical to the income statement in Exhibit 7-30, also prepared at the end of August, because it represents a fiscal period of six months, while the income statement in Exhibit 7-30 is only for a period of one month. Whenever income statements are prepared on a monthly basis, and an annual income statement is required to obtain the operating results for the full year, or other fiscal period, it is necessary to take the separate monthly statements and carefully add up the amounts of each account, to arrive at an income statement which includes operating results for the entire fiscal period. This is because an income statement gives the results of operations over a specified period of time.

No such additions need be performed on the balance sheet, however, because a balance sheet gives us the financial position of a business at a particular point in time. Thus, the balance sheet at the end of August is already in its final form, notwithstanding the fact that it was prepared as part of a set of monthly financial statements.

It may not be apparent at first glance that the amount of net income after dividends and income taxes is equal to the increase in owner's equity as a result of profitable operation of the business.

This is because owner's equity from the proprietorship has been transferred, or rolled-over, to the corporation. To prove that the results of operations of the business correspond to the changes in equity on the balance sheet, these changes are detailed in Exhibit 8-5, where it can be seen that when the amount of retained earnings is calculated using detailed arithmetic, the balance $4,122 equals the amount of retained earnings shown on the balance sheet at the end of August.

Exhibit 8-3: Combined income statement for fiscal period March 1, 1997, to August 31, 1997.

Pacific Printers Mart Inc.
Income Statement
For the fiscal period ending August 31, 1997

Revenue:				
Commissions				$14,566
Cash Overage				10
Sales			$53,220	
Less: Sales Returns and Allowances		$400		
Sales Discounts		226	626	
Net Sales:				52,594
Cost of Goods Sold:				
Inventory (beginning)			000	
Purchases		30,100		
Add: Transportation-in		550		
Delivered Cost of Purchases		30,650		
Less: Purchase Ret. & Allowances	$600			
Purchase Discounts	206	806		
Net Purchases			29,844	
Cost of Goods Available for Sale			29,844	
Less: Inventory, August 31st			5,000	
Cost of Goods Sold:				24,844

Gross Profit:		$42,326
Expenses:		
Rent Expense	$2,000	
Telephone Expense	231	
Utilities Expense	390	
Automobile Maintenance Expense	110	
Insurance Expense	120	
Office Supplies Expense	343	
Shop Supplies Expense	160	
Advertising and Promotion Expense	1,230	
Interest and Service Charges Expense	410	
Bad Debts Expense	960	
Salaries Expense	11,000	
Pension Plan Expense	62	
Unemployment Insurance Plan Expense	34	
Workers' Compensation Plan Expense	17	
Depreciation Expense: Office Equipment	125	
Depreciation Expense: Furniture and Fixtures	100	
Depreciation Expense: Automobile	750	18,051
Net Income:		$24,275
Less: Income Taxes	$5,954	
Dividends on Preferred Shares	100	
Dividends on Common Shares	860	6,914
Net Income after Taxes and Dividends:		$17,361

Exhibit 8-4: Balance sheet at the end of August.

Pacific Printers Mart Inc.
Balance Sheet
August 31, 1997

Assets

Current Assets:		
Cash		$15,084
Accounts Receivable	$4,940	
Less: Allowance for Bad Debts	250	4,690
Inventory, August 31, 1997		5,000
Unexpired Insurance		240
Government Bonds		3,000

Notes Receivable		1,000	
Total current assets:			$29,014
Plant and Equipment:			
Shop Supplies		$ 640	
Office Equipment	$1,800		
Less: Accumulated Depreciation: Office Equipment	125	1,675	
Furniture and Fixtures	$2,400		
Less: Accumulated Depreciation: Furniture and Fixtures	100	2,300	
Automobile	$7,200		
Less: Accumulated Depreciation: Automobile	750	6,450	
Total plant and equipment:			11,065
Other Assets:			
Goodwill		2,000	
Company Charter		200	
Total other assets:			2,200
			$42,279

Liabilities and Shareholders' Equity

Current Liabilities:		
Accounts Payable	$2,037	
Interest Payable	400	
Unearned Commissions	800	
Sales Tax Payable	1,242	
Income Taxes Payable	1,518	
Dividends Payable on Preferred Shares	100	
Dividends Payable on Common Shares	860	
Total current liabilities:		$ 6,957
Long-term Liabilities:		
Notes Payable:		12,000
Shareholders' Equity:		
Preferred share capital, 10% cumulative, $1 par value, authorized 1,000,000 shares, issued and outstanding 1,000 shares		1,000
Premium on Preferred Shares		1,000
Common Share Capital, without par value, authorized 1,000,000 shares, issued and outstanding 17,200 shares		17,200
Retained Earnings		4,122
		$42,279

Exhibit 8-5: Details of changes in equity resulting from roll over from proprietorship to corporation.

Changes in Equity

Proprietorship:

Jack Fraser, Capital, March 1, 1997			$10,000
Net Income (Proprietorship)		$17,675	
Less: Income Taxes	$4,436		
Drawings	6,300	10,736	6,939
Jack Fraser, Capital, July 31, 1997			$16,939

Corporation:

Preferred Share Capital (subscribed for cash):			$1,000
Premium on Preferred Shares (subscribed for cash):			1,000
Common Share Capital:			
Subscribed for past services		$ 200	
Subscribed for cash		61	
Subscribed for the balance in the equity account,			
Jack Fraser, Capital, July 31, 1997		16,939	17,200
Retained Earnings:			
Net Income (Corporation)		6,600	
Less: Income Taxes	$1,518		
Dividends on Preferred Shares	100		
Dividends on Common Shares	860	2,478	4,122

SMALL BUSINESS LEDGER ACCOUNTS INDEX

A small business ledger accounts index, which may also be referred to as a chart of accounts, is presented in the Appendix of this book. This index was designed to facilitate the accounting process, and comprises 100 accounts. Even so, on some occasions, additional accounts may be required, in a particular section of the index. A good example is the purchase of a franchise. In our list of accounts, there is no such account, so we must replace an existing, unused, account with an account called *Franchise.* A franchise belongs to the category of accounts titled *other assets* so logical candidates for substitution are the Patents account or the Goodwill account. So if a business purchases a franchise but does not own patents then account number 125 may be labeled *Franchise;* account number 126 then must be labeled *Accumulated Depreciation: Franchise;* and account number 598 must be labeled *Depreciation Expense: Franchise.* Whenever you make substitutions, be certain that the substitution occurs within the same kind of account. Thus, in our example, it would be inappropriate to substitute the Franchise account for a current asset account such as Prepaid Rent. New accounts should not be created unless absolutely necessary. For example, do not open a new account to record the purchase of a bag of fertilizer, if fertilizer is purchased once every four or five years. Instead, enter this purchase of fertilizer in the Office Supplies Expense account even though inclusion of this expenditure for fertilizer with office supplies may appear somewhat far-fetched to those unfamiliar with accounting.

INCOME TAX RETURNS

An income tax return must be filed every year by every business. This means filing a form, available from the income tax department, along with a set of financial statements. Some data from the financial statements is transferred to the income tax form and other information is entered on the income tax form as well. Basically, the procedure is straightforward. In other words, once you have reached the stage where you have prepared a set of financial statements, the task of accounting for the year is nearly finished.

How, one may ask, does income taxation interface with accounting? In accounting we learn how to record financial data and how to prepare financial statements in accordance with recognized accounting principles. The way certain financial transactions are treated for accounting purposes may be determined by tax rules. And the income tax department prescribes the rules that apply to the transactions of a business. For example, the way depreciation is recorded is determined by the tax regulations in effect. Some assets are depreciated on a straight line basis; other assets are depreciated on a declining balance basis with the maximum rates prescribed by the tax department. Some jurisdictions allow double-declining balance depreciation, and other jurisdictions forbid depreciation of assets acquired with the aid of funds received from the government.

Regardless of changes that might be made in the income tax act, fundamental to every business is the production of a set of financial statements. Once this set of statements is produced, in the manner in which we learned to produce statements in this book, the rules of taxation may be applied to complete the income tax filing requirements. The rates of income tax are set by federal and state legislatures. The income tax department provides rules and regulations that determine when income tax returns must be filed, penalties for non-compliance, methods and maximum rates of depreciation, limits on certain expenses such as travel to conventions, donations to charities, expenditures on advertising on media in foreign countries, taxation of capital gains, etc. If any of these limits set by the income tax department has been exceeded, then, generally speaking, the excess expenditure charged off as expense must be added back to income so that it may be subject to taxation.

Having learned small business accounting, you now have a foundation on which to pursue the study of taxation, if you wish. But do not get carried away with the study of taxation as you only need to know a few tax rules to function as the owner of a small business. For most small business owners and managers, however, virtually all the knowledge of accounting that you will ever need, and more, has already been presented in this book.

SUMMARY AND CONCLUSION

In this chapter we reviewed the kinds of files, records, and books of account that must be kept and we were introduced to an alternative way of arriving at a set of financial statements through the use of a worksheet. A prerequisite to sound and efficient management of a small business enterprise is the necessity to keep orderly records of financial events, so that the financial position and operating results of the business may be easily computed. This task is easier than it sounds and may be accomplished with very little extra effort than if only bookkeeping itself were done.

If you have studied this book carefully, and have performed the exercises at the end of each chapter and have done the problems, you will have gained a thorough knowledge of the accounting cycle. This text was prepared with painstaking care to ensure that you will have been exposed to virtually every kind of account that you will ever need to understand and deal with. If on occasion you may have thought that some of the transactions were unrealistic you might just be in for a surprise. Success in business is very often achieved by being prepared to deal with financial events that appear to be beyond expectation so do not constrain your imagination by placing artificial bounds on your expectations as reality is not limited in any way or fashion.

If you understand the material in this text (and nothing is stopping you from going over the material a second time if you need to do that to understand accounting) there is every expectation that you will be able to prepare complete and accurate financial statements for your business. When your business has grown to the stage where you no longer wish to be involved in the accounting process itself, you will nevertheless make use of the principles that you have learned in accounting in making financial decisions more efficiently and more effectively. By understanding the nature of every kind of financial transaction, you will immediately realize the implications of these transactions and the impact they will have on the financial statements of the business.

Accounting is the language and the tool for efficient financial decision-making and management, a knowledge of which is essential if the business is to*survive, grow*, and earn a *profit*.

Exercises

1. What is the purpose of a General Correspondence file? Explain.

2. Which businesses should keep a record of assets? What kinds of assets are recorded in this record?

3. Every business must keep an expenditures file. Explain how this file may be organized. What should be done to ensure that the data in this file can be processed efficiently? Explain.

4. In your opinion, is a check register identical to a Cash ledger account? Will they both have the same balances at the end of a particular accounting period if the records are kept up to date? Will the balance in the check register be identical to the balance on the bank statement at the end of an accounting period?

5. Is a sales file that simply consists of carbon copies of all invoices that have been issued adequate for a business whose sales are mainly high value and few in number? What is required for a merchandising business that makes numerous low price sales every day?

6. What is the purpose of a personnel file? Is this file an accounting record?

7. Payroll books may be organized in various ways with the objective of efficiently recording data on salaries, deductions from salaries, and employers' contributions to payroll plans. Do you agree with that assessment? Explain.

8. A student once commented, "you said that books of account and records are available at every stationery store, yet I have searched and could not find any of these books you mentioned." She agreed that the store she visited did have several kinds of books of account and other accounting paper, but she could not find a book of account specifically designated as a journal, ledger, payroll, etc. What suggestions would you make to her to help her in her quest to purchase the appropriate material?

9. An accountant explains to a business owner that she will prepare financial statements from a worksheet at the end of the year. But in the meantime, she would like the business owner to keep certain files and records that require no knowledge of accounting and at most require only an elementary knowledge of arithmetic. Explain which files and records should be kept by the business owner as well as the purpose of each of these files and records.

10. A bookkeeper calls on a newly formed business with five employees and offers to "keep its books and records for only $100 per month." This offer

does not include keeping a journal, ledger, worksheet, or preparing financial statements. Which files and records may be entrusted to the bookkeeper? Explain the nature and purpose of each file and record.

11. Financial statements are prepared for a business every month. However, the income tax department must be provided with only one set of financial statements representing the financial position of the business at the end of the year and the operating results of the business for the year. What must be done to produce one set of financial statements from the twelve separate sets of statements? Provide separate explanations for the income statement and the balance sheet.

12. A fast food operator buys a franchise from a national fast food chain. To his surprise he discovers that *Franchise* does not appear in the small business ledger accounts index. However, it is necessary to record the purchase of this asset and provide accounts in which to record depreciation. How may the accounts in the small business ledger account index be altered to accommodate the needs of this operator? Explain.

Problems

1. From the data below, prepare a worksheet and year end financial statements for Pacific Insurance Agency. John Brown is sole proprietor. The check register reveals a balance of $36,957 at the end of the year. An initial deposit of $20,000 was made by the owner at the time of commencement of the business. The record of depreciable assets, kept by the owner, is shown below:

Record of Depreciable Assets

Asset and Supplier	*Date of Acquisition*	*Cost*
Office desks and furniture; purchased from Superior Office Supplies Inc.	(7-year property) January 2, 1997	$3,598
Photocopier, typewriter and a mailing machine; purchased from Ajax Business Machines Inc.	(5-year property) January 3, 1997	$4,200

No payroll book was kept as the firm did not hire any employees. However, Mr. Brown, the proprietor, made withdrawals of cash throughout the year. The data on drawings, extracted from the check register, is presented below:

January 31	$1,100	July 31	$1,200
February 28	1,000	August 31	1,500
March 31	900	September 30	1,000
April 30	1,400	October 31	1,100
May 31	1,300	November 30	1,200
June 30	1,100	December 31	1,400

All revenue was in the form of commissions. The data below was extracted from the *Commissions* file. No credit was extended.

January	$3,480	July	$4,200
February	8,920	August	3,900
March	4,740	September	4,300
April	3,530	October	2,480
May	3,970	November	3,760
June	4,160	December	3,320

No money was borrowed for the operation of the business.

A file on expenditures throughout the year was maintained in chronological order by pasting the receipt for each expenditure into the file. Care was taken to ensure that only one copy of each receipt was actually filed. Bills that were not paid by the end of the year are marked with an asterisk.

Desks and furniture	$3,600	Rent	$500
Office supplies	80	Electricity	90
Photocopier, etc.	4,200	Telephone	35
Office supplies	32	Yellow pages	12
Office supplies	14	Advertising	94
Insurance	120	Envelopes	46
Advertising	220	Radio spots	140
Office supplies	31	Rent	500
Business license	125	Telephone	40
Telephone	35	Yellow pages	12
Yellow pages	12	Electricity	92
Electricity	73	Business tax	20
Office supplies	14	Office supplies	22
Rent	500	Postage stamps	36
Advertising	130	Telephone	40
Advertising	200	Yellow pages	12
Office supplies	31	Rent	500
Accountant	600	Electricity	102

Fertilizer	4	Advertising	160
Postage stamps	36	Postage stamps	36
Promotional literature	240	Printing	52
Rent	500	Electricity	98
Electricity	84	Rent	500
Telephone	40	Telephone	35
Yellow pages	12	Yellow pages	12
Office supplies	19	Stationery	35
Printing	42	Rent	500
Advertising	180	Telephone	40
Postage stamps	72	Yellow pages	12
Office supplies	21	Electricity	95
Taxi fare	2	Office supplies	47
Telephone	35	Rent	500
Yellow pages	12	Electricity	95
Electricity	80	Telephone	35
Rent	500	Yellow pages	12
Postage stamps	36	Advertising	240
Stationery	42	Electricity	101
Attorney	800	Rent	500
Electricity	89	Telephone	35
Rent	500	Yellow pages	12
Telephone	35	Postage stamps	36
Yellow pages	12	Rent	500
Printing	82	Telephone	40*
Advertising	62	Yellow pages	12*
United Way Charity	50	Electricity	96*
Business tax	20	Advertising	230*

2. Prepare a final set of financial statements, from the worksheet data presented below, for North West Gift Shop Inc. The income tax rate is 20%.

Cash	Accounts Receivable	Inventory	Furniture and Fixtures	Ac. Deprn.: Furn. & Fixtures
126,254	246	beg.: 4,000	7,168	1,024
	90	ending: 3,200		1,024
	400			
	80			
126,254	816		7,168	2,048

Company Charter	Accounts Payable	Salaries Payable	Interest Payable	Sales Tax Payable
240	430	874	2,000	600
	35			
	97			
240	562	874	2,000	600

Income Taxes Payable	Notes Payable	Common Share Capital	Retained Earnings	Income Taxes
____	20,000	50,240	34,859	____
____	20,000	50,240	____	____

Commissions	Sales	Sales Returns and Allowances	Sales Discounts	Purchases
17.28	9,400	40	10	3,400
16.92	8,300	80	8	4,100
14.94	8,700	75	20	3,800
15.66	9,600	30	14	3,200
17.28	7,200	25	24	3,100
12.96	8,100		18	3,400
14.58	8,500		28	2,800
15.30	9,100		12	3,200
16.38	7,300		10	3,600
13.14	7,700		6	3,400
14.28	9,600		24	3,300
17.28	10,000	____	22	3,200
186.00	103,500	250	196	40,500

Transportation-in	Purchase Returns and Allowances	Purchase Discounts	Rent Expense	Telephone Expense
80	140	68	600	35
45	204	82	600	35
65	180	76	600	35
90	50	64	600	42
30		62	600	35
20		68	600	35
		56	600	35
		64	600	40
		72	600	35
		68	600	35
		66	600	35
____	____	64	600	35
330	574	810	7,200	432

Utilities Expense	Insurance Expense	Advertising and Promotion Expense	Interest and Service Charges Expense	Legal Services Expense
102	240	140	2,000	2,400

98		180		
86		390		
97		320		
95		350		
104		380		
124		230		
86		160		
89		220		
92		230		
94		410		
97		410		
1,164	240	3,420	2,000	2,400

Accounting Services Expense	Licenses and Annual Reports Expense	Business Tax Expense	Salaries Expense	Pension Plan Expense
3,500	135	48	1,200	18
	15	47	1,200	18
			1,200	18
			1,200	18
			1,200	18
			1,200	18
			1,200	18
			1,200	18
			1,200	18
			1,200	18
			1,200	18
			1,200	18
3,500	150	95	14,400	216

Unemployment Insurance Plan Expense	Workers' Compensation Plan Expense	Cash Shortage	Depreciation Expense: Furniture and Fixtures
14	72	18	1,024
14			
14			
14			
14			
14			
14			
14			
14			
14			
14			
14			
168	72	18	1,024

Other data:

The authorized share capital of the company is 100,000 common shares without par value; 50,240 common shares have been issued and are outstanding.

Commissions on sales tax are earned in the month in which the sales tax is collected. The sales tax rate is 6%.

Income taxes are due two months past year end.

The loan is due in five years time and is repayable together with interest at the rate of 10%.

This data was taken from the payroll book:

Gross salary for December:		$1,200
Withheld from salary:	Income taxes	$300
	Pension Plan	16
	Unemployment Insurance Plan	10
Employer's Contributions:	Workers' Compensation Plan	72
	Pension Plan	18
	Unemployment Insurance Plan	14

Salary is payable on January 5th; payroll deductions and employer's contributions are due by January 10th (accounts payable).

The telephone and utilities bills for December are due by January 15th.

Appendix

Small business ledger accounts index

BALANCE SHEET ACCOUNTS:

Assets

Current Assets:

101 Cash
102 Petty Cash
103 Accounts Receivable
104 Allowance for Bad Debts
105 Inventory
106 Unexpired Insurance
107 Prepaid Rent
108 Government Bonds
109 Notes Receivable

Plant and Equipment:

110 Office Supplies
111 Shop Supplies
112 Office Equipment
113 Accumulated Depreciation: Office Equipment
114 Furniture and Fixtures
115 Accumulated Depreciation: Furniture and Fixtures
116 Automobile
117 Accumulated Depreciation: Automobile
118 Shop Equipment
119 Accumulated Depreciation: Shop Equipment
120 Leasehold Improvements
121 Accumulated Depreciation: Leasehold Improvements
122 Building
123 Accumulated Depreciation: Building
124 Land

Other Assets:

125 Patents
126 Accumulated Depreciation: Patents
127 Goodwill
128 Accumulated Depreciation: Goodwill
129 Company Charter

Liabilities

Current Liabilities:

230 Accounts Payable
231 Salaries Payable
232 Interest Payable
233 Unearned Commissions
234 Unearned Fees
235 Sales Tax Payable
236 Income Taxes Payable
237 Dividends Payable on Preferred Shares
238 Dividends Payable on Common Shares
239 Dividend Distribution Tax Payable

Long-term Liabilities:

240 Notes Payable
241 Mortgages Payable
242 Bonds Payable

Equity

Proprietorship:

343 Jack Fraser, Capital
344 Jack Fraser, Drawings
(Also account numbers 349, 353, and 354 which are common to both proprietorship and corporation).

Corporation:

345 Preferred Share Capital
346 Premium on Preferred Shares
347 Common Share Capital
348 Retained Earnings
349 Income Taxes
350 Dividends on Preferred Shares
351 Dividends on Common Shares
352 Dividend Distribution Tax
353 Gain and Loss on Disposal
354 Income Tax Penalties

INCOME STATEMENT ACCOUNTS:

Revenue

Revenue:

455 Commissions
456 Fees
457 Miscellaneous Revenue (or Cash Overage)
458 Interest Income
459 Dividend Income
460 Sales
461 Sales Returns and Allowances
462 Sales Discounts

Cost of Goods Sold:

463 Purchases
464 Transportation-in
465 Purchase Returns and Allowances
466 Purchase Discounts

Expenses

Expenses:

567 Rent Expense
568 Telephone Expense
569 Utilities Expense
570 Automobile Maintenance Expense
571 Insurance Expense
572 Office Supplies Expense
573 Shop Supplies Expense
574 Advertising and Promotion Expense
575 Interest and Service Charges Expense
576 Equipment Rental Expense
577 Travel Expense
578 Bad Debts Expense
579 Legal Services Expense
580 Accounting Services Expense
581 Licenses and Annual Reports Expense
582 Business Tax Expense
583 Property Tax Expense
584 Salaries Expense
585 Pension Plan Expense
586 Unemployment Insurance Plan Expense
587 Workers' Compensation Plan Expense

588 Directors' Allowances
589 Miscellaneous Expense (or Cash Shortage)
590 Charitable Donations Expense
591 Political Donations Expense
592 Depreciation Expense: Office Equipment
593 Depreciation Expense: Furniture and Fixtures
594 Depreciation Expense: Automobile
595 Depreciation Expense: Shop Equipment
596 Depreciation Expense: Leasehold Improvements
597 Depreciation Expense: Building
598 Depreciation Expense: Patents
599 Depreciation Expense: Goodwill

Income Summary

600 Income Summary

Bibliography

Abdel-Khalik, A. Rashad (Editor), **The Blackwell Encyclopedic Dictionary of Accounting,** Blackwell Publishing, 1997.

Blake, John, **Accounting Standards,** Pitman Publishing Ltd., 1995.

Boockholdt, James L., **Accounting Information Systems: Transaction Processing and Controls,** Richard D. Irwin, 1995.

Bushong, Joe Gregory, **Accounting and Auditing of Small Businesses,** Garland Publishing, 1995.

Chambers, R.J. (editor), **An Accounting Thesaurus: 500 Years of Accounting,** Pergamon Press, 1996.

Fox Jack, **Accounting and Recordkeeping Made Easy for the Self-Employed,** John Wiley & Sons, 1995.

Gelinas, Ulric J., Jr., Oram, Allan E., **Accounting Information Systems,** South-Western Publishing, 1995.

Gutmann, Jean E., **Accounting Made Easy With Your Computer: Understanding the Buzzwords and Basics of Accounting Using Today's Most Popular Software,** Sourcebooks Trade, 1997.

Internal Revenue Service, **How to Depreciate Property,** Washington, D.C.: GPO, 1996.

Jones, T. Colwyn, **Accounting and the Enterprise: A Social Analysis,** Van Nostrand Reinhold, 1995.

Kurkowski, Lloyd J., **Accumulated Appreciation: Career Advice for Young Accountants,** Sulzburger & Graham Publishing Company, 1997.

Meigs, Robert and Wittington, Ray, **Accounting: The Basis for Business Decisions,** McGraw Hill, 1995.

Meyer, Charles H., **Accounting and Finance for Lawyers in a Nutshell,** West Publishing, 1995.

Schrader, Eleanor, **Accounting for the Small Business,** Richard D. Irwin, 1993.

Solomon, Lanny M. (Editor), Walther, Larry M., and Vargo, Richard J., **Accounting: The Foundation for Business Success,** South-Western Publishing, 1996.

Tracy, John A., **Accounting for Dummies (For Dummies),** IDG Books Worldwide, 1997.

Yarnall, Gerald L. (editor), **Accounting Trends and Techniques 1996,** American Institute of Certified Public Accountants, 1996.

Zimmerman, Jerold L., **Accounting for Decision Making and Control,** Richard D. Irwin, 1996.

Index

D

E

F

G

H

I

J

L

M

N

O

P

U

V

W